NEOPLATONISM AND WESTERN AESTHETICS

NEOPLATONISM AND WESTERN AESTHETICS

Aphrodite Alexandrakis, Editor

Nicholas J. Moutafakis, Associate Editor

INTERNATIONAL SOCIETY FOR NEOPLATONIC STUDIES

Volume 12 in *Studies in Neoplatonism: Ancient and Modern*
R. Baine Harris, General Editor

STATE UNIVERSITY OF NEW YORK PRESS

Published by
State University of New York Press, Albany

© 2002 State University of New York

For information, address State University of New York Press,
90 State Street, Suite 700, Albany, NY 12207

Production by Michael Haggett
Marketing by Fran Keneston

Library of Congress Cataloging-in-Publication Data

Neoplatonism and Western aesthetics / Aphrodite Alexandrakis, editor; Nicholas J.
    Moutafakis, associate editor.
        p.   cm. — (Studies in Neoplatonism; v. 12)
    Includes bibliographical references and index.
    ISBN 0-7914-5279-4 (alk. paper). — ISBN 0-7914-5280-8 (pbk. : alk. paper)
    1. Neoplatonism—Congresses.   2. Aesthetics, Modern—Congresses.
I. Alexandrakis, Aphrodite, 1944–   II. Moutafakis, Nicholas J., 1941–   III. Series.

B645.N47 2001
186'.4—dc21   2001049176

10 9 8 7 6 5 4 3 2 1

Table of Contents

II. Neoplatonism and Representational Design

III. Neoplatonism in Contemporary Aesthetics

PREFACE

R. Baine Harris

One of the best ways to begin a study of Neoplatonism is through a study of its aesthetics. In fact, one of its most serious Twentieth Century students, William Ralph Inge, once referred to the whole system of Plotinus as a "Grandiose Aesthetic." He did so, I think, because Neoplatonism is based upon valuation. It is a philosophy that proposes to evaluate and rank reality in terms of what it judges to be the highest reality. Valuation is necessarily based upon experience, as indeed, is the whole of aesthetics. Whether or not Dean Inge's label can apply depends upon what is to be seen as the legitimate scope of aesthetics. If aesthetic experience is seen as limited only to our sensuous experiences as understood by our intellect, it would not. But if it is extended to include our experience of purely rational concepts, such logical concepts as principles, laws, and numbers, and extended even further to include direct experience of the divine, it would. Plotinus certainly appealed to a wide range of human experience, sensuous, rational, and religious as the basis of his ontology, as did most of his admirers in later centuries. A multi-leveled scheme of valuation is the basis of his ontology; and his ontology figures into almost every other subject he treats, and especially so in his psychology, theology, and aesthetics. An understanding of his aesthetics and the way he establishes it will aid in understanding other elements of his philosophy and the way he establishes them.

Neoplatonism is based upon an axiomatic presupposition that the world that we experience through our senses is not the real world. Behind it lies something that is more real than it is, which, in turn, is based upon something that is still even more real than it, so that the Most Real is quite removed from what we ordinarily experience. It is a theme found in ancient Greek philosophy and in numerous Hindu writers throughout the centuries. It is only a presupposition and not a scientific fact. It is a hypothesis and a point of faith, since its verification is beyond that which can be scientifically ascertained. It is a presupposition that many people would like to believe, and some find they are able to do so, and some find that they are not. In any case, it is a theme of great historical importance in the intellectual history of the West, and India, and one that is not inconsistent with, and is even relatively amenable to, the major theologies of the Greeks, Indians, Hebrews, Romans, Christians and Muslims. One mode of demonstration of this point is to be found in the religious artifacts of these major cultural traditions. A study of the religious art of the West, for example, could hardly be done without some understanding of the basic themes of Neoplatonism as they were interpreted in various centuries, and the same would apply to religious art in other venues.

One distinctive feature of the Neoplatonic interpretation of this theme is a mapping or ranking of reality into a series of levels of reality so that anything at any given lower level is only relatively real. It can be concretely real as an individual thing while also being real as a lower level of something of a higher level. According to Plotinus, for example, man is most apparently real as a body, but he is also real as a soul, and as some element of the divine.

Another distinctive feature of Neoplatonism is that in contrast to many themes in the major theologies of the West is that it is mystical without being other-worldly. Plotinus was quite concerned to combat other-worldliness and once said "All things there are here," which I interpret to mean there is no "there" except "here." He was concerned with the same world that Aristotle was concerned with, the same individual real, but he saw different levels of reality in any given individual. His mysticism results from the mystery we encounter when we consider the various sorts of reality inherent in any concrete individual, and in his case, in particular, the various levels of reality inherent in it. This point is especially important in considering the history of religious art in the West, a notable instance being the artifacts influenced by Renaissance Neoplatonism, a specific case being the works of Michelangelo.

The essays in this book are not specifically intended to present a comprehensive picture of Neoplatonic aesthetics, but rather to show how elements of the aesthetic views of Plotinus and later Neoplatonists have had a role to play in the history of Western Art. Certain papers do focus on certain themes in the aesthetics of Plotinus and some later Neoplatonists, while others deal mainly with the appearance and reappearance of those themes in the writings and artifacts of later philosophers and artists throughout the centuries. Again, they are not presented as a comprehensive treatment of the subject but rather as typical significant examples to illustrate the way in which Neoplatonic aesthetic teachings continued to be influential in various venues in various centuries, including even our own time.

All of the papers in this volume were first presented in an earlier form in an international conference of the International Society for Neoplatonic Studies held in Rethymnon, Crete in the summer of 1998 under the sponsorship of the University of Crete. The idea for the conference was conceived by Professor Aphrodite Alexandrakis of Barry University in Miami, who also arranged for its funding and served as its able conference director. She also served as the editor of this volume and was assisted in this function by Professor Nikolas J. Moutafakis of Cleveland State University in Cleveland, Ohio. Altogether they present a well-balanced scholarly brief introduction both to Neoplatonic aesthetics and to its significance in Western Art.

August, 2000
Department of Philosophy and
Religious Studies
Old Dominion University

Editors' Introduction

It is interesting to note how Greek philosophy achieved one of its most lasting impressions through Neoplatonism. From modest adaptations by the early fathers of the Church, to the bolder christianization of aspects of the Neoplatonic system by Saint Augustine and Dionysius the Aeropagite, as well as by later efforts, one encounters the seeds of Neoplatonism blossoming again and again throughout the long history of Western thought. One needs only cite the works of Scotus Erigena, Hugo and Richard of St. Victor, Eckhart, Böhme and Bruno to appreciate the far reaching influence of this tradition. Even as late as the nineteenth century Friedrich Shelling sought to infuse Neoplatonism with Intuitionism, percipitating new insights into the philosophy of history, which in turn became a prelude to Hegel's philosophy of mind.

Not only are the origins of Neoplatonism significantly diverse, involving a wide array of thinkers as its founders, *e.g.* Plotinus, Iamblichus, Longinus, etc. to mention a few, but the scope of its influence has penetrated deeply into a broad ranging field of philosophical inquiry, encompassing issues familiar in areas relating to the formal study of metaphysics and epitemology, as well as in lesser known areas concerning the nature of art, the contemplation of the beautiful, the essence and function of artistic objects, the knowing of nature as an aesthetic experience, etc. It was felt by several members of the Society that attention should be directed finally to the latter and relatively unchartered territory. Thus, as a means of exploring the scholarly community's most recent understanding of how key Neoplatonic concepts play a seminal role in aesthetics, the International Society for Neoplatonic Studies and the University of Crete cosponsored the 1998 International Conference on the theme of "Neoplatonism and Western Aesthetics" in Rethymnon, Crete.

1

Apart from the superbly beautiful surroundings of the island's natural setting and the gracious accommodations and support provided for the conference participants by his Grace Anthimos, Metropolitan of Rethymnon and Avlopotamos, Mr. Dimitris Archondakis, Major of Rethymnon, the Vice Rector Dr. Christos Nicolaou and Dean Dr. Alexis Politis of the University of Crete, the Hellenic Ministry of Culture, the GrecoTel company and the hospitality of the people of Crete, the conference was uniquely endowed with a fine collection of papers pertaining to its central theme. What follows is an arrangement of these contributions under four broad headings.

In the first grouping: "Neoplatonism and the Concept of the Beautiful,'" the theme of each contributor centers about the concept of "the beautiful" itself, as it is addressed in the works of various Neoplatonists from Plotinus to Proclus, and how in some instances this theme plays a central role for later Christian writers.

In "Neoplatonism and the Image in Visual Art," the emphasis shifts to how historically the Neoplatonic concept of beauty is investigated and utilized by certain renowned artists and architects, "concretizing," so to speak, the Neoplatonic concept of beauty in space and time.

The third grouping, "Neoplatonism in Contemporary Aesthetics," contains papers focused specifically upon the influence of Neoplatonism in contemporary discussions involving the creative process and the aesthetic experience generally. Here the tradition of Neoplatonism is found to be underlying the thinking of such seminal twentieth century figures as Kazantzakis, Heidegger, and Santayanna.

Finally, in "Neoplatonism and Cosmic Genesis" the theme centers on how the concept of the beautiful plays a central role in discussions involving processes governing the generation of the world in Plotinus' works. It is the sincere hope of the International Society for Neoplatonic Studies that these contributions will achieve their major objective, which is to stimulate further research and study in the area of Neoplatonism and the study of aesthetics.

The editors also wish express their gratitude to Jonathan Raymon for the wonderful job he did in preparing the camera-ready manuscript for publication.

Nicholas J. Moutafakis [Associate Editor]

Aphrodite Alexandrakis [Editor]

Action, Contemplation and Interiority in the Thinking of Beauty in Plotinus[1]

Jean-Marc Narbonne

Beauty as a state of affairs

The thinking of Beauty in Plotinus is intimately related to his philosophy, primarily because the very undertaking of a spiritual elevation is at the same time, for Plotinus, an aesthetic undertaking, an experience of beauty experienced in itself; and, moreover, even prior to the slightest will toward a higher reality, our very experience of the world is already, for Plotinus, an experience of beauty.

Let us begin with the second point, that of our very own experience of the world which is declared as fundamentally an experience of beauty. This latter declaration might seem striking once we remind ourselves of Porphyry's opening statement in his *Life of Plotinus*, relating that his master "seemed ashamed of being in the body,"[2] and also, once we acknowledge that Plotinus is the philosopher of the *aphairesis* par excellence, professing the retrenchment and detachment from all that is sensible. Shame of one's body and will to detach oneself from the sensible does indeed presuppose a certain disavowal of the world and of its beauty.

We must immediately reply that nothing is more alien to Plotinus than the condemnation of the world for its lack of beauty. On the contrary, as Plotinus points out, we do not see, by reflecting, just how such diversity which is our world, could have been as artfully arranged as it is indeed in reality: "if anyone could plan rationally as well as possible, he would wonder at it because planning could not have found out another way to make it" (III, 2, 14, 2-4). And again:

> Will anyone be so sluggish in mind and so immovable that, when he sees all the beauties in the world of sense, all its good proportion and the mighty excellence of its order, and the splendour of form which is manifested in the stars, for all their remoteness he will not thereupon think, seized with reverence, "what wonders, and from what a source?" (II, 9, 16, 51-55)

We are, then, from the start, according to Plotinus, in beauty and are attracted by it. The proof, *a contrario*, is that the ugly is unendurable for us, our soul "when it encounters [it] shrinks back and rejects it and turns away from it and is out of tune and alienated from it" (I, 6, 2, 5-6); cf. *Symposium*, 206 d). But what is ugliness for Plotinus? It is the absence of form in that which is destined to receive one. The ugly, then, is the unformed with which the soul has no affinity, in front of which it can receive no guidance, that which presents itself as the undetermined and unattainable. And it is not just that the soul judges ugly that which is in a state of indistinctness, but it is also that the soul cannot endure the spectacle as if it was facing nothingness, emptiness, an abyss devoid of the least trace of intelligibility from which it must protect itself (cf. II, 4, 10). This peculiar effect that the ugly has on us is described by Plotinus as "an impression of the shapeless" (typon tou amorphou II, 4, 10, 23).

On the other hand, the beautiful is obviously that which, first of all, is the bearer of form, shape and just proportions, in other words, that which the world profusely displays and that to which our soul is naturally directed. How can this natural attraction be explained? What is it, in harmony, that attracts us? Plotinus' explanation is straightforward and precise: there is a kinship between the soul and the beautiful, or more precisely, an original belonging to one another:

> Our explanation of this is that the soul, since it is by nature what it is and is related to the higher kind of reality in the realm of being, when it sees something akin to it or a trace of its kindred reality, is delighted and thrilled and returns to itself and remembers itself and its own possessions. (I, 6, 2, 7-11)

Beauty in the lower world is, then, a trace of a higher beauty. Manifestly beautiful in itself, without a doubt, but as a trace, it bears witness to its superior, its archetype and its source.

We might ask though, why insist on the reference to a higher reality on seeing sensible beauty as a trace of something else, and not be content with sensible beauty as such, beauty as it presents itself in the here and now? It is because, for Plotinus, the aforementioned affinity between the soul and beauty is explainable only by a common origin shared by these two realities, and not by haphazard chance. The universal nature of man's search for beauty and his astonishment before it could not possibly be explained without admitting that such an attraction was prepared beforehand; such a communion is too profound, too intimately felt to be the fruits of fortuitous links and accident; hence, such a communion is only understood by assuming a mysterious belonging, a pre-existent belonging, since it is not immediately given in the diversity of our sense experience. Beauty simultaneously appeases and astounds the soul, since the soul recognises in the trace of truth, of purity, of a unifying principle, to which the soul senses its belonging and to which it aspires. Indeed, our pleasure experienced through the intermediary of art results entirely from the impact of such a discovery.

The soul is delighted in beauty because through the recognition of the imprint of that in which it participates and finds the source of its being, it comes to recognise itself. In noticing the form which unifies and structures the diverse parts of a certain work; in perceiving the concept shaping otherwise insignificant matter, the soul discovers in nature or in the artifact the cohesive force of the Idea, the organising principle which communicates symmetry, measure, and beauty to the object. And in its own self-recognition it is lightened, because it now can aspire to its own inner harmony and seek to re-ascend to that principle inside itself which regulates, unifies and appeases. Is it not precisely the soul which is unstable and intemperate, whimsically oscillating between every inclination, drawn in every direction, which, in mood and in deed, is incapable of constancy, unity or harmony, which we qualify as ugly? And is it not because of a work's firm unity and basis that we qualify it as beautiful?

Beauty as above symmetry

Let us immediately dispose of a first possible misunderstanding in the comprehension of Plotinus' stance on the question of Beauty.

For the latter, the beautiful can in no way be reduced to the symmetry of parts because this might lead to the erroneous conclusion that only the composite can be beautiful and that whatever is simple, like the sun or a unique sound, is devoid of beauty, when in fact the parts of a composite are not always beautiful. Moreover, "though the same good proportion is there all the time, the same face sometimes appears beautiful and sometimes does not, surely we must say that being beautiful is something else over and above good proportion, and good proportion is beautiful because of something else?" (I, 6, 1, 37-40).[3] Who would dare profess—unless one desired to eradicate the ethical dimension in the consideration of Beauty—that a funeral procession, no matter how symmetrical and justly proportioned it presented itself to be, evokes beauty? Symmetry of the parts in sensible objects, then, is the bearer of beauty only when it manifests the marvel of the Idea. The object, then, is beautiful only as the epiphany of the Idea, the latter being what is first called beautiful, since it is itself responsible for irradiating the object with beauty and ultimately communicating symmetry and just proportion to it. "It is as if it was in the presence of a face which is certainly beautiful, but cannot catch the eye because it has no grace playing upon its beauty" (VI, 7, 22, 22 ss.). This applies, as much to artistic productions as it does to natural productions: it is the "inner form" (endon eidos, I, 6, 3, 8) of the artist, or of the architect (I, 6, 3, 6 ss.) which is beautiful even before the material manifestation, which is beautiful only insofar as it lends itself to the original idea. Hence, we can understand Plotinus saying that art in itself, or preferably, the artistic process itself, is superior to its product:

> If art makes its work like what it is and has—and it makes it beautiful according to the forming principle of what it is making—it is itself more, and more truly, beautiful since it has the beauty of art which is greater and more beautiful than anything in the external object. (V, 8, 1, 22-26)

It might well be beautiful and harmonious, but a work cannot abandon its status as trace: "well, then, are the things made and the forming principle in matter beautiful, but the forming principle which is not in matter but in the maker, the first immaterial one, is that not beauty?" (V, 8, 2, 16-19).

Beauty as above imitation

There is a second misunderstanding that must be avoided when interpreting the aesthetics of Plotinus: since the value of the artistic production depends on the value of the inner concept (endon eidos) in the artist, it goes without saying that, for Plotinus, who on this point drops the platonic interpretative framework,[4] artistic production could vie with and perhaps sometimes supersede nature's own productions:

> But if anyone despises the arts because they produce their works by imitating nature, we must tell him, first, that natural things are imitations too. Then he must know that the arts do not simply imitate what they see, but they run back up to the forming principles from which nature derives; then also that they do a great deal by themselves, and, since they possess beauty, they make up what is defective in things (V, 8, 1, 32-38).

In the same way, borrowing Plotinus' example, "Pheidias too did not make his Zeus from any model perceived by the senses, but understood what Zeus would look like if he wanted to make himself visible" (V, 8, 1, 32-40).[5]

If, then, symmetry in the sensible order is beautiful as an expression of the Idea working within nature and the artist, then, we can include as beautiful certain actions, occupations, ways of being, in so far as they can be referred to the Idea which engenders them. Consequently, a single term, a single concept, can be predicated of otherwise heterogeneous realities: a beautiful painting, a beautiful melody, a beautiful action, a beautiful sentiment, a beautiful virtue, a beautiful science, a beautiful soul. The following question which Plotinus had asked himself is thus answered: "how does the bodily agree with that which is before body?" (I, 6, 3, 5-6); there is agreement because both participate in the Idea (2, 13). From here, the aesthetic ascendence, which is also an ethical and metaphysical one, can begin; as Plato taught,[6] from wordly beauty, the beauty of the work used as a "stepping stone" (I, 6, 1, 20), we may advance progressively toward the Idea of the Good in itself, which allows us to see the beauty of all beautiful things. But what an arduous task it is for us to learn to reascend the emotional path leading from the beauty of works of art and nature to the inner principle that gives them life! As Plotinus remarks, "but we, because we are not accustomed to see any of the things within and do not know them, pursue the external and do not know that it is that within, which moves us" (V, 8, 2, 32-34). We must waken the inner vision from its stupor, teach it to recognise the true bearer of beauty, that original reason "which is no longer in anything else but in itself" (V, 8, 3, 7-8).

Beauty as contemplation

The soul, then, is naturally inclined towards Beauty, since both belong to each other. The clearest statement on this point is without a doubt V, 8 [31], 3, 1 ss.: "There is therefore in nature a rational forming principle which is the archetype of the beauty in body, and the rational principle in soul *is more beautiful* than that in nature, and it is also the source of that in nature. *It is the clearest in a nobly good soul* and is already advanced in beauty; for by adorning the soul and giving it light from a greater light which is primarily beauty [*scil.* the Intellect] it makes us deduce by its very presence in the soul what that before it is like, which is no longer in anything else but in itself."

When the soul wanders away from Beauty, when it can no longer recognise it, it is a sign of its straying into the distractions of the multiple. And by forgetting the true status of sensible beauties as *images, traces, shadows* (I, 6 [1] 8, 7), the soul confounds veritable beauty with its signs, like the man who wished to catch his "beautiful reflection playing on the water" (8,9). And when the soul is thus weakened by its submersion in the sensible diversity, it can no longer see the links existing between corporeal beauty, consisting in the exteriority of the parts, and incorporeal beauty, that, primarily, of the soul and of the sciences and virtues which relate to the virtue of the soul, that are, as Plotinus says, katharseis, "purifications" (I, 6 [1] 6, 2).

The fact that the beauty found in the soul predominates over that embedded in the sensible *lógos*, itself over the accomplished *érgon* which derives from it, is an implication of plotinian metaphysics, which holds that sensible reality is but a trace, a lower form of a higher activity which is one of thinking (*noêsis*), of contemplation (*theôria*) or of wisdom (V, 8 [31], 5, 1 ss.). Plotinus professes that all beings are in fact by-products (*parergon*) of contemplation (III, 8 [30], 8, 26); or, as he expresses differently: "every life is a thought, but one life is dimmer than another" (*ibid.* 8, 17), and " all things come from contemplation and are contemplation, both the things which truly exist and the things which come from them" (*ibid.* 7, 1-3). As a universal rule, Plotinus states that "everywhere ... making (*poiesis*) and action (*praxis*) are either a weakening or a consequence of contemplation" (*ibid.* 4, 39-40). In the first instance, then, action and making are *substitutes* of contemplation; unable to contemplate because of the weakness of their soul, men turn to practice and action, the sensible counterparts of contemplation; in the second instance, action and making are, so to speak, naturally superadded to contemplation. It is so for nature, since, being a result of contemplation, it produces by means of contemplation: "my act of contemplation makes what it contemplates, as the geometers draw their figures while they contemplate. But I do not draw, but as I contemplate, the lines which bound bodies come to be as if they fell from my contemplation" (4, 7-10). But even in this second type of contemplation, what is produced is weaker than its source: "that which is produced must always be of the same kind as its producer, but weaker through losing its virtue as it comes down" (*ibid.*, 5, 24-25).

It is obviously in this general economy that the particular beauty of the sensible object must be interpreted and ranked; in itself beautiful, the artifact is nonetheless a shadow of a higher and purer contemplation, that can at best remind us of the beauty from which it emanates, but must never be taken as an ultimate goal in itself. Amidst our action, we again long for contemplation: "for men of action too, contemplation is the goal, and what they cannot get by going straight to it....they seek to obtain by going round about it" (*ibid.*, 6, 1-4). The purification, in this context, is necessarily a purification *from the sensible*, a process of detachment by which the human soul recognises the secondary status of the bodily beauties to which it is driven.

Beauty as an inner quest

How, then, can we catch a glimpse of that unique Beauty reigning above all others? By entering into ourselves. Entering into ourselves means ceasing to be the mirror that reflects the changing images of the external world so that the image of Beauty which lies inside of us may appear, for the Idea of Beauty is, so to speak, everpresent inside the whole of our soul. But its reflection becomes visible only if the endless glittering of external objects is interrupted (cf. I, 4, 10, 6 ss.). Plotinus insists that we "not look. Shut your eyes, and change to and wake another way of seeing, which every one has but few use" (I, 6, 8, 24 ss.).

The quest for Beauty becomes what it, in fact, always was, an inner quest. "For one must come to the sight with a seeing power made akin and like to what is seen. No eye ever saw the sun without becoming sunlike...." (I, 6, 9, 29-30); "just as in the case of the beauties of sense it is impossible for those who have not seen them or grasped their beauty—those born blind, for instance,—to speak about them, in the same way only those can speak about the beauty of ways of life who have accepted the beauty of ways of life and kinds of knowledge and everything else of the sort" (I, 6, 4 9 ss.).

And, as we have seen, a beautiful thing, be it corporeal or incorporeal, is such by virtue of that inner element with which it is imbued, that Idea in which it participates, that which allows us to call "beautiful" heterogeneous realities, a beautiful painting, a beautiful melody, a beautiful action, a beautiful senti-ment, a beautiful virtue, a beautiful science, or a beautiful soul. All beautiful things can be rendered so because of one common element; a single and unique word appears in our minds when we see them: beautiful. And all of them at-tract us.

> "What then are we to think, if anyone contemplates the absolute beauty which exists pure by itself, uncontaminated by flesh or body, not in earth or heaven, that it may keep its purity?" All these other things are external additions and not primary, but derived from it. If then one sees that which provides for all and remains by itself and gives to all but receives nothing into itself, if he abides in the contemplation of this kind of beauty and rejoices in being made like it, how can he need any other beauty? ... Here the greatest, the ultimate contest is set before our souls; all our toil and trouble is for this, not to be left without a share in the best of visions. The man who attains this is blessed in seeing that *blessed sight*, and he who fails to attain it has failed utterly. A man has not failed if he fails to win beauty of colours or bodies, or power or office or kingship even, but if he fails to win this and only this. (I, 6, 7, 21-36)

At this stage of our inquiry, we can understand the following: "the treatises Plotinus had devoted to Beauty are not aesthetical treatises, but metaphysical treatises."[7] The splendour of Beauty moves us deeply because it wakes us to ourselves, to that transcendent beauty in which we participate. We can reflect on Joyce's statement in *A Portrait...*: "I desire to press in my arms the loveli-ness which has not yet come into the world."[8] But why does the Beauty to which we aspire, inspire us so? There is, for Plotinus, one lone answer. Beauty is an offshoot of the Good, which is more ancient, as Plotinus remarks, "not in time but in truth, and has the prior power" (V, 5 [32], 12, 38).

Beauty as *bonum*

We can, so to speak, briefly summarise the thought of Plotinus with a single formula: "he who seeks beauty seeks goodness". The common element in all that is beautiful, be it music, a deed, a soul, a disposition or a virtue, is their achievemnt of a certain good, and can be called beautiful only because they are inspired by the Good. A beautiful symmetry is beautiful only when it derives from the Good, not when it derives from Evil or that which is destructive.

But the relationship between Beauty and the Good, *pulchrum* and *bonum*, is rather complex in Plotinus. The Good is clearly above Beauty. The soul seeks Beauty so that it may attain the Good, and not the other way around: "the Good itself does not need Beauty, though Beauty needs [the Good]"[9]. But, and this goes without saying, the Good itself is by no means devoid of Beauty: "Anyone who has seen [the Good] knows what I mean when I say that it is beautiful" (I, 6, 7, 2-3). In essence Plotinus is here reproducing in his own words Plato's thought, especially as it is expressed in the *Philebus* (64 e 5): "And now the power of the good has retired into the region of the beautiful; for measure and symmetry are beauty and virtue all the world over". In the *Republic* 509a 6, Plato states: "What a wonder of beauty that must be which is the author of science and truth, and yet surpasses them in beauty"[10]. The infinite power of the Good, the Measurer (VI, 7 [38], 30, 34) above all measure, is the first and immeasurable condition of all measurable beauty: "so his beauty, explains Plotinus, is of another kind and beauty above beauty. For if it is nothing, what beauty can it be? But if it is lovable, it would be the geometer of beauty. Therefore the productive power of all is the flower of beauty, a beauty which makes beauty" (VI, 7 [38], 32, 27-29). The Good is, then, the flower of beauty, and as the beautiful things of this world are the *sensible manifestations* of Beauty in itself or the Idea of Beauty, we might say that Beauty in itself is, in a certain analogical way, the *intelligible manifestation* of the absolutely transcendent Good.

Moreover, the soul, Plotinus says, is "skilled in finding what it loves, and not leaving off till it catches it" (31, 28-29). Why are we so driven toward the object of our love? In order to revive the vision of the incommensurable Good that lives inside of us:

> The experience of lovers bears witness to this, that, as long as it is in that which has the impression perceived by the senses, the lover is not yet in love; but when from that he himself generates in himself an impression not perceptible by the senses in his partless soul, then love springs up. But he seeks to see the beloved that he may water him when he is withering. (VI, 7 [38], 33, 22-27).

Or again: "Then the soul, receiving into itself an outflow from thence, is moved and dances wildly and is all stung with longing and becomes love....But when a kind of warmth from thence comes upon it, it gains strength and wakes and is truly winged; and though it is moved with passion for that which lies close by it, yet all the same it rises higher, to something greater which it seems to remember. And as long as there is anything higher than that which is present to it, it naturally goes on upwards, lifted by the giver of its love. It rises above Intellect, but cannot run on above the Good, for there is nothing above" (VI, 7 [38], 22, 8 ss.).

Beauty as inward openness

We might think, in light of the preceding descriptions of the quest for Beauty and the Good, that the coveted object of the soul lies outside of it. This is not so. Plotinus reminds us that what is "really worth aspiring to for us is our selves, bringing themselves back for themselves to the best of themselves; this is the well-proportioned and beautiful and the form which is not part of the composite and the clear, intelligent, beautiful life" (VI, 7 [38], 30, 36-40).

In what does this clear and beautiful life consist? What is this "best" of ourselves toward which we ought to tend? A certain clarification might be forthcoming if we look at Plotinus' representation of consciousness. The "I" contains all levels of reality which we can distinguish in "external" nature, from the ineffable One-Good down to the Intellect and to the Soul. "And just as in nature there are these three of which we have spoken [the One, the Intellect and the Soul], so we ought to think that they are present also in ourselves" (V, 1 [10], 10 5-6; see III 8 [30], 9, 23). The Good and Beauty are, therefore, always in us,[11] although we are not always conscious of the fact, as when we are unaware of that part of ourselves responsible for the beating of our heart and our other bodily processes. Our consciousness, then, is but a fraction of our total selves, lodged, as it were, between two extremes of which we are, for the most part, unaware:

> Why then, when we have such great possessions, do we not consciously grasp them, but are mostly inactive in these ways, and some of us are never active at all? They are always occupied in their own activities, Intellect, and that which is before Intellect, always in itself, and soul, which is in this sense "ever-moving." For not everything which is in the soul is immediately perceptible, but it reaches us when it enters into perception; but when a particular active power does not give a share in its activity to the perceiving power, that activity has not yet pervaded the whole soul. We do not therefore yet know it, since we are ac-

companied by the perceptive power and are not a part of soul but the whole soul (V, 1 [10], 12, 1 ss.).

Entering into ourselves, then, means becoming open to that which lies deepest in us, the Good, which is shrouded by the multiple external objects, of which we, for the most part, bear the reflections.

But how can this openness be imagined? I shall take a very simple example to describe the openness to the Good which is, in itself beyond all acts of consciousness. I am sitting and reading at my desk; the telephone rings, and I make an appointment with a friend to lunch at one, remembering that I must also stop at the bookdealer to pick up a book that I need; but, pursuing my reading, I absorb myself in it, forgetting my meeting and the bookdealer; I am no longer hungry nor thirsty, I feel no need for anything, time has vanished, and I am no longer aware what I am doing, I am totally swallowed up by my reading totally absent to myself, to my body, to the passing of time; the fact is, at the very moment when I am no longer conscious of my activity, it is then that I am truly reading; and when I slowly become conscious of my surroundings, once my consciousness accompanies my act, I am no longer truly reading, at least not with the same intensity. This absence to ourselves which unleashes our inner activity and intensifies its power, is the veritable openness and presence for Plotinus: "Often I have woken up out of the body to myself and have entered into myself, going out from all other things; I have seen a beauty wonderfully great...; Then after that rest in the divine, when I have come down from Intellect to discursive reasoning, I am puzzled how I ever came down..." (IV, 8, 1 ss.).

In the midst of such pure activity, in this unconscious immersion of ourselves into our very depths, we might ask, "who is it that is reading?," since no one is present to state: "it is I who is reading." Plotinus himself exclaims "but we—who are we?" (VI, 4, 14, 16), when confronted with this type of presence, the experience of reading being but a pale reflection.

As P. Hadot explains, we are here faced with "the whole paradox of the human self...: we are only that of which we are conscious, yet we are conscious of no longer being ourselves precisely when, lifting ourselves to a greater inner simplicity, we have lost consciousness of ourselves."[12] This is by far what is most singular for us modern thinkers in the plotinian conception of the true presence: the idea that what is most intimate to us is, in a sense, what is most impersonal. Inwardness is openness, not withdrawal; it lies not at the root of personality but of wholeness which takes us beyond any restrictive notion of individuality. From this point of view, all of Plotinus' philosophy, is "directed against anthropomorphism,"[13] as the following reflection describes to perfection: "For he has ceased to be the All now that he has become man; but when he ceases to be man he 'walks on high and directs the whole universe'[14]..." (V, 8, 7, 33-35).

Thus, we can find in Plotinus many passages professing the surpassing of the self, or the forgetting of the self:

> Conscious awareness, in fact, is likely to enfeeble the very activities of which there is consciousness; only when they are alone are they pure and more genuinely active and living; and when good men are in this state their life is increased, when it is not spilt out into perception, but gathered together in one in itself (I, 4, 10, 28 ss.).

> The reader is not necessarily aware that he is reading, least of all when he is really concentrating (I, 4, 10, 24-26).

> The more it presses on towards the heights the more it will forget....so that if anyone said that the good soul was forgetful, it would be correct to say so in this sort of sense. For the higher soul also flies from multiplicity, and gathers multiplicity into one and abandons the indefinite; because in this way it will not be [clogged] with multiplicity but light and *alone by itself* (IV, 3, 32, 13 ss.).

The soul, then, is its true self only when it detaches itself from everything, including consciousness, which fragments it, and distracts it from its proper activity. It is a well-known fact. We can cite as an example Braque commenting on his art: "I had learned to paint in accordance with nature, and when convinced that I had to liberate myself from this model [Plotinus would have said "....of the world"], it proved anything but easy. But I set myself to work and with intuitive leaps, the *detachment* that progressively separated me from the model was thus achieved. In such moments, *we adhere to virtually unconscious imperatives,* not knowing what they may bring forth. It is an adventure. *Consciousness is not involved.*"[15]

This presence of non-consciousness within us is that which, for Plotinus, gives us access to our internal beauty which alters and enriches our vision, since we have seen, "one must come to the sight with a seeing power made akin and like to what is seen" (I, 6, 9, 29-30). And hence, we can cite the following exhortation: "Go back into yourself and look; and if you do not yet see yourself beautiful, then, just as someone making a statue which has to be beautiful cuts away here and polishes there and makes one part smooth and clears another till he has given his statue a beautiful face, so you too must cut away excess and straighten the crooked and clear the dark and make it bright, and never stop 'working on your statue'..." (I, 6, 9, 7-13).

The aesthetics of Plotinus is thus, above all, a purification of the soul, an ethical and metaphysical experience where the soul contemplates that Beauty which is penetrated by the Good. This contemplation culminates in the grace and the delight *vis-à-vis* what is and what, inside of what is, shines from a unique fire. We can also say, from a different angle, that the contemplation of Beauty is a sort of exercise, an initiation to ecstasy. Innumerable artists and writers have spoken of the deep-felt need to continually reimmerse themselves into their work, into their creative activity, which appeals to them as the abode of their most profound identity, an identity though that they themselves cannot seize, or at least, about which they cannot cannot say anything precise except may be that it somehow renders them free. It is within this singular identity, this identity without point of reference, that the artist confesses both his greatest detachement from, and his greatest communion with everything, in other words, the sense of the greatest universality.

This state which brings us closer to divinity is what Plotinus, more or less, conceives as grace, a state of perfect happiness and sufficiency. So, his aesthetics, like that of Ficin, Schiller, Ravaisson and most notably Bergson, is one of grace. Bergson wrote:[16] "In all that is graceful, we sense a sort of surrender, like a condescension. Likewise, whoever contemplates the world with the eyes of an artist, it is grace that is traceable in Beauty, and it is goodness that shows itself through grace."[17]

Summary

The aesthetics of Plotinus proceeds, according to the ancient alliance between pulchrum and bonum, from sensible beauty to the beauty of the incorporeal and then culminates in the pure vision of Beauty as such, itself invested with the infinite power of the Good, the true object of the quest. But this aes-

thetic is, above all, an inward odyssey toward oneself, for the path opened by
the Good is the one that our soul must itself open, hence, the task rests on each
of us to cease being the mirrors of evanescent realities and to veritably want to
attain to grace.

Notes

1. I am greatly indebted for the pages that follow to the translation-commentary of P. Mathias, *Plotin. Du Beau, Ennéades I, 6 et V, 8*, Paris, 1991, and to P. Hadot's, *Plotin ou la simplicité du regard,* Paris, Gallimard, 1997.

2. *Life of Plotinus,* 1, 1-2. The English translations of Plotinus throughout this paper are those of A. H. Armstrong, Plontinus, *Enneads*, in seven volumes, Harvard University Press, 1966-1988.

3. *Cf.* E. Panofsky, *Idea. Contribution à l'histoire du concept de l'ancienne théorie de l'art,* trad. H. Joly, Paris, Gallimard, 1983, 44: "Plotinus, for whom the progression that leads from unity to multiplicity also leads from perfection to imperfection, is explicitly and passionately opposed to this definition of beauty which was associated with 'the balance of proportions' and 'the beauty of coloris', by classical antiquity and the Renaissance.'"

4. *Cf.* E. Panofsky, *ibid.,* 39: "the philosophy of Plotinus undertakes to obtain for the 'inner form' the metaphysical right to merit the status of a 'perfect and supreme model.' Plotinus had, in effect, deliberately protested against the attacks Plato had formulated concerning 'mimetic art.'"

5. The Zeus of Pheidias, an attempt by Pericles to embellish the athenian image, was considered as one of the "seven wonders of the world" in antiquity.

6. *Cf. Symposium,* 211c.

7. P. Mathias, *op. cit.,* 5.* As Plotinus teaches, it is equally true that being and beauty accompany each other, their very nature being identical (V, 8 [31], 9, 42). In this sense, we can say that Plotinus does not hold a specific concept of Beauty, and indeed, as we have seen when he disallows its identification with the concept of symmetry, he omits any such possibility. So, the beautiful cannot really be a characteristic or attribute of being, or something that can be representative of a certain category of being; rather, beauty is being, or otherwise, it is the expression or the name for the plenitude of being as such.

8. *A Portrait of the Artist as a Young Man*, The Modern Library, New York, 1916, 297.

9. V, 5, 12, 32-33. The proof of the Good's higher independence and value is as Plotinus says a little earlier (19-20): "All men think that when they have attained the Good it is sufficient for them."

10. In the *Symposium,* 211c, it is Beauty, rather, that is given as the supreme goal of the soul's ascendence.

11. *Cf.* IV, 8, 8, 1 ss.: "And, if one ought to dare to express one's own view more clearly, contradicting the opinion of others, even our soul does not altogether come down, but there is always something of it in the intelligible."

12. *Op. cit.,* 40.*

13. P. Hadot, *Plotin, Traité 38,* Paris, Cerf, 1988, 68.

14. Plato *Phaedrus,* 246 c.

15.   D. Vallier, *L'intérieur de l'art*, Paris, Seuil, 1982, 33, cited by P. Mathias, *op. cit.,* 36.*

16.   Henri Bergson, *La Pensée et le Mouvant.* Essais et conférences, Paris, Presses Universitaires de France, 1941, 280.*

17.   On the subject of the aesthetics of grace, see P. Hadot, *op. cit.,* 76 ss.; and from the same author, *Plotin. Traité 38,* Paris, Cerf, 1988, 55 ss.

*.   The above translations of the French texts are a joint effort between myself and Kiriakos Katakos.

Personal Beauty in the Thought of Plotinus

Joseph Sen

ὁ μὲν γὰρ καλὸς, ὅσον ἴδην, πέλεται [καλὸς],
ὁ δὲ κἀγαθὸς αὔτικα καὶ καλὸς ἔσσεται.
— Sappho

I. Introduction

If the contemporary literature on aesthetics were taken as a gauge, personal beauty might appear of peripheral significance to human life. For the predominant concern is works-of-art, objects rather than subjects. The interests of philosophers here diverge from the everyday, where the beauty of other persons stands as one of the most immediate and primordial experiences we can have. By contrast, the joys of art may often pass unnoticed. Why this neglect exists is a question that can only be touched upon here. Perhaps the fear is that anything will go in this area, that attention to the subject would herald an embarassing collapse into subjectivism. Another concern might be the gratuitous quality which seems to surround personal beauty, especially when this is just taken in physical terms. It may then appear as a feature either brutely given or not and so incapable of provoking the kind of admiration which matches the sense of *achievement* found in a work of art. Platonic thought has, however, always challenged the assumption that this is a subject too flimsy to warrant philosophical notice. While Plotinus may differ from Plato in the unreservedly positive status he assigns to art, both share a conviction about the philosophical vitality of personal beauty.[1] The distinctive way in which Plotinus articulates this conviction will be treated here, but Plato will never be far away from our reflections. These will centre on two themes. We will first look at the

19

way Plotinus encourages us to move away from thinking of personal beauty in physical terms by emphasising its relation to interiority. This is a familiar move in the *Enneads* . But the second theme is less documented, and needs more unfolding. It has to do with the way this understanding leads to a tacit role for *time* as the form of experience in which personal beauty comes to view.

II. Picture Imperfect

There is a tendency to take personal beauty as a fixed quota, something possessed unbrokenly, for a definite period of life. The view is taken by Aristotle in the *Rhetoric*:

> Beauty is different for different ages (ἡλŋκία). A youth's beauty consists in having a body that is serviceable for exertions in running and physical force, and pleasant to look at for gratification. This is why the all-round athletes are the most beautiful, since they are naturally suited both for physical force and for speed. Beauty in someone in the prime of life consists in having the body serviceable for exertions in war, and in being both pleasant and formidable to look at. Beauty in an old man is having a body adequate for necessary exertions, and not painful to look at, because it has none of the deformities that mark old age (*1361b7-14, trans. Irwin and Fine*).[1]

Aristotle here links beauty with three factors: the body, visuality and time. Beauty remains consistently bodily and visual but varies according to the age of the body we are considering. By so permitting each stage of life its own beauty Aristotle avoids ageism. He would not go along with the rather monochrome view prevalent in our times which allows the beauty of youth to exercise a tyrannical sway. But while allowing for this diversity Aristotle still takes the beauty of these different periods of life to be *enduring*. For example, the beauty of youth remains for a continuous stretch of time and does not just "come and go." It is as constant as the physical setting in which it is found.

Plotinus has something to say about this:

> The same bodies appear sometimes beautiful, sometimes not beautiful, so that their being bodies is one thing, their being beautiful another (*I.6.1.14-16*).[2]

Plotinus is not merely repeating Aristotle and saying that the criterion of beauty varies for different stages of life. It is a narrower temporal span to which he refers, a matter, we might say, of moments rather than years. According to

Plotinus the same physical face can appear beautiful at one time, and not beautiful at another where these times follow closely upon one another. Crucial here is that while the spatial proportions of the face remain invariant, its beauty wavers. Plotinus is suggesting that even if a face has perfect bone structure, this is neither a sufficient nor even a necessary condition for beauty, since there are times when the beauty "comes through" and others when it does not.

We may disagree with Plotinus if we think that a face is beautiful unconditionally—*over* time rather than *at* a time. Commonsense might also favour Aristotle to the extent it construes personal beauty as physical and as a constant. When beauty is present, it is there in a strong sense, for several years at a go, it has a continuous presence. It is this attribution which Plotinus is questioning.

A suggestion here why Plotinus' view might look strange to us. Perhaps when it comes to beauty the tendency is to assume that it is all the same, whether we are dealing with works of art or persons. The beauty of a painting, for example, might seem to be a property present once and for all—barring fire and vandalism. This lends the beauty a certain immobility. Emmanuel Levinas, a rather unsung Platonist, puts this well:

> Within the life, or rather the death, of a statue, an instant endures infinitely: eternally Laocoon will be caught up in the grip of serpents; the Mona Lisa will smile eternally. Eternally the future announced in the strained muscles of Laocoon will be unable to become present. Eternally, the smile of the Mona Lisa about to broaden will not broaden. An eternally suspended future floats around the congealed position of a statue like a future forever to come. The imminence of the future lasts before an instant stripped of the essential characteristic of the present, its evanescence. It will never have completed its task as a present, as though reality withdrew from its own reality and left it powerless. In this situation the present can assume nothing, can take on nothing, and thus is an impersonal and anonymous instant.[3]

Levinas here collates two arts—sculpture and painting—which Plotinus would want to keep separate. But instructive here is the claim that these works of art lack genuine temporality. The beauty of the Mona Lisa is striking but static, subject neither to change nor development. It remains interminably present within the space of the painting.

It might be retorted that this point is downright trivial! Of course, the beauty of a painting doesn't change: otherwise we wouldn't be talking about a painting![4] But the question here is whether our attitude to paintings influences our appreciation of personal beauty. For perhaps when it comes to personal beauty we tend to transpose our way of thinking about paintings to living beings. On analogy, we thereby easily but mistakenly assume that personal beauty is also a property which is spatially and statically present in a person. Thus thinking a face beautiful, we take this beauty as inalienable like the smile on the Mona Lisa. But Plotinus encourages further thought. Personal beauty may be more a *temporal* than a spatial property, and one which can come and go within moments rather than years. The perception of personal beauty here becomes more a matter of witnessing an *event* than seeing a *thing*.[5]

III. Beauty and Life

On what then does the appearance of beauty depend? What brings it to view? If we leave aside talk of "form" a more accessible lead is found in *Ennead* VI.7:

> . . . here below beauty is what illuminates good proportions rather than the good proportions themselves, and this is what is lovable. For why is there more light of beauty on a living face, but only a trace of it on a dead one, even if its flesh and its proportions are not yet wasted away? And are not the more lifelike statues the more beautiful ones, even if the others are better proportioned? And is not an uglier living man more beautiful than the beautiful man in a statue (*VI.7.22.24-32*)?

The argument is controversial but sound granted the premise that whatever has life has beauty. To the extent then that a body is animated it possesses a minimum of beauty. This means that anything which has soul is beautiful since soul is, on Platonic terms, the bearer of life. Plotinus even goes further than this, claiming that the activity of soul is causally responsible for every kind of beauty found in actions, ways of life and bodies—everything, that is, apart from Intellect and the Good where beauty and life have their proper residence.[6]

But we might still want more explanation how one living being can be more beautiful than another. Animation won't suffice here, since this only accounts for a beauty which effectively amounts to the lowest common denominator. Plotinus himself wants to make room for judgments of a higher order than this by indicating elsewhere that soul is not beautiful by itself, since otherwise it would not be possible for one soul to be wise and beautiful, and another stupid and ugly.[7] Both we might say are beautiful relative to the corpse but when compared one soul can still be more beautiful than the other.

In what then does this "additional" beauty consist if not animation? It needs to be emphasised that the concept of life is not superfluous for an explanation here so long as we keep in view the semantic depth it assumes in Plotinus's hands. For life in this context is by no means exhausted by its manifestation in living beings which only represent its tail end, so to speak.[8] Crucially for Plotinus, when we come to a richer understanding of life we see its synergy with thought:

> And every life is a thought, but one is dimmer than another, just as life . . . But perhaps men may speak of different kinds of life, but do not speak of different kinds of thought but say that some are thoughts, but others not thoughts at all, because they do not investigate at all what kind of thing life is. But we must bring out this point, at any rate, that again our discussion shows that all things are a by-product of contemplation. If, then, the truest life is life by thought, and is the same thing as the truest thought, then the truest thought lives, and contemplation, and the object of contemplation at this level, is living and life, and the two together are one (*III.8.8.17-30*).

Once again we find Plotinus turning everyday conceptions on their head. We are not to think of thought as a manifestation of life but life as a manifestation of thought. Thought here does not mean deliberate, discursive thought. It is a more effortless and holistic kind of thought which Plotinus has in mind.[9]

This identity of thought and life is usually hard for us to grasp given their apparent disjunction in the physical world.[10] It is only in Intellect that their full identity is realised. According to Plotinus this heightened thought-life comes to operate in a wise soul. And given the co-extension of life and beauty, greater beauty is therefore displayed:

> Intellect and the things of intellect are its beauty, its own beauty and not another's, since only then is it truly soul (*I.6.6.17-18*).[11]

The insistence that the soul is only truly soul when living from Intellect reminds us of the axiological dimension which the concept of soul has for Plotinus.[12] A wise soul is soul in its fullest sense so far as it shares more in the greater life and beauty of Intellect where its higher identity is found. In fine, the wise soul is more beautiful than the stupid not because the latter lacks life but because of the former's greater, indeed "abundant" (ἄγαν) life.[13]

IV. Beauty and Time

The life to which Plotinus refers so exuberantly is inwardly realised, by moving into the self, towards the beauty of Intellect and the Good. But what is discovered inwardly is diffusive. Once realised the inner life has power to appear and enliven the external which means it is no longer merely "inner." If we bear this in mind we gain a better handle upon the following remark:

> But perhaps it is not really possible for anything to be beautiful outwardly but ugly inwardly; for if the outside of anything is wholly beautiful it is so by the domination of what is within. Those who are called beautiful and are ugly within have an outward beauty, too, which is not genuine. But if anyone is going to say that he has seen people who are really beautiful but are ugly within, I think that he has not really seen them, but thinks that beautiful people are other than who they are (*II.9.17.40-46*).

Commonsense takes its bearings from physical beauty and would only grudgingly allow the concept an inward dimension. But Plotinus takes an equally one-sided stance, insisting so firmly on the priority of inner beauty that a merely external beauty is left struggling for recognition. Plotinus' thought is radical and revisionary here. He is not describing what normally passes for beauty but telling us how mistaken the usual view is and putting another in its place. He does not merely subordinate physical beauty, but denies its status altogether. The task is not to weigh priorities—the inner with the outer—for the error lies in assuming two alternatives to begin with. Only interior beauty *is* beauty.

But what are we to make of this? Plotinus is after all making sham of everyday judgments. Surely we can call someone beautiful irrespective of the wisdom and virtue in their souls? Can we make any sense of Plotinus' inversion? We would be hard pressed to make a compelling case for Plotinus given his normative tone. Even he admits that his approach is not for everyone.[14] But his perspective may not be so alien as it at first appears. Clearly there is no *patent* way in which we connect beauty with goodness or virtue. But is there an *implicit* association? Consider the case of someone initially taken for beautiful turning out on closer acquaintance to be deceitful or vicious. Would we thereafter still feel inclined to call them beautiful? We might want to stay with "attractive" but "beautiful" might no longer seem so fitting a description. Of course, we may go on using the term should we find no positive, ethical grounds for doubt: beauty in this sense is innocent until proven guilty. But might not the perception of a serious flaw warrant a change in our understanding ?

Plotinus presents another scenario. A man with an ugly face may come to be judged beautiful once we discover his virtue.[15] This brings to mind Alcibiades' eulogy to Socrates in the *Symposium*. Socrates, he tells us, is like one of those statues of the god Silensus which contain little figurines within:

> Whether anyone else has caught him in a serious moment and opened him, and seen the images inside, I know not; but I saw them one day, and thought them so divine and golden, so totally beautiful (πἁγκαλα) and wondrous, that I simply had to do as Socrates bade me (*216E- 217A*).[16]

It should be noted here that Alcibiades' discovery hardly comes in a flash but dawns upon him over time. If all he ever had to go on was Socrates' physical appearance he might well have remained repelled by the sight of the old man with the squashed nose and squinting eyes. But subsequent acquaintance brings to his notice a beauty in Socrates' words, actions and even his nonactions which, invisible to first sight, remains so to all who do not go through a like experience. But without the movement of time this acquaintance presumes Alcibiades would have never transcended his first impression.

This offers a way of uncoupling merely external beauty from its genuine, inward counterpart. While the first grabs us immediately and is largely a matter of effortless "spotting" in space, the second only makes a gradual appearance and requires discovery through the course of time. Related to this is the fact that external beauty is available to one and all; to this extent it is egalitarian but also commonplace. By contrast, insight into personal beauty is a kind of privileged access *won* through acquaintance. It is by no means given to all, its recognition being a matter of time and individual experience. Recall that Alcibiades draws attention to Socrates' beauty not by pointing in space but by recounting his various experiences with Socrates, a *history*, in other words, the details of which only he can fully know.[17]

V. Conclusion

We have so far seen how Plotinus encourages a shift away from a physical, "spatial" understanding of personal beauty to one centred on interiority. But we have also observed - and perhaps unexpectedly - how far recognition of this beauty depends upon time, although Plotinus never makes an explicit theme of this.[18] Now the goal for Plotinus is not to remain enraptured by any object of vision, however impressive. The reflexive turn is always imminent.[19] Plotinus emphasises how appreciating the beauty of another's virtue is difficult unless we have realised the same in ourselves.[20] But this requires a work of its own much akin to the artist's. Each of us must work on our own statue and this is a project which is quite senseless outside of a temporal context.

Still, the beauty eventually unveiled is always present within the self. It is not so much created as *realised*. [21] The difficulty for us here is coming to terms with Plotinus' insistence that it is not only the *feeling* but the *content* of the experience of beauty which lies within. Fathoming the mystery of this proximity is a challenge Plotinus has left to us.

Let me close with a refrain: "Isn't an ugly living man more beautiful than a beautiful man in a statue?" The rhetorical tone might look naïve since Plotinus takes for granted what is far from obvious. Some might not want to mention the two men in the same breath, so great appears their disparity. But pause for a moment and consider a world where this thought did ring true, where the ethical took precedence over the aesthetical while remaining the domain of beauty, where our living contemporaries were always more important to us than any work of art. Perhaps such a world was a reality for Plotinus. Were it to become so for us I venture to say that ours would not only be better, but even on the whole more beautiful.

Notes

1. In *Aristotle: Selections*, (Indianapolis, Ind.: Hackett, 1995), 528.
2. Translations from Plotinus' *Enneads* follow those of A.H. Armstrong in the Loeb Classical Library edition, 7 volumes, (Cambridge, Mass.: Harvard University Press, 1966-1988). *Ennead*, chapter and line numbers follow P. Henry and H.R. Schwyzer's *Plotini Opera*, 3 volumes, (Oxford: Clarendon Press, 1964, 1976, 1982).
3. "Reality and its Shadow," in *The Levinas Reader*, Sean Hand (ed.), Cambridge University Press, 138.
4. Our appreciation may, of course, change; but this is a matter of recognising what we take to have been previously present but unnoticed. There is realism here, perception is never invention.
5. This claim appears trivial if taken to mean that *eventually* personal beauty is subject to time. But Plotinus' point is stronger, personal beauty is constantly related to time, and specifically, as we shall see, the life of the soul which manifests itself in time.
6. Plotinus, *Enn.*, I.6.6.27-33; see also I.6.9. 3-7: "So that the soul must be trained, first of all to look at beautiful ways of life: then at the beautiful works, not those which the arts produce, but the works of men who have a name for goodness; then look at the souls of the people who produce the beautiful works." The drive here is from the objective to the personal. While the concern with beauty remains a shift takes place from the aesthetical to the ethical. This suggests a measured stance towards art which is close in spirit to Plato.
7. Plotinus, *Enn.*, V.9.2.18-20.
8. For the mulivalence of life see I.4.3.
9. This interplay between life and thought might be understood more concretely. Sometimes we find ourselves in a rather indifferent state of mind which is broken by a thought coming upon us suddenly. Perhaps we hear a remark or grasp an idea which gives a sort of jolt to our system, waking us up and making us feel more invigorated. Or think of the animated gestures of someone deeply engaged by what they are saying. The point here is that the presence of the thought *shows* itself in heightened animation. The proper word for this is *vivacity*.
10. "For as in the portrait (εἰκόν) of a man many things are wanting, and especially the decisively important thing, life, so in the things perceived by sense being is a shadow of being, separated from that which is most fully being, which was life in the archetype" (VI.2.7.11-14).
11. "So beauty in the soul comes by wisdom. And what is it, then, which gives wisdom to the soul? Intellect, necessarily an intellect which is not sometimes intelligent, and sometimes not intelligent, but the true intellect" (V.9.2.20-22).
12. See also V.9.13.7-8.

13. Plotinus, *Enn.,* I.4.3.24-26. See also I.4.3.33-37: "We have often said that the perfect life, the true, real life, is in that transcendent intelligible reality and that other lives are incomplete, traces of life, not perfect or pure and no more life than its opposite. Let us put it shortly; as long as all living things proceed from a single origin, but have not life in the same degree as it, the origin must be the first and most perfect life."

14. Plotinus, *Enn.,* V.8.2.45.

15. Plotinus, *Enn.,* V.8.2.38-41. A question here is whether our respective judgment alters our perception of the face by a sort of "looping" effect so that it no longer really seems so ugly. Continuing to speak of its ugliness might then be more of a concession to the common understanding of beauty rather than an expression of individual experience.

16. Trans. W.R.M. Lamb [modified], Plato, Loeb Classical Library, vol. 3, (Cambridge, Mass.: Harvard University Press, 1925).

17. Which reminds us that Alcibiades' knowledge of beauty comes through acquaintance, while ours is gained only through the description he provides.

18. Given the strong links between beauty and life we might expect some such reference to time. Ordinarily, the life of an embodied being is understood to be *its* time. We might, of course, expect more connection between beauty and eternity within a Platonic context. But we should bear in mind that eternity is not a static condition for either Plato or Plotinus. Both are keen for any notion of a transcendent reality to accomodate life, movement and activity — categories which certainly have a temporal ring to them. Plato's clearest statement of this comes in the *Sophist*: "But tell me, in heaven's name, are we really to be so easily convinced that change, life, soul, understanding have no place in that which is perfectly real — that it has neither life nor thought, but stands immutable in solemn aloofness, devoid of intelligence?" (*Sophist*, 249a, trans. Cornford). On this question A.H. Armstrong has argued that there may be a way in which the motion in the intelligible world belies the presence of a form of time (see his "Eternity, Life and Movement in Plotinus' account of Nous," in *Le Neoplatonism*, Colloque International du Centre National de la Recherche Scientifique, 1969, Royaumont, 67-74; 73).

19. Generally, Plotinus tells us that whenever we admire the beauty in another, we admire the beauty in ourselves (V.1.2.50-51).

20. Plotinus, *Enn.,* V.8.2.41-44.

21. Plotinus indicates this by employing the analogy of sculpture rather than painting for the procedure of taking away (ἀφαίρεσις) which brings the ideal self to view (see, for example, I.6.9.6-15). Sculpture is no less a creative art than painting but the activity involved is distinct. The sculptor is more concerned with the removal of the obstructions which prevent a vision of the work-to-be. The physical activity involved is negative, for its end somehow seems more present in the

stone. It's as if the sculptor is simply exposing to view what was already latent. As Aristotle remarks, we can speak of seeing Hermes in the uncarved stone (*Metaphysics* V, 1017b6-7); but could the same be said of the picture in the bare canvas?

The Beautiful According to Dionysius

Dimitrios N. Koutras

The concept of the "beautiful" (καλόν) in Dionysius' teaching is developed primarily in his treatise *"De divinis nominibus."* The influence of Plato's philosophy and of Neoplatonism, of Plotinus and particularly of Proclus, is obvious. Thus, M. Beardsley[1] is right when he says that Dionysius' view that the sensible is the correlative of the invisible derives from Plato's doctrine of Ideas, while his theory of emanation originated with Plotinus.

What we should particularly notice in Dionysius' teaching on the beautiful is the functional nature of the icon, of the symbol in the metaphysics of light, and of his doctrine of emanation.

According to ancient Greek philosophy the concept of καλόν, "beautiful," must be examined both in itself and in relation to the *good* (ἀγαθὸν). The categories of the *beautiful* and the *sublime*, as is well known, became a controversial issue during the 18th century in Western Europe. However the concept of the "beautiful" in ancient Greek philosophy had a universal meaning, which, in the field of Metaphysics, the general doctrine of Being, was not confined to the narrow framework of aesthetics.

The "beautiful" in Plato's work was found to be closely related to the *Good* as "καθ' αὐτό αἱρετόν," *i.e.* as that which should be chosen as an end-in-itself. Everything else is subjected to it as a means. The "beautiful" should never be considered as a means to something else.

In Plato's philosophy one can see that there is not only a close relationship between the Idea of the *Good* and that of the *beautiful*, but also that often the former is replaced by the latter. Both Ideas are of overriding importance in Plato's philosophy. In the *Symposium* the loving soul only meets true "beauty" at the end of its journey. It passes first through the variety of Forms of the beautiful, up to the level of the One, the μονοειδές, exactly as it appears in the

31

Republic, where the Idea of the *Good* surpasses everything, abiding beyond them all. It seems that the idea of the *beautiful* in Plato's philosophy surpasses every other being in degree, just as the Idea of the Good. One can also see that the gradation of Being, in the journey undertaken by the loving soul towards it, is found to correspond with that of the beautiful.[2]

The question, however, is: Does Plato's description in the *Symposium* of the soul's ascent through every grade of the beautiful and the lonely passage of the "sensible" on its way to the intelligible beauty, really aim at showing the gradation from the merely *beautiful* to true *beauty* or simply a parallel gradation of the Being, which is identified by him with the beautiful?

As indicated above, for the ancient Greeks the idea of the *beautiful* has a metaphysical character. This explains its close relation to, or even its identification with, the *Good* in Plato's work. There is no doubt that for Plato the *beautiful* differs from the *Good*, since the latter is beyond intellect and essence, and therefore inaccessible. Thus the "beautiful" in Plato, and later in Neoplatonism, constitutes the external appearance of the Good as well as that of Being. In fact, it is the value dimension which is actualized in the ascending process of the loving soul in every teleological approach to the beautiful.

The beautiful as an idea, according to Plato, is "ἐκθανέστατον"[3] and "ερασμιώτατον" (most "revealing" and "lovable"). By its nature, it tends to unfold on the horizon of the senses; it appears and manifests itself as light. This property motivates the love (ἔρως) of the soul. Love, as Proclus says, is "επιστρεπτικός,"[4] a return to the "beautiful."

From the preceding it becomes clear that in the anagogic function of the beautiful, as described strikingly by Plato in the *Symposium*, lies one of its ontological structural elements. At the same time, the "beautiful" also reveals a universal structure of Being, which, in opposition to the "Good," is manifested and unfolded in the sensible world, in such a way that it plays the role of mediator between the idea and the sensible reality, Being and Becoming, *appearance* and *participation*.

I consider the preceding discussion to be a necessary prerequisite for the understanding of both the Neoplatonic and Dionysian teaching on the "beautiful." It should be pointed out, however, that the image (εἰκών) plays an important role in their approach. In Plato's philosophy the *image* constitutes the *eidolon* and the *imitation* of the idea. On the contrary, in Neoplatonism, the *image* obtains an ontological significance. It does not imitate the Idea in the manner of a shadow, but reveals it.

The *image* is the product and offspring of the Form (εἶδος, ἰδέα), although it has a different character. Ontological dependence means affinity and not identity. The *paradigm*, as a formative principle, acts on the underlying matter of the image. The image is the potency and the potentiality. The paradigm is itself the actuality. The image is also found to be in a dynamic relation to the archetype; it tends to assimilate itself to it, as much as possible. At the same time the image is a kind of resemblance (ὁμοίωσις). It exists on account of its affinity with the archetype. The resemblance minimizes the degree of difference. Nevertheless, the resemblance does not remove their radical difference. Archetype and image never coincide, that is, they are never identical with each other, because, as we know, similar things always include difference.

The Neoplatonists and Dionysius repeatedly and figuratively refer to the idea of light, in order to point out the relationship between the paradigm and the image. Without light, and object not only does not seem to be beautiful, but it cannot be beautiful. Thus, the beauty of the beautiful object appears, as *splendour* (ἀγλαΐα). Light is not exclusively identified with its brightness. Light is visible, when it renders the other objects visible.

"Light," for Plotinus, distinguished as it is by its ability to approach the limits of the incorporeal[5], is placed at the top of the sensible and intelligible world. For Dionysius light and the sun are God[6] himself, who, by his rays radiates the hierarchical orders of the Angels and of the Church. Everything is immersed in the light of the superessential goodness. Light grants them life and saves them. It recalls all things from darkness. When they are illuminated through the divine light, they acquire boundaries and form. Entering the sphere of light they obtain ontological significance. By illumination they escape darkness.

Darkness is the enemy of light. The presence of light drives away darkness. Darkness is entirely *non-being*; it has no essence, nor is it a principle; it is a lack and privation of light, a sub-hypostasis (παρυπόστασις)[7] and false idea.

In connection with light, the Neoplatonists employ the notion of emanation. According to their theory beings flow from the profusion of the inexhaustible source, which does not itself undergo any ontological diminution. What is new in the Neoplatonic theory of emanation, is that it goes beyond the limits of previous Greek philosophy on substance, due to its conception of the process of emanation of the *many* form the *One*. The *One* does not only diminish in its substance, but also it contributes to the increasing of Being. Thus light, though shining upon its objects, does not undergo any diminution[8] of its substance.

The objects participating in the properties of the light-giving source, participate also in light itself and in its illuminating rays. The presence of the source allows communication with it and renders visible the surface of the objects. The colours which are visible on the surface of bodies are derived from the existing conflict between light and darkness. The visible objects convey the *splendour* (ἀγλαΐα) of their brightness from their contact with light, while, at the same time, light itself remains indivisible (ἀμερὲς)[9] and above everything else.

The concept of the icon involved in Dionysius' teaching on the *beautiful* merits particular examination. Undoubtedly his aesthetic theory follows the Neoplatonic tradition. He shares Plotinus' and Proclus' understanding of the beautiful, but his contribution to aesthetics is not so significant as that of these authors. In my view, the personal contribution of Dionysius is to be found in his efforts to reveal the symbolic and anagogic nature of the icon.

The icon, according to Dionysius, is the symbol of the intelligible world and of divinity. Plotinus expresses the same belief, but does not state it so clearly. Besides, in Dionysius the emphasis is on the principle of the "beautiful." In Plotinus, the *beautiful* originates in the *One*, or Beauty (καλλονή)[10], but emphasis is placed on the role of the *intellect* (νοῦς).[11] In Dionysius, on the contrary, the source of the beautiful is God.[12] Sensible beauty is a theophany, projected on the horizon of phenomena.

In Plato's philosophy, artistic beauty occupies a lower level than natural beauty. The physical form is closer to the idea of the "beautiful" than the artist's image. The image as an imitation is, for him, far removed from the truth and the idea of the beautiful. Aristotle, later on, will restore art, because he does not consider it to be a simple imitation; the *form*[13] of the work of art and of art itself exists not in nature, but in the artist's soul. The work of art, according to Aristotle, bears the mark of form, which derives from the soul of the artist.

It is Plotinus who first discusses the subjective nature of the work of art. The work of art as an intentional object, no longer constitutes an imitation of natural objects, but is an intellectual achievement. Art acquires a metaphysical dimension; it is a reflection of intellectual intuition, expressed in solid form. The classical conception regarding beauty as harmony and symmetry, is rejected by Plotinus.

According to Plotinus, sensible beauty is not derived from the external form of matter. Not the external, but the internal form, existing in the artist's soul is that which, completed by the intellectual intuition, manifests itself in sensible matter. Beauty, for him, is "μᾶλλον τὸ ἐπὶ τῇ συμμετρία ἐπιλαμπόμενον ἢ τὴν συμμετρίαν."[14] Thus, art, at this stage, is considered to be the hierophant of the intellect[15]; it does not imitate natural forms; it simply uses them to express metaphysical contents.[16] In this way he places the Idea in the domain of the senses, i.e. the universal in the particular. Hence for Plotinus the image becomes the sensible presence of the paradigm; it is both a *shadow* (σκιά) and a sensible form (εἴδωλον) of the idea.

In Neoplatonism "beauty" itself is the *intellect* (νοῦς), the domain of Being and truth. The intellect, according to Plotinus, constitutes the basis of intelligible beauty, the principle from which derives the beauty of the soul and of the body. The "Good" (ἀγαθόν), *i.e.,* beauty in itself (καλλονή)[17] is the transcendental principle of intelligible beauty.

As has already been suggested, the "beautiful," according to Plato, depends directly on the Idea of the "Good," on the Idea of "Goodness." The beautiful is, for him, a medium through which the good manifests itself. In the *"Philebus"* Socrates, searching for the Idea of the Good, is forced to have recourse to the *"nature of the beautiful."*[18] He attempts, through the image, the offspring, to approach its creator.

As pointed our earlier, according to Plato, beauty possesses two properties: it is "revealing" and "lovable" *par excellence* ("ἐκφανέστατον")[19] and ("ἐρασμιώτατον"). It radiates and shines like the light. Beauty and light have the capacity to display their presence; they illuminate the surrounding world. They descend on objects and make them translucent. They appear and reappear, expand and multiply in the illuminated bodies. The enlightened bodies, in turn, rise up and aim towards light and beauty. They are stimulated by beauty in the same way as the sense of sight is stimulated by light. Sight becomes the desire of illuminated bodies, the contemplation of the source of their origination, that is, Beauty in itself.

"Beauty" and "light," according to the Neoplatonists and Dionysius, have an attractive nature. Their appearance excites admiration. They attract and captivate vision as long as they do not fully reveal themselves, but simply appear in the lighted bodies. Their fascination is mainly due to the way in which they summon objects to their presence, while, at the same time, revealing and concealing themselves. The *splendour* (ἀγλαΐα) of the bodies tacitly declares their presence and invites (καλεῖ).[20] In Dionysius, in particular, light and beauty have attractive attributes. They invite everyone to a common vision.

The visible icon in Dionysius is the presence of the divine light. The light ray which originates in the divine is present in the icon. The divine itself is within the icon and the icon is the manifestation (ἔκφανσις)[21] of the divine. The icon is possessed by the divine light. The divine is entirely present in the icon, its stamp is on each impression.[22]

The relation between the divine and the icon, according to Dionysius, is analogous to that of light and its appearance. The icon is a representation of divine light, of divine beauty. It appears through its light. Without light there can be no appearance. The appearance is the manifestation of light. Light[23] is manifested in its appearance and, in some way, is diffused through it.

As a figure which reveals the divine[24] the icon refers to it in the same way as oral speech refers to internal thoughts. It becomes a symbol, i.e. a confluence of two different factors. The confluent factors join in the symbol. In the icon the confluent factors are mater and light. Through its *splendour* (ἀγλαία) the enlightened *matter* expresses perfectly its contact with the divine light.

Every symbol has, by its nature, a dual function. It functions both as a sign and as an image. As a sign it points to the signified and as an image it constitutes a self-contained reality. A national symbol, for example the flag, points to the idea of the nation, but, at the same time, the nation exists within the flag which represents it. From this point of view the icon, according to Dionysius, supports the divine. It expresses it sensibly. In the material shape the particular co-exists with the universal, the finite with the infinite.[25] The divine become sensible intuition and matter discards its humiliating nature. As a symbol of the divine the icon expresses God's concession to save the believer's senses, in a way analogous to the Logos made flesh.

The icon is metaphysically dependent on the divine, but is, moreover, enriched in its very being as representation of the divine. The incarnation of the divine through the icon symbolizes the incarnation by Christ of the eternal nature of divinity. In this way through divine consent, the divine represented by the icon somehow becomes incarnate, removing the weight of matter form the sensible form. This is the reason why the sensible beauty of the icon escapes decay, rises up and leads us to the sanctuary of the divine. It becomes the bridge connecting earth with heaven.

In reality the icon with its beauty constitutes the principle of ascending[26] return to the divine. The ascending function of the icon is due to God's illumination through the process of emanation. Again, the emanation of light from God constitutes for the icon a real ascent (ἀναγωγή).[27] which is analogous to the actualized reception of light by it. The more light the icon receives from the ocean of divine light, the easier it ascends to the divine and the brighter and more elevated it becomes.

The icon, according to Dionysius, through the sensible forms of matter and through anthropomorphic figures, guides the believer towards intelligible and immaterial divine beings. Their symbolic and anagogic character of the icon indicated the weakness of the human intellect in approaching the supersensible essence of divinity, accustomed as it is to the sensible world. It is impossible for man to know God other than through sensible objects. This is the reason for which the accidental human shapes and symbols reveal and, at the same time, conceal the divine.[28] God is hidden in the transcendent nature of his essence, within his darkness (γνόφος). The sensible symbol is unable to have a complete correspondence with the divine; it lacks the power to represent it fully. It is a constant, but fruitless effort to approach the divine. On account of this, the symbol expresses absolutely the theology of Dionysius. As a being preeminently beyond affirmation and negation in the symbol, God is affirmed and negated at the same time.

From what has been said so far it follows that, for Dionysius, the icon, in becoming a finite symbol of the divine, undertakes the task of guiding[29] and elevating man to the divine through materal shapes. This guidance, however, is difficult becuase all that the guide can do is to facilitate the wandering of our ignorance in search of the divine. The path taken is that of sensible figures,[30] but the divine remains inaccessible. Without the sensible form of the divine, the aforementioned guidance would be impossible. The form would be something indifferent, like the rest of the sensible shapes. That which intuitively leads towards the divine is its own presence.[31] In descending to the icon the divine consecrates it. The presence of the divine in the icon is similar to that of Jesus in the sacraments of the Church.[32] The worshipping character of the icon is sanctioned by its presence. As an imitation of the divine, the icon is ontologically dependent upon it. The divine descends[33] into the icon and the icon ascends to the divine. The believer's soul enters the domain of the divine symbolically and anagogically (συμβολικῶς and ἀναγωγικῶς)[34] through the icon. Thus, the icon constitutes a factual way for the soul to liberate itself from earthly things and to reach the domain of the divine.

Through the presence of the icon in its symbolic function, the fallen soul is delivered from the deceiving world of the senses and from sin, because it recognizes the divine[35] in the icon.

The unique and sacred character of the icon is grounded for Dionysius in its function as revealing the beauty of divinity. The icon, in its symbolic function, does not constitutes an arbitrary and accidental sign, but a metaphysical relation of the visible to the invisible divine, where the sensible form is indissoluble linked with the meaning and presence of the divine.

The positive evaluation of the significance of the icon, as presence and product of emanation from the *One*, the divine, from the point of view of Neoplatonism and Dionysius, seems to have persuaded the Fathers of the Greek Church to overcome the declared hostile attitude of the Old Testament towards icons. There is no doubt that Christology favored icon worship, especially the doctrine of the New Testament regarding the incarnated divine Logos. Through the incarnation of the son of God, the sensible and visible constitute the horizon, in which the invisible and the divine appear. In this way art is legitimated and the possibilities of its development are wide open in the Christian East and West.

The later Fathers of the Church have fully accepted Dionysius' universe. Icon worship finds in his person the most ardent supporter and apologist. Byzantine Churches and the Cathedrals in the West, influenced by the Neoplatonic and Dionysian doctrine, express magnificently the aesthetic climate of both doctrines. Through their tendency to elevation and attainment of power and internal lighting these Church buildings have become the icons of the intelligible and supra-intelligible world. In them we still hear the faint echo (ἀπήχημα) of a new Celestial Hierarchy.

Notes

1. M.C. Beardsley, *Histoire des théories esthétiques*, translated into Greek by D. Courtrovic and P. Christodoulidis, Athens, Nefeli, 1989, 105.
2. Plato, *Symposium*, 210d.
3. Plato, *Phaedrus*, 250d, 7-8.
4. Proclus, in *Alc.*, 30, 14, 59, Westerink.
5. Plotinus, *Enn.*, I, 6, 3, 18.
6. Migne, *PG3, De div. non.*, 1, 6, 596 A, God has the qualifications of ἀρκίφωτος πατὴρ and of φῶς.
7. *PG3, De div. nom.*, 4, 31, 732 C.
8. *PG3, De coel. hier.*, 15, 2, 329 C. Cf. Plotinus, *Enn.*, VI, 9, 9, 1-6: ...ἀμείωτον ἐν πάσαις ταῖς πανολβίαις ἑαυτοῦ μεταδόσεσι.
9. *PG3, De coel. hier.*, 15, 2, 329 A. Fire, the father of light ἔστι μὲν ὡς εἰπεῖν ἐν πᾶσι καὶ πάντων ἀμιγῶς φοιτᾷ καὶ ἐξήρηται πάντων.
10. Plotinus, *Enn.*, I, 6, 6, 21-22.
11. Plotinus, *Enn.*, I, 6, 9, 40-43.
12. *PG3, De div. nom.*, 4, 7, 701 C: God is καλὸν and κάλλος; *cf. ibid.*, 701 C-D: He is πάγκαλον ἅμα καὶ ὑπέρκαλον καὶ ὑπερούσιον καλὸν.
13. Aristotle, *Met.*, Z7, 1032, 232-1032b1.
14. Plotinus, *Enn.*, VI, 7, 22, 25-26.
15. Plotinus, *Enn.*, VI, 3, 16, 18-19: ἐπεὶ καὶ τὸ καλὸν τὸ ἐν σώματι ἀσώματον.
16. Plotinus, *Enn.*, VI, 2, 22, 36-44.
17. Plotinus, *Enn.*, I, 6, 6, 21.
18. Plato, *Philebus*, 64e, 6.
19. Plato, *Phaedrus*, 250d, 7.
20. *PG3, De div. nom.*, 4, 7, 701 C-D: καλὸν μὲν εἶναι λέγομεν τὸ κάλλους μετέκον, κάλλους δὲ τὴν μετοχὴν τῆς καλλοποιοῦ τῶν ὅλων καλῶν αἰτίας. Τὸ δὲ ὑπερούσιον καλὸν κάλλος μὲν λέγεται, διὰ τὴν ἀπ' αὐτοῦ πᾶσι τοῖς οὖσι μεταδιδομένην οἰκείως ἑκάστῳ καλλονήν, καὶ ὡς τῶν πάντων εὐαρμοστίας καὶ ἀγλαΐας αἴτιον, δίκην φωτὸς ἐναστράπτον ἅπασι τὰς καλλοποιοὺς τῆς πηγαίας ἀκτῖνος αὐτοῦ μεταδόσεις, καὶ ὡς πάντα πρὸς ἑαυτὸ καλοῦν (ὅθεν καὶ κάλλος λέγεται) καὶ ὅλα ἐν ὅλοις εἰς ταὐτὸ συνάγον.
21. *PG3, ibid,* 4, 967 C: διὸ καὶ φωτωνυμικῶς ὑμνεῖται τ' ἀγαθόν, ὡς ἐν εἰκόνι τὸ ἀρχέτυπον ἐκφαινόμενον.
22. *PG3, ibid,* 2, 5, 644 A: Images are ἐκτυπώματα τῆς νοητῆς διαδόσεως καὶ τῆς ἀύλου φωτοδοσιας.
23. *PG3, ibid,* 2, 588 C-D: ταῖς ἑκαστασχοῦ τῶν ὄντων ἀναλόγοις ἐλλάμψεσιν ἀγαθοπρεπῶς ἐπιφαίνεται.

24. *PG3, De coel. hier.*, 1, 3, 121 C-D: ...ὑλαία χειραγωγία χρήσαιτο τὰ μὲν φαινόμενα κάλλη τῆς ἀφανοῦς εὐπρεπείας ἀπεικονίσματα λογιζόμενος.
25. *PG3, De eccl. hier.*, 1, 2, 373 B: ῾ημεῖς δὲ αἰσθηταῖς εἰκόσιν ἐπὶ τὰς θείας, ὡς δυνατόν, ἀναγόμεθα θεωρίας.
26. *PG3, De coel. hier.*, 2, 4, 144 B: ...ἐπεὶ καὶ αὐτὴ (sc. ἡ εἰκών), πρὸς τοῦ ὄντως καλοῦ τὴν ὕπαρξιν ἐσχηκυία κατὰ πᾶσαν αὐτῆς τὴν ὑλαίαν διακόσμησιν ἀπηχήματά τινα τῆς νοερᾶς εὐπρεπείας ἔχει καὶ δυνατόν ἐστι δι᾽ αὐτῶν ἀνάγεσθαι πρὸς τὰς ἀΰλους ἀρχετυπίας.
27. *PG3, ibid.*, 2, 5, 145 B: The icon is an ἀναγωγὴ ὥς τι προσεθίζον ἱερῶς ἀνατείνασθαι διὰ τῶν φαινομένων ἐπὶ τὰς ὑπερκοσμίους ἀναγωγάς.
28. *PG3, ibid.*, 4, 1, 473 C: καὶ δείξει τὸ ἀληθὲς ἐν τῷ ὁμοιώματι, καὶ τὸ ἀρχέτυπον ἐν τῇ εἰκόνι, καὶ ἑκάτερον ἐν ἑκατέρῳ παρὰ τὸ τῆς οὐσίας διάφορον.
29. *PG3, ibid.*, 2, 2, 397 C: ...τὰ μὲν αἰσθητῶς ἱερὰ τῶν νοητῶν ἀπεικονίσματα καὶ ἐπ᾽ αὐτὰ χειραγωγία καὶ ὁδός, τὰ δὲ νοητὰ τῶν κατ᾽ αἴσῐησιν... ἀρχὴ καὶ ἐπιστήμη.
30. *PG3, ibid.*, 1, 5, 377 A: The symbol needs sensible forms as δεομένη τῶν αἰσθητῶν εἰς τὴν ἐξ αὐτῶν ἐπὶ τὰ νοητὰ θειοτέραν ἡμῶν ἀναγωγήν.
31. *PG3, ibid.*, 2, 2, 137 B: The divine is present in the icon ὡς τῶν ἁπλῶν ἐφ᾽ ἑαυτῶν ἀγνώστων τε καὶ ἀθεωρήτων ἡμῖν ὑπαρχόντων.
32. *PG3, ibid.*, 3, 9, 437 C: ...ἐπιτεθέντων τῷ θείῳ θυσιαστηρίῳ τῶν σεβασμίων συμβόλων, δι᾽ ὧν ὁ Χριστὸς σημαίνεται καὶ μετέχεται.
33. *PG3, ibid.*, 1, 3, 121 D: Ας ἐκτυπώματα τῆς διαδόσεως καὶ τῆς ἀΰλου φωτοδοσίας. *PG3, ibid.*, 1, 3, 124 A: They lead us διὰ τῶν αἰσθητῶν ἐπὶ τὰ νοητὰ καὶ ἐκ τῶν ἱεραπλάστων συμβόλων ἐπὶ τὰς ἁπλὰς τῶν ἱεραρχιῶν ἀκρότητας.
34. *PG3, ibid.*, 1, 2, 121 A.
35. Cf. Proclus, *in Tim.*, II, 246, 7-9: ἔστι γὰρ καὶ ἐν ταῖς εἰκόσι τὰ παραδείγματα θεωρεῖν καὶ διὰ τούτων ἐπ᾽ ἐκεῖνα μεταβαίνειν.

The Experience of Beauty in Plotinus and Aquinas: Some Similarities and Differences

Patrick Quinn

Introduction

The similarities and differences in the writings of Plotinus and St. Thomas Aquinas on the experience of ultimate beauty specifically emerge when we compare Plotinus's account of his out-of-body experience in *Ennead IV.8.1* with St. Thomas Aquinas's attempts in *De Veritate 13.1* and *ST.II-II.175.1* to analyse St. Paul's experience of rapture described in *2 Corinthians 12.1-6*. The implications for human bodiliness is a feature of both approaches and concerns the way in which the out-of-body state in which ultimate beauty is experienced is said to affect the relationship between soul and body and to determine the kind of intellectual activity that can then take place. All this raises questions about what it is to be a human soul, to be a human body, and about how it would be possible to function cognitively in the absence of the body. As a Platonist, Plotinus typically wonders how he ever came to "descend" from his out-of-body state back down into one of human bodiliness characterised by discursive reasoning, whereas for Aquinas, as a self-proclaimed Aristotelian, what is important is to know how the human mind can function independently of the sensory faculties. This difference of emphasis suggests a much more fundamental opposition between the Platonist, Plotinus, and the Aristotelian, St. Thomas, which is characterised by the former's primary interest in a non-sensory based form of intellectual activity with all the implications that this has for the nature and destiny of the human soul, whereas, for Aquinas, what always remains important throughout is the bodily-based nature of human life and thought.

41

The Platonic Context

Plotinus's description of his out-of-body experience in *Ennead IV.8.1* is shaped by his assumption that there is a psychic link between the changing corruptible and bodily world of appearance "here" and the unchanging immortal and spiritual realm of intelligible reality "There."[1] This is depicted in various ways in Plato's writings. In *The Symposium*, for example, we are told that love provides such a bonding. Diotima informs Socrates that divine love is "halfway between mortal and immortal" (*202D*), "a very powerful spirit, halfway between god and man." (*202E*). Love is a spirit of mediation, according to Diotima, and, like other such spirits, flies "upward with our worship and prayers, and (descends) with the heavenly answers and commandments" (*202e*). It forms part of the

> medium of the prophetic arts, of the priestly rites of sacrifice, initiation, and incantation., of divination and of sorcery, for the divine will not mingle directly with the human, and it is only through the mediation of the spirit world that man can have any intercourse, whether waking or sleeping, with the gods. (*Symposium, 202e-203a*).

That there is a very definite religious aspect to such mediation is clear from the above passage and this is linked to mortality and immortality and to ignorance and wisdom.[2] In Plato's *Republic*, for example, the philosopher, who is metaphorically depicted in the Cave Allegory as the released prisoner, is vocationally obliged to mediate the vision of what lies beyond the darkness of the cave to those still trapped within (*515c-519c*). In this domain of "the in-between", the objective is always to transcend this world to what is beyond and this is described in Plato's *Phaedo* as the psychic journey of release from human bodiliness towards intelligible reality. The philosophic life facilitates this possibility by mediating what is beyond to those who live in the world of change and this is given central political importance in *The Republic* as a core value of the ideal society.

These ideas, which are typically reflected in those thinkers who came after Plato and were sympathetic to his views, are consequently found in Plotinus's writings where they are represented and reformulated but, perhaps, more importantly, are attested to in the form of a personal experience in Plotinus's own life. This is the real significance of what is set out in IV.8.1.

Plotinus

Before considering his description of his out-of-body experience of beauty, it is worth recalling that Plotinus makes many references to the domain of the "in-between". The ability of the soul "to live by turns the life There, and the life here" (Enn.IV.8.4) is a frequent theme in Plotinus's writings, for example, in the following passage:

> Since this nature is twofold, partly intelligible and partly perceptible, it is better for the soul to be in the intelligible, but all the same, since it has this kind of nature, it is necessarily bound to be able to participate in the perceptible... it occupies a middle rank among realities, belonging to that divine part but being on the lowest edge of the intelligible... (and has) a common boundary with the perceptible nature...(IV.8.7).

Plotinus describes a kind of split-level form of human existence in *Ennead III.4.2* characterised, on the one hand, by an involvement in the sensory and vegetative biological processes that pertain to animal and plant life accompanied, on the other hand, by a constant reaching towards "the upper world" of pure intelligibility. He remarks on the human tendency to indulge one's animality at the expense of the higher life. The majority of us occupy a position midway between animality and divinity, he states, which lies between the extremes of those who "become like gods and others like beasts." (*Enn. III.2.8*) This mixture that we are, enables us to remain in contact with the worlds above and below and defines each of us as an intelligible universe, according to Plotinus.[3] The following passage explains this point in more detail:

> For the soul is many things, and all things, both the things above and the things below down to the limits of all life, and we are each one of us an intelligible universe, making contact with this lower world with the powers of the soul below, but with the intelligible world by its powers above and the powers of the universe; and we remain with all the rest of our intelligible part above, but by its ultimate fringe we are tied to the world below...(*Enn. III.4.3*).

This ability of the soul to remain linked to these two worlds denotes a psychic state of both equilibrium (*Enn. IV.4.3*) and tension and is reflected in a polarity of time and eternity, both of which we touch, moving up and down, as it were, between them (*Enn. III.4.3*). The tension is resolved when we are completely removed from the bodily world and this is what occurs (if only paradoxically for a time) in the kind of out-of-body state described by Plotinus in *Ennead IV.8.1* and from which, perhaps understandably, he is reluctant to withdraw.

Plotinus's Out-of-Body Experience

Plotinus describes his out-of-body experience as follows:

> Many times it has happened: lifted out of the body into myself; becoming external to all other things and self-centred; beholding a marvellous beauty; then, more-than ever, assured of community with the loftiest order; enacting the noblest life, acquiring identity with the divine; stationing within It by having attained that activity; poised above whatsoever within the Intellectual is less than the Supreme: yet, there comes a moment of descent from interception to reasoning, and after that sojourn in the divine, I ask myself how it happens that I can now be descending, and how did the Soul ever enter into my body, the Soul which, even within my body, is the high thing it has shown itself to be (*Enn.IV.8.1*).

Plotinus finds support in the Platonic writings for his own views concerning these movements of ascent and descent respectively and gives some examples of texts where Plato approves of the former and disapproves of the latter. One such reference is to *The Republic* where the released prisoner in the Cave Allegory metaphorically represents the journey of the soul from the world here below to the transcendent realm of the ineffable above. Plotinus detects Plato's disapproval in the myth of the winged soul in *Phaedrus 246b et seq.* which has shed its wings (that would have enabled it to journey on high) and sinks down to earth, settling there to take to itself an earthy and mortal body. What is clear, if we are to believe Plotinus, is that he seems to have experienced out-of-body states more than once and these were characterised by an experience of ineffable beauty and divinity which, for some reason, ceased after some time. What is interesting about Plotinus's account of these extraordinary experiences is his matter of fact style of setting out what he believes has occurred and the brevity of the description of what transpired. This may be due to the limitations of language and to the sense of awe that such a vision might inspire.

In his treatise on Beauty, he describes the kind of context in which the vision of non-sensory beauty can be experienced:

These experiences must occur whenever there is contact with any sort of beautiful thing, wonder and a shock of delight and longing and passion and a happy excitement (*I.6.4*).

We must recognise our own inner beauty, he tells us (*Enn.I.6.5*) and cultivate the right kind of disposition through purification and self-control. "Greatness of soul", according to Plotinus, "is despising the things here: and wisdom is an intellectual activity which turns away from the things below and leads the soul to those above." (*Enn.I.6.6*) It is by ascending to what is good that we are lead to the vision of beauty and leaving "all that is alien to the God" behind us, and can then see "with one's self alone" (*Enn.I.6.7*) Seeking the good necessarily means reaching the vision of primary beauty and the path to it involves a form of self-training where we become sensitive to all that is beautiful in life. We need to purify our vision and "concentrate (our) gaze and see". (*Enn.I.6.9*). Becoming good, God-like, and beautiful are identical processes for Plotinus.[4] Good and the primal beauty are on the same level and beauty exits in the intelligible world.[5]

The elegiac treatment of beauty in Ennead I.6 echoes Plato's views in *Symposium* and *Phaedrus*, with the notable difference that Plotinus claims to have experienced what he describes. Separation from the bodily world is a precondition for such ultimate experience although for Plotinus, as a Platonist, the non-bodily dimension of such an encounter does not present any serious philosophical problems. For Aquinas, however, who also accepted the validity of out-of-body experiences of this kind, albeit in a limited number of cases, there are difficulties which must be addressed, given the Aristotelian position he is happy to adopt on the natural relationship between body and soul. It is to this view that we shall now turn.

St. Thomas Aquinas on Out-of-Body Experiences

Aquinas's account of religious ecstasy is an attempt to analyse, from a philosophic point of view, the Pauline account set out in *2 Corinthians 12.1-6* which goes as follows:

> I know a man still in Christ who, fourteen years ago, was caught up—whether still in the body or out of it, I do not know; God knows—right into the third heaven. I do know however, that this same person—whether in the body or out

of the body, I do not know; God knows — was caught up into paradise and heard things which Must not and cannot be put into human language.

This extraordinary passage is taken by Aquinas to represent an actual description by St. Paul of a personal experience. Although no specific mention is made to the vision of God, Aquinas understands the Pauline event as a kind of limited beatific vision and, for our purposes here, it seems fair to say that this also would imply a vision of ultimate beauty.[6] St. Thomas's task is to try to philosophically explain how such an event could have occurred, given that, as a Christian Aristotelian, he is supposed to subscribe to the view that knowledge can only take place on the basis of a relationship between intellect and senses. The texts in which Aquinas's analysis is found are *De Veritate Q13* and *Summa Theologica II-II.Q175* and they are revealing in terms of the obstacles that confront St. Thomas when he tries to explain how such a noetic experience could occur.

The Argument

Aquinas cites the authority of St. Augustine in support of his own belief that St. Paul actually had a vision of God during the experience described in *2 Corinthians*.[7] However, Thomas is also aware of objections to the possibility of religious ecstasy, chief among which is the claim that human beings cannot act in a way that is contrary to their own nature.[8] He answers this latter objection by claiming that it is quite appropriate for human beings to be uplifted to divine reality since they are made in God's image and are therefore intellectually oriented towards God in any case although they require supernatural help to reach their goal. The same theme is pursued in *De Veritate 13.1* where rapture or religious ecstasy is defined as a state of elevation contrary to nature.[9] What is interesting in both *De Veritate 13.1* and *Summa Theologica II-II.175.1* which deal with this issue is the underlying assumption of a subsistent human soul capable of functioning intelligently in partnership with the sensory powers or independently of them, as the case may be. This is an important point to note in the writings of Aquinas since it suggests that his Aristotelianism had to be supplemented with a contribution from Platonism on certain key issues, notably with regards to how the mind continues to function in the absence of any sensory input.[10] In fact, the Thomistic treatment of the Pauline experience is strikingly Platonic in certain key respects, as we shall see.

In *De Ver.13.1*, Aquinas begins his main approach to the question of how it was possible for Paul to see God in life before death, by suggesting that, for this to happen, the human mind must be capable of transcending the physical limitations of everyday life where the intellect crucially depends on sensory experience. Indeed, in the state of rapture, the mind is able to focus its attention on intelligible realities because of something divine within us rather than because of any human disposition as such. Aquinas claims that Aristotle put forward such a view in *The Eudemian Ethics VII.14.1248a* although one might also argue that this is a very untypical Aristotelian position and represents Aristotle at his most Platonic. What is certainly true is that the claim that human beings possess an inner God-like disposition reflects a form of Platonism, and brings to mind the kind of cryptic remark attributed to Plotinus on his deathbed by Porphyry in his life of Plotinus.[11] The notion of divine illumination is also relevant here, as found in the writings of St. Augustine and later in Aquinas's own texts, especially where the latter puts forward his views on the kind of mechanism that operates during the mind's vision of God.[12]

Aquinas next proceeds (*De Ver.13.1*) to make a distinction between this divine inner disposition and sensory activity, stating that the latter does not specifically pertain to being human as such but is something shared between humans and animals. Compared with the transcendent impulse of the mind to seek out intelligible reality, the ability to grasp what is sensory is merely a function of our animality, claims Aquinas. The impression here, once again echoing Plotinus, is of a split-level quality to human life, a boundary between the divine and human animality. The tension is between an immersion in physical life and bodily concerns, and a continuing advance towards the divine realm and the vision of God. As St. Thomas describes it later in *De Ver.13.3 & 4* there is a definite conflict of interests between the mind and the senses and a competitiveness between them that can only be resolved in favour of the intellect during rapture by excluding sensory activity altogether which is consequently suspended by divine intervention during the event. The victory of intellect over the sensory powers is crucial for this process to occur at all, according to St. Thomas. He was also aware of spurious forms of rapture that seemed to replicate religious ecstasy.[13] However, he argues that these deaden and stupefy the senses rather than enhance and elevate the individual. In fact, Aquinas regards rapture as a self-authenticating form of experience but this claim also has its own difficulties.

Visio Dei in Rapture

One of the problems with regards to whether or not St. Paul could have seen God when enraptured relates to how it could ever be possible for any human being to experience the beatific vision before death. Although a number of quite formidable objections argue against the possibility of a Pauline vision of God before death,[14] it is clear from the *sed contra's* of both *De Ver.13.2* and *ST.II-II.175.3* that Aquinas relies heavily on St. Augustine's authority to justify his own conviction that Paul had had such an experience. Aquinas explains his conclusion by comparing the temporary beatific state of St. Paul to a ray of sunlight that passes through the air and then departs although how he could maintain that the vision of God could function in such a way must remain questionable. If the mind is so engrossed in God and fixated on this ultimate objective (which one presumes must be the case in the beatific vision), then surely such an experience cannot be regarded as a passing phenomenon.[15] In any case, it does seem that Aquinas was satisfied enough with his own account in which he claims that some sort of mental withdrawal is necessary if rapture is to occur. On the one hand, he insists that this abstraction does not imply that the mind is wandering (*ST.II-II.175.1*) and, on the other hand, this state of withdrawal is not identical with the kind of separation of soul and body that signifies death (*ST.II-II.175.5*). Somewhere between these two extremes, the human intellect can somehow function in a state of rapture so that the sensory powers are present but suspended, so to speak, leaving the intellect free to operate at the highest level possible, under the extraordinary influence of God.[16] This, of course, echoes the kind of view put forward in Plato's *Phaedo* (*e.g. 80c-81a*).

St. Thomas begins his discussion in *De Ver.13.3* by claiming that the relationship between the mental and physical powers is such that intense activity on the part of the mind will correspondingly weaken the effect of sensory activities. It is like someone who is so engrossed in watching something that s/he cannot hear what is being said.[17] Rapture represents a state of imbalance where the mind's focus on God occurs at the expense of sensory activities:

> But for the understanding to be raised up to the vision of the divine essence, the whole attention must be concentrated on this vision, since this is the most intensely intelligible object, and the understanding can reach it only by striving for it with total effort. Therefore, it is necessary to have complete abstraction from the bodily senses when the mind is raised to the vision of God (*De Ver.13.3*).

It is typical of Aquinas's Platonism that he should use it in this way, namely, to explain how it is possible to function intelligently in the absence of the senses or, as in the case of rapture, where the sensory powers are seen to be a hindrance to the vision of God.[18] The kind of intense intellectual activity which is required for rapture means that a withdrawal from bodily and sensory activity is intrinsic to this experience, even though bodily existence still occurs.[19]

Some Differences between Aquinas and Plotinus

One of the differences that we find in the Pauline account as compared with what Plotinus writes about his own experience is that Paul is not sure whether he was in an out-of-body state whereas Plotinus seems quite clear about what has occurred. Aquinas agrees that Paul is unsure and has argued earlier in *De Ver.13.3 ad 4* that the vision of rapture does not occur in the memory which is linked to the sensory faculties, but rather takes place in the intellect itself since it is a purely intellectual activity wholly independent of any kind of sensory input. This explains why Paul had some difficulty knowing what precisely had happened to him when he "returned" to his natural way of knowing things, *i.e.* through sensory input, memory and imagination. Plotinus does not need to address this point since he seems to be confident that his soul could function intelligently in a separate way by itself "even when it is in the body" (in a mystic state, presumably), although the mechanism by which this could occur remains unclear *(Enn.IV.8.1)*. Perhaps another difference lies in Aquinas's claim that authentic rapture can never be self-induced but is always involuntary and comes about by a special divine dispensation *(ST.II-II.175.1)*. It is possible to argue that Plotinus's writings suggest that one could train oneself, so to speak, to acquire the correct disposition to recognise beauty in itself.[20] This is not a position that Aquinas could support since he regarded the attainment of the beatific vision as a gratuitous gift rather than an ultimate goal that becomes possible to achieve by following a certain path. This is the Thomistic (and Christian) view of grace assisting nature which proclaims that human beings can have access to the supernatural.

What both Plotinus and Aquinas certainly have in common on the subject of religious ecstasy is an approach based on Platonism but whereas this is clearly acknowledged in the writings of Plotinus, this it is not the case in the Thomistic texts.[21] Recent Thomistic scholarship, however, now recognises Aquinas's Platonism, while not denying the importance of his debt to Aristotle.[22]

This Platonism arrived from a variety of sources including Pseudo-Dionysius, Proclus and Islamic philosophers such as Avicenna and Averroes whose thinking was in certain important respects shaped by Neoplatonism.[23] Without acknowledging these influences, it is very difficult to understand why St. Thomas took the approach he did in his treatment of rapture since it seems to be so much at variance with his Aristotelianism. The fact is that when Aquinas was confronted with questions about how any form of knowledge can occur in the absence of the sensory powers, he came up against the limitations of Aristotelian theory and instead found in Platonism, solutions to problems that would otherwise remain largely unresolved, at least from a philosophic point of view. This is certainly true about significant aspects of his concept of mind.[24] Perhaps it is apt to conclude by referring to Inge's comment on this point in his work on Plotinus where he suggests that "Aquinas was much closer to Plotinus than to the real Aristotle."[25] What is certainly true is that St. Thomas's analysis of rapture is an important contribution to the literature on the subject on an area of experience with which Plotinus seems to have been personally so familiar.

Notes

1. *Cf.* Patrick Quinn, Aquinas, *Platonism and the Knowledge of God*, Avebury, Aldershot, 1996, 56-57.

2. Love is said to be "neither mortal nor immortal"(*Symp.203e*) and "midway between ignorance and wisdom"(*Symp.203e-204a*).

3. *Cf. also Aquinas's concept of minor mundus in II.Sent.d.1.q.2.a.3.*

4. "You must become first of all godlike and all beautiful if you intend to see God and beauty." (*Enn.I.6.9*).

5. *Ennead I.6.9.*

6. "Beauty and the beautiful - these are one and the same in God" *De Div.Nominibus iv.lect.5*, quoted in Thomas Gilby (transl.), *St. Thomas Aquinas Theological Texts*, Oxford University Press, London, 1955, 41.

7. *Cf. De Ver.13.2* and *ST.II-II.175.3.*

8. *Cf.* the three objections cited in *ST.II-II.175.1.*

9. *"Raptus id est contra naturam elevatum" (De Ver.13.1).*

10. I have dealt with the Platonism in Aquinas's thinking in my book, *Aquinas, Platonism and the Knowledge of God* and in "Being on the Boundary: Aquinas's Metaphor for Subject and Psyche," in Karl Simms (ed.), *Ethics and the Subject*, Editions Rodopi B.V., Amsterdam, 1997, 165-172. Also cf. "The Interfacing Image of the Soul in the Writings of Aquinas," *Milltown Studies*, No.32, Autumn 1993, 70-75.

11. "Try to bring back the god in you to the divine in the All." Porphyry, "On the Life of Plotinus and the Order of his Books," in A.H. Armstrong (trans.), *Plotinus Vol.I*, Harvard University Press, Cambridge, Mass. & William Heinemann Ltd., London, 1966, 7.

12. See Vernon Bourke (ed.), *The Essential Augustine*, Hackett Publishing Company, Indianapolis, 1974, 97 and Aquinas's *Summa Contra Gentiles III.53* and *Summa Theologica I.89.1 ad 3.*

13. In *De Ver.13.1*, he says that insanity can induce states of mind in which the intellect seems to be detached from the senses. The same is true for certain kinds of illness and he also cites demonic possession as bringing about conditions which simulate out-of-body states. Aquinas was also aware of the hallucinatory effects of certain herbs.

14. A number of objections in *De Ver.13.2* relate to this point, specifically Objections 1, 3 and 4. These deny the possibility of a Pauline vision of God on the grounds that St. Paul's body was not glorified. The point here is that such an experience would have left long-term and clearly observable effects and would have had enhancing bodily consequences. Objections 2, 7 and 8 deny that Paul could have had some kind of temporary beatific vision. In *ST.II-II.175.3*, Objections 1 and 4 suggest that Paul must have imagined the event while Objection 2

bluntly states that if he had really seen God, he would never have returned to the unhappiness of this life.

15.   Aquinas may have simply assumed that it is only in the incorruptible beatified bodies of the resurrection that *visio Dei* remains a permanent phenomenon whereas in the corruptible bodies prior to death, this was not possible. *Cf. ST.I-II.4.6 ad 3.* Also *cf. Aquinas, Platonism and the Knowledge of God,* 72-73 for more on this.

16.   *De Ver.13.3 & 4* and *ST.II-II.175.4 & 5.*

17.   There are further echoes here of *Phaedo 66b-67b.*

18.   *Cf.* Endnote 10 above.

19.   There are some interesting questions here in relation to Aquinas's analysis of bodily resurrection. *Cf. ST.I-II.4.5 & 6.* Also, *Aquinas, Platonism and the Knowledge of God,* 77-78, 81-90.

20.   *Cf.Enn.VI.6.6,7 & 8.*

21.   *Cf.* Little's conclusion: "The reluctance of Thomists to acknowledge the Platonic affiliation of Thomism is founded on St.Thomas' own reluctance to acknowledge it." Arthur Little, *The Platonic Heritage of Thomism,* Golden Eagle Books Ltd., Dublin, 1949, xv.

22.   *Cf. Aquinas, Platonism and the Knowledge of God,* 1-5.

23.   *Cf.* Mary T. Clark (ed.), *An Aquinas Reader,* Fordham University Press, New York, 1988, 25.

24.   Patrick Quinn, "Aquinas's Model of Mind," *New Blackfriars,* May 1996, Vol.77, No.904.

25.   William Ralph Inge, *The Philosophy of Plotinus Vol.I* Longman, Green & Co. Ltd., London, 1918, 15.

Translations of Plato's writings are taken from Edith Hamilton and Huntington Cairns (eds.), *The Collected Dialogues of Plato,* Princeton University Press, New Jersey, 1964. The translation of *Ennead IV.8.1* is taken from Stephen McKenna (trans.), *Plotinus: The Enneads,* abridged with notes by John Dillon, Penguin Books, London, 1991. All other quotations are taken from A.H. Armstrong (trans.), *Plotinus* Vols.I-VII, Harvard University Press & William Heinemann Ltd., Cambridge Mass & London, 1966-88. Passages taken from Aquinas's *Summa Theologica* is taken from The Fathers of the English Dominican Province (trans.), *Summa Theologica,* Burns & Oates, London, 1947-48. Quotations from Aquinas's *De Veritate* taken from James V. McGlynn SJ. (trans.), *St. Thomas Aquinas The Disputed Questions on Truth,* Henry Regnery Company, Chicago, 1952-54. The Pauline Corinthian Text is taken from Alexander Jones (gen.ed.), *The Jerusalem Bible,* Darton, Longman & Todd, 1966.

The Sense of Beauty (κάλλος) in Proclus the Neoplatonist

Christos Terezis and
Kalomoira Polychronopoulou

I. Introduction

In the whole framework of Proclus' attempt to explain the way in which the metaphysical and natural world exist and function, description and interpretation are used as methodological instruments. His aim is to formulate a theoretical system which is not based merely on scientific analysis and research, but also —or perhaps mainly— on interpretative approaches. As a true metaphysician he is not thoroughly satisfied with cognitive schemata which are introduced by the scientific logos, although he respects and uses them. He believes that the scientific logos does not constitute a sufficient grounding for those presuppositions, which when interpreted could satisfy a consciousness that does not remain at the same level of perceptive facts. Of course he recognizes the necessity of such a rational description, but he mainly argues for a transcendental reality, which makes this consciousness possible and provides it with its final and substantial meaning. It concerns that entity, which is at the same time the primeval and the final cause of the world.[1] The main factor of Proclus' vision is beauty, as a fundamental and not as an acquired element of beings. Proclus elaborates on this issue in many of his discourses and mainly in his comments on Plato's *Timaeus* (Τίμαιος). In that work he presents beauty as a means or a component which the creator gives to the created.[2] He briefly analyses the general principles of this gift in his commentary Plato's *Alcebiades I* (᾿Αλκιβιάδης Α᾿). There he attempts to relate Aesthetics with Ethics and Ontology. The present paper focuses on the relationship between Ontology, Aesthetics and Ethics in Proclus.

II.

First, Proclus maintains that every metaphysical entity which has order and symmetry, also comprises the qualities of justice (defined as equality) and beauty. For Proclus, beautiful entities possess these moral properties since the beginning of time. He also claims that entities which have equality also possess beauty. On the other hand, unequal entities are regarded by Proclus as non-symmetrical and ugly. Proclus further adds that such entities lack inner cohesion.[3] Furthermore, he attempts to describe the relation between the metaphysical and the natural world. According to Proclus, beauty is not ascribed to anything else but to the archetypical "form"(εἰδῶν), which has predominated over matter. So, if we approach matter in its original condition, then we realize that it is obscene and totally without beauty. Consequently, whenever "form" is dominated by matter, then according to Proclus, it has been governed by disgrace and lack of shape. This also means that the conditions of matter have been imposed upon it and the "form" exists now in a way similar to that of the matter which then in turn constitutes its reception place in the formation of the body. Therefore, "forms" don't exist in the condition they should exist from their own nature. So, the metaphysical archetypes lose their strength and are no longer able to accomplish their formative mission.[4]

It is also obvious that Proclus is a dualist in the sense that his system provides both an ontological account and evaluating criteria. Every body is comprised of shape which has been received from the "form" and by the matter, which has received the shape. So, the body becomes aesthetically significant only then, i.e. when the ontological purity and authenticity of the "form" destroys or transforms the disorder and the lack of restraint which is attributed to matter. Consequently, the natural world becomes a negative force when it fails to receive the abilities and perspectives provided by the "form" In addition he highlights the aesthetical dimension of the bodies through a peculiar combination of Platonism-Aristotelianism. This combination is consonant with his aesthetic theory. According to him matter adheres to the "form," either from the beginning, on the strength of its own nature or at a later stage. Matter cannot "form" a body on its own; on an aesthetic level it can be nothing but deprivation.[5]

Consequently, Proclus remarks that beauty is not only to be found in bodies, but also exists in the intellectual realm of human existence. In order for beauty to reveal its aesthetic value and potential in this area, it is absolutely necessary that some of the hierarchies and interventions mentioned above come into force. So, beauty appears in the soul only when logical powers predominate over illogical ones. Human life has certain attributes which must be dominated by the power of logos and prudence in order for them to dismiss their ugliness and the disproportion. But the main reason why beauty exists in the soul is justice, because justice contains moderation, limit and perfection.[6] These three elements are given to the soul by justice. Apparently, what is implied here is that logical elements are alien to passions and instincts and that mental purity is gained only when man overcomes his animal nature. The beauty of the soul arises from a morally righteous life, which on the one hand provides true proportions in volition and action and on the other hand eliminates chaotic situations with regard to choice and behavior.

For Proclus, all those attributes which guarantee a logical organizing dimension of things do not differ from each other in the quality of their natural origins. They all reflect the natural and authentic state of those things which arise from a common ontological source. That can be ascertained not only by the close affinity and interrelation between the effects of the attributes mentioned above, but also by their range. Justice, for example, ensures analogy, harmony and unity, not only on the anthropological but also on the cosmological level. The creator used justice as his instrument and thus ensured the coherence to the cosmological function. In this way beauty became sensible.[7] This account leads us to assume that this Neoplatonic philosopher indirectly claims that there should be a holistic consideration of the things as far as their positive existence is concerned. Beauty needs in any case the three following presuppositions: a) natural state, b) precise coherence, c) an integrated effect. Similar presuppositions must be noticed on the other values as well.

Consequently, Proclus examines the issue of the question of whether beauty is by nature (φυσει) or by convention (θεσει).Thus posing the question of whether beauty is substantial or accidental. In other words does beauty exist *a priori* or is it formed *a posteriori*? Is it or is it not in relation to the attributes which have been set out by human understanding? Proclus remarks that if we accept the statement that it is by human by convention, then it means that it is proper (πρεπον) and perhaps that it derives from the human belief, that it is an opinion based on the criteria of a surface perception.[8] At this point there is a clear reference to an *a posteriori* subjectiveness or an idealism, whose criteria and origins are purely gnosiological. The thinking subject sets its presuppositions in anteriority to the object and defines it with its attributive determinations. Proclus rejects gnosiological anteriority and ontological relativism and so he believes that beauty is lovable on its own nature. For man beauty is compulsively lovable. It can be noticed that there is a human inclination to show interest and to accept whatever provokes love and admiration. This inclination is not only noticeable in relation to authentic beauty. It is also noticeable in relation to the beauty of lowest ontological and aesthetical levels. This beauty, although it is bound up with images, also has the ability to motivate the human soul to admiration. And although it is not real, it is surprising as a phenomenon, because its depiction of divine beauty is sensible, *i.e.* visible.[9] At this point it is also obvious that Proclus revaluates the world of experience, at least in relation to its authentic potentialities and their preconditions. But we should keep in mind that Proclus still believes in the unstable and changeable character of this world. He accepts that "appearances," up to a certain degree, are authentic reactions of "being." For Proclus, appearance is connected with those values which can cause genuine emotional reactions and movements in the human consciousness.

In the following stage of his argument Proclus attempts to support his viewpoint by an etymological analysis of the term of beauty. He further remarks that beauty is defined as that which attracts to itself, as that which attracts those who behold it and as that which is intrinsically loveable. Therefore, it is essential for man to express his interest in beauty because this is the only way to reach it aesthetically using the superior elements of his being or soul. The most genuine expression of man's inner nature is love, which firmly and with no deviation leads to the enjoyment of beauty.[10] Proclus believes that whatever is worthy of desire, is good and thus lovable. Consequently, the real good is the subject of real interest and love, namely it has the highest priority in the scale of ontology and in the scale of values.[11] Therefore, if beauty is particularly lovable as a phenomenon, this applies all the more so to the case of referring to what is genuinely beauty. Thus formulating some logical combinations, the philosopher observes that, if whatever is beautiful is particularly lovable then it is the object of human reference and if this object is decent then whatever is good is decent, too.[12] Of course the combination above is based on what Proclus considers as real facts. However, through this combination, beauty is given authentic ontological features, which stimulate the human inner nature to possess the virtue of fulfillment.

In addition, Proclus establishes a gradation from lower levels of beauty to higher ones. This of course follows the Platonic models and hierarchical principles. He remarks that we should be interested in beauty since in the first place it exists in the phaenomena, in our actions, in our professional occupations, in the sciences and in our virtues. It is very important to consider all these phaenomena and activities not simply as such, but from the aesthetic point of view. The next step is the beauty of the mind and the highest point is divine beauty which is in itself beauty.[13] With such a grading it is clear that Aesthetics is not an autonomous theoretical discipline, but is to be viewed in relation to Ethics, Gnosiology and Ontology. In other words these three disciplines comprise Aesthetics as a fundamental and supplementary element.

In conclusion, it must be noted that Proclus insists on the distinction between beauty in itself and acquired beauty. By beholding beauty in itself we behold elements of the highest level. Beauty is good in itself. Beauty in itself is the cause of symmetry in the soul. Whenever symmetry exists in the soul, it ensures the predominance of the superior conditions over the inferior ones. The former ones are reforming and purifying conditions that provide the grounds for expiation.[14] It is the ground for the perfection and purity of the soul of the humans. So the anthropological issue acquires a highly aesthetic dimension as long as man has become a carrier of metaphysical principles or he has at least come closer to them.

III. Conclusions

According to all we have examined above, we come to the three following confirmations:

I. When Proclus extends the beauty as a superior aesthetical category, he is not only referring to the existence of beings, but also to the way in which they exist. When he describes the metaphysical and the natural world with beauty as their substantial property, he reveals them as ontological systems, which are characterized by logical order and organization, from which anything, having to do with chaos and lack of rhythm is absent.

II. He emphasizes that the right aesthetical vision of beings presupposes the understanding of their special and profound quality. He therefore suggests an approach which will be raised to the substance of beings by exceeding the level of the phenomena. The question here deals not only with the identification of beauty, but also concerns the search for the way elements which express fullness are interrelated on their own or in combination to one another.

III. He believes that beauty has an authentic value, meaning that it is found in the level of the absolute. Beauty is not influenced by fortuitous or occasional events, but possesses an archetypical character. Its sources are in the metaphysical, from which it derives its definitions. By claiming that the metaphysical beauty is the presupposition of the natural world the philosopher gives a positive attribute to the beings which exist in the world of experience. In this frame Plato is preserved. The natural world makes sense because it participates in the metaphysical world. The former world is not autonomous and it does not provide its conditions, in order to construct itself to a logical system.

Finally, we will try to give a definition of aesthetics based on the text of Proclus, which we have analyzed: Aesthetics is the theoretical branch, which transcends the world of ''appearance'' and tries to find the world of "being." It starts from the confirmation that there is an archetypical system of values, which is fixed and absolute, and so it offers the principles and the rules of perfection. He maintains that the metaphysical world is comprised of rules and therefore human consciousness is obliged, to adopt and use regulated schemata of thought and interpretation, so as to function aesthetically. This occurs not only when consciousness comprehends but also when it enjoys the metaphysical world itself and its results in the natural world. Consequently, aesthetical interpretation means searching and formulating rules which regulate, ontologically speaking, the composition of metaphysical and natural beings and, from a gnosiological point of view, giving to the human thought the strict criteria for understanding.

Notes

1. This is a reference to the "One" ("Εν) or the "Good" ('Αγαθόν). For further comments see the second book of Proclus' work *About Plato's Theology* (Περί τῆς κατά Πλάτωνα Θεολογίας). Also, A. J. Festugière; *La Révélation d' Hermès Trismégiste*, vol. IV, Paris 1994, 1-140.

2. See *Commentary on theTimaeus of Plato* ('Υπόμνημα εἰς τόν Πλάτωνος Τίμαιον), II, 328.16-402.12.

3. See *Commentary on the First Alcibiades of Plato* ('Υπόμνημα εἰς τόν Πλάτωνος Πρῶτον 'Αλκιβιάδην), 326.8-11. For the metaphysical bases of the justice in Proclus, see *About Plato's Theology*, IV, 43.24-45.15.

4. See *Commentary on the First Alcibiades of Plato*, 326.12-17: "Τό ἐν σωματι καλόν οὐκ ἄλλως ὑφέστηκεν ἤ ὅταν τό εἶδος ἐπικρατῇ τῆς ὕλης. "Ακαλλης γάρ αὕτη καί αἰσχρά, καί ὅταν κρατηθῇ τό εἶδος ὑπ' αὐτῆς, αἴσχους ἀναπιμπλαται καί ἀμορφίας καί οἷον ἀνείδεον γίνεται τῇ ὑποκειμένη φύσει συνεξομοιούμενον." For the theory of "forms" in Proclus' work, see L.J. Rosan, *The Philosophy of Proclus*, New York 1949, 158-163; S. Gersh, *From Iamblichus to Eriugena*, Leiden 1978, 86-106; J. Trouillard, *La mystagogie de Proclos*, "Le belles lettres," Paris 1982, 143-186.

5. For the way in which Proclus approaches in a synthetical manner the views of Plato, Aristotle and the other ancient Greek philosophers, see A. Kojève, *Essai d' une histoire raisonée de la philosophie paienne*, vol. III, Paris 1973.

6. See *Commentary on the First Alcibiades of Plato*, 326.17-25. Also,*Commentary on the Timaeus of Plato*, III, 234.9-238.29.

7. See *Commentary on the First Alcibiades of Plato*, 327.2-20: " "Αμα τό δίκαιον τέλειόν ἐστι καί μέτριον καί ὡρισμένον καί καλόν καὶ οὐ διέστηκε ταῦτα ἀπ' ἀλλήλων κατά φύσιν ..." Also, *Commentary on the Timaeus of Plato*, I,409.7-30.

8. See *Commentary on the First Alcibiades of Plato*, 327.21-328.5; *Commentary on the Parmenides of Plato* ('Υπόμνημα εἰς τόν Πλάτωνος Παρμενίδην), 809.28-811.31.

9. See *Commentary on the First Alcibiades of Plato*, 328.5-11: "Τό καλόν ερἀσμιόν ἐστι κατά τήν αὐτοῦ φύσιν, ὅπου γε καί τό ἔσχατον κάλλος ὡς ἐν εἰδώλοις φερόμενον ἐραστόν ἐστι καί κινεῖ τάς ψυχάς πρός αὐτό καί ἐκπλήττει φαινόμενον, ἴνδαλμα φέρον τοῦ θείου κάλλους." Also *About Plato's Theology*, I, 108.9-109.2. A similar view is encountered in the platonic dialogue *Symposium*, 204 c4.

10. See *Commentary on the First Alcibiades of Plato*, 328.14-17 "Διάτό καλεῖν εἰς ἑαυτό κέκληται καλόν εἴτε διά τό κηλεῖν καί θέλγειν τά πρός αὐτό δυνάμενα βλέπειν, ἐραστόν ἐστι κατά φύσιν. Διό καί ὁ ἔρως πρός τό καλόν ἄγειν λέγεται τό ἐρῶν." Also, *About Plato's Theology*, I, 87.4-24. A

similar etymological analysis is encountered in the Platonic dialogue *Kratulos*, 416b6-c11.

11.   See *Commentary on the First Alcibiades of Plato*, 328.17-329.21. Similar views are found in Platos (*Menon*, 77b2-78b2) and Aristotle (*Nicomachean Ethics*, A.1,1094 a 3).

12.   See *Commentary on the First Alcibiades of Plato*, 330.1-9. about the relationship between the beauty and the good, see *About Plato's Theology*, I, 109.10-16.

13.   See *Commentary on the First Alcibiades of Plato*,332 10-17. The variety and the hierarchy with which Proclus presents beauty reminds the Platonic dialogue *Republic*, 210a4-211c9. Similar views are also found in Plotinus, *Enneads*, I, 6(1),4.7-9;5.2-5; 9.3-6. See also Ev. Moutsopoulos, *Les structures de l'imaginaire dans la philosophie de Proclos*, "Les belles lettres," Paris 1985, 48-51.

14.   See *Commentary on the First Alcibiades of Plato*, 333.13-334.18 and 338.14-339.7.

The Vigil of the One
and Plotinian Iconoclasm[1]

Frederic M. Schroeder

Introduction

In a dream, the dreamer sees himself as in a dream landscape. Yet the self that he sees is not himself as sentient subject, but himself as dream object, as one among the objects in the landscape of reverie. The suspension of the ego belongs to the pleasure of a dream. To understand this, we may engage in the following thought experiment. I have a daydream of travelling to Crete to see Knossos. When I in fact take that trip and go to visit Knossos, there will be many differences between the real life experience and the dream, most occasioned by the vagaries of ego awareness. I shall at the same time be thinking of whether there is time to catch the bus back to Rethymno, try to remember whether I left something at the hotel, or worry about a person or situation at home. In the daydream, all of these factors are missing, because the ego that is occupied with such things will have been suspended: only the dream image of myself, a part of the idyllic landscape, will make the journey.

Plotinus engages in the following experiment (5.8.10-11). He invites us to self-knowledge. If we are unable to see ourselves, perhaps a god will help us toward that vision:

> Further, one of us, being unable to see himself, when he is possessed by that god brings his contemplation to the point of vision, and presents himself to his own mind and looks at a beautified image of himself; but then he dismisses the image, beautiful though it is, and comes to unity with himself, and, making no more separation, is one and all together with the god silently present, and is with

him as much as he wants to be and can be. But if he returns again to being two, while he remains pure he stays close to the god, so as to be present to him again in that other way if he turns again to him. (5.8.11.1-9).[2]

Bréhier comments that this passage is like a dream state in which the dreamer, half awake, is aware of his dream and wishes to re-enter it.[3] Gurtler, recalling Bréhier's dream comparison, remarks on the similarity of the experience described in this passage and the appreciation of Byzantine art, in which the viewer of the art is no mere spectator, but is himself absorbed into the community created by its inverse perspective, with the vanishing point behind him, interacting with the objects within it.[4] Presumably Gurtler sees a similarity between the Byzantine painting and the dream experience in the inclusion of the self as one among the objects of the icon. We notice in this passage that the self seen in the state of consciousness that precedes total loss of self-consciousness is an image, an image rendered preturnaturally beautiful. That icon of the self must be iconoclastically dismissed before union with the ground of the empirical self is achieved.

In fact, Plotinus does not accord to dreaming the positive role that Bréhier's use of it might suggest. He does use dreaming to illustrate the relationship between our ordinary waking consciousness, as a dream, and noetic awareness, which is an awakening.[5] Nevertheless, when we make the necessary equation, our thought experiment about dreaming has its uses for our understanding of noetic conscsiousness in Plotinus.[6]

In the above passage, surely the god who helps the contemplative to self-knowledge is that contemplative's own higher self.[7] Yet that self has, as it were, an objective presence among the Forms (I shrink from introducing the subject-object distinction into this context, but wish only to suggest the absence of aesthetic awareness). Plotinus suggests that when we enter into union with that god, we have no awareness of the god as other. Indeed our consciousness transcends all duality, just as as a healthy person need have no awareness of health, while a sick person will have an acute awareness of health (or its absence) (5.8.11.24-33).

Where the experience of waking consciousness can, in Plotinus' description in 5.8.11, resemble what we would think of as a dream experience, what is for Plotinus a lapse into the dream world of sense might seem to us like waking up:

Many times it has happened: lifted out of [awakened out of (ἐγειρόμενοc)] the body into myself; becoming external to all other things and self-encentred; beholding a marvellous beauty; then, more than ever, assured of community with the loftiest order; enacting the noblest life, acquiring identity with the divine; stationing within It by having attained that activity; poised above whatsoever within the Intellectual is less than the Supreme: yet, there comes the moment of descent from intellection to reasoning, and after that sojourn in the divine, I ask myself how it happens that I can now be descending, and how did the Soul ever enter into my body, the Soul which, even within the body, is the high thing it has shown itself to be (4.8.1.1-11). [8]

Here Plotinus describes his waking consciousness of the world of Platonic Forms and his fall from that vigil into the sleep or dream of the world of sense.

Plotinus applies to wakefulness language that would apply well to the dream experience as we have explored it in our thought experiment:

If then he [the One] did not come into being, but his activity was always and a something like being awake, when the wakener was not someone else, a wakefulness and a thought transcending thought which exists always, then he is as he woke himself to be (ἔστιν οὕτως, ὡς ἐγρηγόρησεν). But his waking transcends substance and intellect and intelligent life; but these are himself. (6.8.16.30-35).

Here the awakener and the awakened are one and the same, the self does not exist apart from the experience of waking. There is a total absence of distraction. The vigil of the One, of course, would be the summit of wakefulness.

Plotinus encounters a difficulty in explaining how the soul, which is by nature impassive, can be affected by passions (3.6.5). The source of the affections is not in the external world, but in the soul itself. If the soul turns from the world of sense to the higher world of Forms, it will be free of affections just from this new orientation. The process is compared to an awakening in which the soul realizes that it is itself that generates the images in its dreams and at that moment is awakened:

It is as if someone who wanted to take away the mental pictures seen in dreams (τὰς τῶν ὀνειράτων φαντασίας ἀναιρεῖν) were to bring the soul which was picturing them to wakefulness (ἐν ἐγρηγόρσει), if he said that the soul had caused the affections, meaning that the visions as if from outside were the affections of the soul (3.6.5.10-13).

In the experience of awakening, the dream images are abolished. This awakening of the soul demands a purification. However, the purification is not simply a freedom from the body, but a fundamental change in the soul's attitude:

> The purification would be leaving it alone (καταλιπεῖν μόνην), and not with others, or not looking at something else or, again, having opinions which do not belong to it—whatever is the character of the opinions, or the affections, as has been said—and not seeing the images (μήτε ὁρᾶν τὰ εἴδωλα) nor constructing affections out of them (3.6.5.15-19).

We should notice here, for the sake of the rest of our argument, the association of the word "alone" (μόνην) with the dismissal of images. For the soul to be "alone" is to be free of images.

Background in Plotinus' Rhetorical use of Imagery

Everyone knows that Plotinus makes an abundant and compelling use of images. Let us consider a rhetorical (as opposed to philosophical) use of imagination.[9] Marcus Aurelius makes a use of imagery designed to overcome passion (*Meditations* 4.32). The disciple is invited to an act of imagination in which he summons before his mind the court of Vespasian and all of its intrigues. He then is further invited to reflect that Vespasian and all of his court are now dead. The effect of this meditation is to create an affective displacement. As he returns to his own world, the objects of his hatred or envy will no longer arouse his passions. Engagement with one's own passions is replaced by engagement of the mind and soul with the image of Vespasian and his court. That engagement induces a detachment from one's own passions. Plotinus makes a similar use of imagery in ethical contexts.[10] He makes use of a rhetorical, as opposed to a philosophical, use of imagination.[11]

Observing the conventions of negative theology, Plotinus will advance an image of intelligible reality, only to subtract from it those features which would suggest that it is corporeal. Thus in 6.4.7, Plotinus, to demonstrate the omnipresence of Soul, advances the image of a transparent sphere containing a luminous centre. The centre of the sphere illumines the circumference without itself being divided over the surface that it illumines. Then Plotinus asks us to subtract the corporeal nature of the luminous source to avoid the associations of corporeality.

Then Plotinus, having generated the image of the sphere, puts it to another use:

> Suppose that someone took away the bulk of the body but kept the power of the light, would you still say that the light was somewhere, or would it be equally present over the whole outer sphere? You will no longer rest in your thought on the place where it was before, and you will not any more say where it comes from or where it is going, but you will be puzzled and put in amazement when, fixing your gaze now here and now there in the spherical body, you yourself perceive the light (6.4.7.32-9).

Now we are seeing the omnipresence of the Soul, not as objective observers, from without, but from within. The image, which was meant to serve the purposes of discursive thought, has now become a contemplative instrument. It has something of the character of a Iamblichean *sunthêma*.[12] What was intended to serve the purposes of negative theology has become a means of purgation and affective displacement as the image is advanced and withdrawn.

Plotinus argues against the sceptical position that self-knowledge must lead to infinite regress (5.3.6). If mind consists of a knowing part and a known part, then the knowing part must know itself as knowing part and subdivide again. This process leads to infinite regress. Yet discursive thought (διάνοια) means to think through or by means of Intellect (διὰ νοῦ) and in Intellect there is no division between knower and known. Now apodeictic argument will have necessity (ἀνάγκη), but it will lack persuasion (πειθώ). Yet if we become truly conscious of the iconic nature of our own thought, we will transcend discursive thought and enter into union with Intellect. By bringing the operations of the discursive mind to awareness and gaining detachment from them, we become engaged in noetic awarenss. In that state, since we no longer think discursively, but noetically, we will be persuaded of the truth of a discursive argument no longer even part of our awareness. Persuasion and necessity will have joined hands. The image of our own intellection has served as a vehicle of transcendence and union. This persuasion is verbal. Yet it consists in an *ekphrasis* of an image already advanced by reason.

Imagination, Perspective, and Iconoclasm

In 5.8.9 Plotinus asks us first to imagine[13] that the universe is set inside a transparent sphere and then to substract from the sphere its corporeal mass and all sense of place. Plotinus urges us to invoke the god who created that of which we have a mental picture:

> And may he come, bringing his own universe with him, with all the gods within him, he who is one and all, and each god is all the gods coming together into one; they are different in their powers, but by that one manifold power they are all one; or rather, the one god is all; for he does not fail if all become what he is; they are all together and each one again apart in a position without separation, possessing no perceptible shape—for if they did, one would be in one place and one in another, and each would be no longer be all in himself—nor does each god have parts different from himself, nor is each whole like a power cut up which is as large as the measure of its parts. (5.8.9.14-24).

In late antique and early medieval art, the vanishing point is located behind the spectator, rather than in the painting itself, so that perspective is measured, not from the viewer, but from the central figure in the piece. The picture provides an aerial view of the scene in which all the objects are encompassed in their own world. The effect of this is to include or enclose the spectator within the horizon of the painting and among its objects. By contrast, in the art of the Renaissance, the vanishing point is located in the painting, so that the spectator has an "objective" view of the scene and stands outside it. The late antique and early medieval perspective is known to art historians as the natural perspective, the perspective of Renaissance art as the artificial perspective.[14]

Grabar argues that the natural perspective represents Plotinus' view of visual perception.[15] Gurtler finds a text that better supports Grabar's position than the ones that he advances:

> But as it is, the whole object is seen, and all those who are in the air see it, from the front and sideways, from far and near, and from the back, as long as their line of sight is not blocked; so that each part of the air contains the whole seen object, the face for instance; but this is not a bodily affection, but is brought about by higher necessities of the soul belonging to a single living being in sympathy with itself (4.5.3.32-38).

Gurtler remarks:

> Plotinus is actually arguing that sight is not some affection in the air that presents us with an image that is like a picture in the classical renaissance perspective, with everything plotted out in a geometric grid to indicate relative distance

and size. Rather, sight sees the whole object, but from the object's point of view. That is, as wholly visible from any vantage point. Or, more precisely, both object and observer are seen or seen from any possible perspective because they are both involved in a living being much greater, the universe as a whole. Thus, one cannot have the situation of classical renaissance perspective with subject and object frozen in time and space as if in a photograph. For Plotinus, the subject cannot be a mere observer, but must be involved in their very environment he perceives, and the object, on the other hand, cannot be a mere datum of perception, but must constitute with the subject the perceivable world.[16]

In the image of the sphere in 5.8.9, Plotinus is presenting us with a noetic universe in which there is no fixed point of observation: all is transparent to all. In another passage, Plotinus shows the theurgic purpose of art:

> And I think that the wise men of old, who made temples and statues in the wish that the gods should be present to them, looking to the nature of the All, had in mind that the nature of soul is everywhere easy to attract, but that if someone were to construct something sympathetic to it and able to receive a part of it, it would of all things receive soul most easily. That which is sympathetic to it is what imitates it in some way, like a mirror able to catch [the reflection of] a form. (4.3.11.1-8).

Gurtler remarks on "the explicit character of the complex of temple and statues as a microcosm, a miniature of the sense world that focuses the presence of the divine."[17] We can only think that it is a sensible image of the noetic sphere of 5.8.9. In this passage, as in 5.8.9, the image contains the seeds of its own destruction, even as it realizes its anagogical purpose. Both the temple and the human mind reflect intelligible beauty, *i.e.*, the relationship is vertical as well as horizontal (if we must use spatial metaphors). Thus the end of the temple is to make the human mind reflect the intelligible beauty that it itself reflects, thus introducing its own obsolescence. The very presence of the divine that the sensible beauty of the temple summons induces the absence or vanishing of the image. That the temple and statue complex forms, together with the human observer, a community effects the transition to the world of noetic awareness in which there is no fixed point of observation and the community is created by the continual establishment of the vanishing point behind the spectator. In another passage, 4.3.9.29-38, Plotinus compares Soul in its creation of the sensible world to an architect:

> There came into being something like a beautiful and richly various house which was not cut off from its builder, but he did not give it a share in himself either; he considered it all, everywhere, worth a care which conduces to its very being and excellence (as far as it can participate in being) but does him no harm in his presiding over it, for he rules it while abiding (μένων) above. It is in this sort of way that it is ensouled; it has a soul which does not belong to it, but is present to it; it is mastered, not the master, possessed, not possessor. The universe lies in soul which bears it up, and nothing is without a share of soul.

The house, then, is in the architect and the world is in the Soul that creates it. If we interpret 4.3.11 in the light of this passage, we may see that, while Plotinus says that the gods are present to the complex of temples and statues, it is really they that are in the gods, *i.e.*, the gods are their place. The divine is the place which contains both the art and ourselves and our experience of the art is one in which the angle of vision and distance are measured from the divine and not ourselves. If I may return to the dream image with which I began, our presence in the visionary landscape is, not that of a sentient subject, but of an objective dream figure contained by the landscape itself.

Plotinus always uses art in metaphor and never addresses the subject directly. The reason is that the object of art has its place in the divine and vanishes into the luminosity that contains it. Plotinus illustrates the soul's vision of the One:

> Like a man who enters into the sanctuary and leaves behind the statues in the outer shrine; these become again the first things he looks at when he comes out of the sanctuary, after his contemplation within and intercourse there, not with a statue or image but with the Divine itself (οὐκ ἄγαλμα οὐδὲ εἰκόνα, ἀλλὰ αὐτό); they are secondary objects of contemplation. But that other, perhaps, was not a contemplation, but another kind of seeing (οὐ θέαμα, ἀλλὰ ἄλλος τρόπος τοῦ ἰδεῖν) (6.9.11.17-23).

I have argued elsewhere[18] that by the phrase ἄλλος τρόπος τοῦ ἰδεῖν Plotinus means, not that our way of looking at things is altered by our experience of the One, but that perpspective is measured from the One. The One is not one among the things that we see. Rather, it is the source of perspective for all the images of itself including ourselves. It is in the iconoclastic moment of abandoning all images that we may achieve *henôsis*.

Armstrong's translation of ἁρπάζειν at 4.3.11.7 as "catch" ("like a mirror able to catch [the reflection] of a form") is too mild and the supply of the words "the reflection" attenuate the sense of the passage. The mirror is rather able to "rape form."[19] In the following chapter (4.3.12), the souls of men who see their images in the mirror of Dionysus are violently severed and plunged into the world of sense, presumably as the body of Dionysus is severed by the Titans in the Orphic myth. It is the genius of a mirror to be something other than what it is, water, silver, glass and mercury, etc. It is also its ability to receive colour and shape in real presence, rather than merely to be a representation. So the moments of presence and self-transcendence are, in the mirror, one and the same. For this reason, the mirror is a suitable symbol for the sacramental character of Plotinian art in its generation of the vanishing image.

Art then is for Plotinus sacramental. Now sacrament may function as a memorial, as exercising a symbolism appropriated to the uses of philosophical *paideia*, to educate intellect and emotion and lead them anagogically toward their proper objects. Yet it may also work *ex opere operato*, or objectively. It is in this latter sense that Plotinian art is sacrament. Why? Because the absence of aesthetic consciousness, of awareness of the other, is precisely the end of Plotinian contemplation.

The Spiritual Director as Artist

It is crucial to understand that, while the natural perspective is to be found in Plotinus' theory of perception, he is not putting himself forward as a theorist of art, nor indeed is his primary interest in perception as such. The use that he makes of natural perspective is to overcome the distortions of sense perception so that we may learn the ways of noetic intuition. Art is of importance for Plotinus because of its anagogical character. The beauty of nature has the same transcendent purpose. The artist is both a producer and a breaker of images. So is nature. They both produce images of intelligible beauty that must dissolve if the soul is to transcend them.

I wish here to contend that that image and its withdrawal, in the grand anagogy of art, nature, and spiritual direction, has a contemplative purpose apart from its demonstrative value in negative theology. In his own creation and destruction of images, Plotinus is every bit as much the artist as the sculptor, the painter, or the architect. The artist and nature are both dependent upon the vision of Form for their creations. So is it also with the spiritual director who by a rhetorical advancement and withdrawal of images leads his disciples from their engagement with sense, discursive reason, and passion to the fathomless beauty of the intelligible world. Plotinus states that the artist "goes back again to the wisdom of nature, according to which he has come into existence, a wisdom which is no longer composed of theorems, but is one thing as a whole." (5.8.5.4-6) Perhaps, we may surmise, the spiritual director is also the child of nature and our guidance back to the intelligible world a part of universal cosmic rhythm.

Formless Form

In the *Treatise on Virtue*, Plotinus argues that the relationship of imitation that prevails between Form and particular is asymmetrical. The relation of similarity between two particulars is symmetrical. However, virtue in this world (civic virtue) imitates virtue in the intelligible world that is not virtue (1.2.2). When sensible reality imitates Form, it imitates that which is formless (καθ' ὅσον δὲ μεταλαμβάνει εἴδους, κατὰ τοσοῦτον ὁμοιοῦται ἀνειδέῳ ἐκείνῳ ὄντι, 21-2).[20]

When we think of the anagogical, mimetic, and erotic ascent recommended by Diotima in Plato's *Symposium*, we might imagine that we advance from one object of contemplation to another, until finally we come to the Form of Beauty as the final object of our ascent. We would be ever more conformed to something which is itself the perfect and defined version of the beautiful. However, for Plotinus the Form of Beauty is formless, while beautiful things are formed (6.7.32.6-9).[21] What this must mean is that, as we approach Beauty, we must ourselves become free of forms and images. The approach to Beauty is through a breaking of images and an iconoclasm. Thus in 5.8.11 the route to the intelligible world lies first in constructing, then in destroying, an image of oneself. We are familiar with that passage in Plato's *Republic* 509b9, so basic to the spirit of Neoplatonism, that declares that the Good is "beyond substance" (ἐπέκεινα τῆς οὐσίας). For Plotinus, the human soul must itself become "beyond substance" if it is to know the first principle (6.9.11.42).

The Nocturne of the Soul and the Vigil of the One

The very formlessness of the One informs the restless eros of the soul. The soul cannot stay with the One, because of its very formlessness, of a lack of a place to stand:

What then could the One be, and what nature could it have? There is nothing surprising in its being difficult to say, when it is not even easy to say what Being or Form is; but we do have a knowledge based upon the Forms. But in proportion as the soul goes toward the formless, since it is utterly unable to comprehend it because it is not delimited and, so to speak, stamped by a richly varied stamp, it slides away and is afraid that it may have nothing at all (6.9.3.1-6).

The advent of the One is a mystery:

> But one should not enquire whence it comes, for there is no "whence": for it does not really come or go away anywhere, but appears or does not appear. So, one must not chase after it, but wait quietly (ἡσυχῇ μένειν) till it appears, preparing oneself to contemplate it, as the eye awaits the rising of the sun; and the sun rising over the horizon (τοῦ ὁρίζοντος) ("from Ocean", the poets say) gives itself to the eyes to see (5.5.8.1-7).

When the nocturne of the soul is ended, to participate in the vigil of the One, to know its sunrise, is to dismiss all that would limit or define it. The horizon here is anything that would define or delimit (ὁρίζειν). As the One is the abyss of formlessness, it is only in this freedom from definition that we may know it.

The One creates while remaining what it is (μένοντος αὐτοῦ) (5.4.2.21-2) and Intellect, which proceeds from it, is an image (μίμημα καὶ εἴδωλον) of it (26). It is precisely a problem of this chapter how such an image can derive from the One while it remains what it is above all images (26-27).

We have seen earlier (3.6.5) that, in a discussion of purification, the word "alone" (μόνος) is associated with the soul's freedom from images. In a discussion of purification, Plotinus associates μόνος, "alone," with μένειν, "remain":

> This is the soul's ugliness, not being pure and umixed, like gold, but full of earthiness; if anyone takes the earthy stuff away the gold is left, and is beautiful, when it is singled out from (μονούμενος) other things and is alone by itself (συνὼν μόνῳ). In the same way the soul too, when it is separated from (μονούμενος) the lusts which it has through the body with which it consorted too much, and freed from its other affections, purged of what it gets from being embodied, when it abides alone (μείνασα μόνη) has put away all the ugliness which came from the other nature (1.6.5.50-58).

In its "remaining" or "waiting" the soul rehearses the creative activity of the One and thus returns to its source (as in 5.5.8.1-7 above). For the soul to remain alone is for it it dismiss all images so that it might become one with its source, itself free of all images and forms.[22]

The One, when it manifests itself, will not brook any limit we might impose upon it. It is this resistance to definitive argument or legtimized images which arouses the hatred of all positivists, dogmatists, or enemies of artistic abstraction to the vision of Neoplatonism. For the rest of us, the sense of undisclosed and continuing mystery, of the surplus of meaning, is what attracts us again and again to the pages of Plotinus and to art inspired by his philosophy.

NOTES

1. By "iconoclasm" here I do not mean that Plotinus advocates the destruction of religious images. On the contrary, he finds them of the greatest value for the spiritual life. By "iconoclasm" I am referring simply to Plotinus' dismissal of intelligible images of his own creation.

2. With the exception of the passage from 4.8.1, all translations of Plotinus shall be from A. H. Armstrong, *Plotinus.* 7 vols. (London and Cambridge: Heinemann, 1966-88). Reference is to P. Henry and H.-R. Schwyzer, *Plotini Opera.* 3 vols. (Oxford: Oxford University Press, 1964-82).

3. E. Bréhier, *Plotin Ennéades*, vol. 5 (Paris: Les Belles Lettres, 1956) 123. Bréhier also notes that in lines 33-39, Plotinus offers a more rationalistic account of why we do not perceive ourselves.

4. G. M. Gurtler, "Plotinus and Byzantine Aesthetics," *The Modern Schoolman* 66 (1989) 275-283 at pp. 282-3.

5. 5.5.11.19-22; 3.6.5.1-13.

6. I am most gratefull to Gregory Shaw who has permitted me to read his paper, "Dreamwork as Theurgy," who makes a similar use of dream imagery to understand Iamblichean theurgy.

7. In 5.8.10.43 the exercise is described as seeking the vision of the god in oneself.

8. Trans. Stephen MacKenna, *Plotinus, The Enneads,* third edition revised by B. S. Page (London: Faber and Faber, 1962). I have favoured this translation over Armstrong's because MacKenna brings out the sense implicit in Plotinus' use of participles that the soul is in a state of contemplation which is interrupted by the descent: Armstrong sees the moment of contemplation as an interruption of normal waking consciousness, *cf.* D. J. O'Meara, "A propos d'un témoignage sur l'expérience mystique chez Plotin," *Mnemosyne* 27, series 4 (1975) 238-44..

9. I pursue this theme in "Contemplation and the Contemplative Image in Plotinus," *Mediterranean Perspectives* (1998), 7-19.

10. *Cf.* 3.2.15.43-47; 3.2.15.56-62.

11. For the rhetorical sense of φαντασία as purposely imagining what is not before us, see Marcus Aurelius 10.28; Longinus 15.1.

12. See G. Shaw, *Theurgy and the Soul. The Neoplatonism of Iamblichus* (University Park, Pennsylvania: The Pennsylvania State University Press, 1995) 189-215.

13. See the instances of φαντασία (5, 8) and φάντασμα (12).

14. E. Panofsky, *Die Perspektive als symbolische Form*, in *Vorträge der Bibliothek Warburg* 1924-1925 (Leipzig and Berlin 1927) 258-330; reprinted in *Aufsätze zu Grundfragen der Kunstwissenschaft* ed. H. Oberer and E. Verheyn (Berlin 1974) 99-167; L. Brion-Gierry, "'L'espace et les perspectives," *Annales d'Esthétique. The Hellenic Society for Aesthetics, Athens* 13-14 (1974-1975) 18-44.

15.   A. Grabar, *L'Art de la fin de l'antiquité et du moyen âge* 3 vols., I: 15-29 (Paris: Collège de France, 1968), 17-20; *cf.* 2.8.1 and Grabar, 17-18; 4.6.1 and Grabar, 19-20; *cf.* my *Form and Transformation: A Study in the Philosophy of Plotinus* (Montreal and Kingston, London, Buffalo: McGill-Queen's Press, 1992) 21-23.

16.   Gurtler, 279.

17.   Gurtler, 281.

18.   "Plotinus and Interior Space," forthcoming in *Neoplatonism and Indian Philosophy. Being, Becoming and Knowing*, ed. Paulos Mar Gregorios, Voume 9 in *Studies in Neoplatonism: Ancient and Modern*, ed. R. B. Harris (Norfolk, Virginia: International Society for Neoplatonic Studies).

19.   The verb has this violent sense unequivocally in 3.1.2.5; 3.2.8.19; 3.2.15.41. In 6.9.11.12 the soul, in its experience of the One, is ἁρπασθείς, arguably "carried off" (like Ganymede?). J. H. Sleeman and G. Pollet, *Lexicon Plotinianum* (Leiden:Brill, 1980), col. 151 translate "plunder, carry away, catch." The translation as "catch" may be Armstrong's source.

20.   *Cf.* C. D'Ancona Costa, "ΑΜΟΡΦΟΝ ΚΑΙ ΑΝΕΙΔΕΟΝ. Causalité des Fomres et causalité de L'Un chez Plotin," *Revue de Philosophie Ancienne* 9 (1992), 69-113 and F. Regen, *Formlose Formen. Plotins Philosophie als Versuch, die Regressprobleme des Platonischen Parmenides zu lösen* (Göttingen: Vandenhoeck and Ruprecht in Göttingen, 1998) for the view that the formlessness of form responds to the introductory arguments if Plato's *Parmenides* by rendering Form unlike the particulars so that it is not confused with them.

21.   *Cf.* D'Ancona Costa, 98.

22.   In 1.6.7.9, the soul in its purification sees itself alone with the principle which is alone and freed from everything alien to itself (αὐτῷ μόνῳ μόνον); the soul which is free from form (μορφή) can receive the One, which is formless, 6.7.34.7-8) μόνη μόνον. Of course, we may also think of the famous words at then end of the *Enneads* as arranged by Porphyry: φυγὴ μόνου πρὸς μόνον (6.9.11.51).

Neoplatonic Influences on Eastern Iconography: A Greek-rooted Tradition

Aphrodite Alexandrakis

In this short study, I will examine the tradition of Greek aesthetics in relation to religious iconography. I will begin by discussing some Platonic and Plotinian concepts, and proceed with a selection of certain early Christian theologians, who as iconophiles, had been influenced by Plotinus and Neoplatonism. I will not deal with Photius' theory for it is well known that he defended icons from an aesthetic point of view. I will defend the position that the iconophiles appealed to aesthetics and concepts that were rooted in the classical Greek tradition. Contrary to the iconophiles, however, the iconoclasts rejected icons by appealing to conservative religious beliefs.

Scholars have taken two opposing views regarding Plotinus: one side places him outside the Greek tradition, while the other identifies him as the mediator between Christianity and the classical world. I will side with, and attempt to provide evidence for, the latter view. My position will be based on Plotinus' own writings on images, which date back to Plato and the art of his time.

Throughout time, people have felt the desire and emotional need to be close to God, and this has led to the practice of creating images of deities. The practice of praying before a god's statue, for example, is an old custom which frequently appears in Herodotus, Euripides, and other Greek authors, and extends to the Greek novelist Heliodor, third century A.D.[1] The Greco-Roman world tended to fuse the god and its image as if they were one, a tradition that formed the basis of image worship for Christianity. The Greeks, however, as lovers of beauty in addition to an emotional need for a god, possessed the need

75

of, and a special feeling for creating *beautiful* statues of their gods. Quintilian, for example, comments on Pheidias' statue of Zeus by saying that the majesty of this figure "is thought to have added something to the impressiveness of received religion; so exactly did the nobleness of that work represent the god."[2] Lucian also pointed out to the "overall beauty" of the same statue.

There are several examples in classical Greek sculpture in which "the visual qualities inherent in the concept of the God—lifting become manifest, and where the notion of pagan theology is applied to real works of art." [3] What was important in classical Greek sculpture was the rendering of (*morphē*:shape) *form*: the *form* of the gods was crucial to the making of a particular statue, although a few critics, like Xenophanes (sixth century B.C.) and later Heraclitus, were opposed to giving the gods any form at all. For example, in his *Elegy*, Xenophanes, admits that "it is proper for men who are enjoying themselves first of all to praise God," but he added that human beings shape god in their own image.[4] Thus, the gods appear with characteristic features of their human counterparts' races such as Aethiopian gods having snub noses and black hair, while Thracian gods have gray eyes and red hair.

With the exception of the above two criticisms, the Greco-Roman view of images remained dominant. There was almost an identification of the image with the god. But even during that time, there were some Iconoclasts. Xenophanes and Heraclitus have already been mentioned. In *The Battle of the Frogs and the Mice*, which is an ancient parody of the *Iliad* (178-87), but composed in the third century B.C.," Athena complains to Saturn that mice have nibbled away her mantle..."[5] This same mental picture of mice destroying the statue of a god from within, is also reflected in the Christian literature of the third century A.D. in which Arnobius says: "...do you not see the newts, mice, and cockroaches, which shun the light, build their nests and live under the hollow parts of these statues?..."[6] Thus, both Christianity and Paganism reacted to the same stimulus, but in a different way. The response, however, was the same: the creation of images. While for Paganism the causes of the natural images are the forms (shape), in Christianity the causes are concepts in the artist's mind.

These views in turn, lead to the question of how the Greeks approached the sacred image. M. Barasch suggests that two attitudes pertained to the statues of gods: "One tends to identify the image with the god, and the other denies any kind of relation between the two."[7] As for the concept of "image," it always existed in Greek culture, and there are various aspects to it. One is that the image (*eidolon*) can be seen, but cannot be touched, for it has no material substance, but it does have form (shape), and its shape is an imitation of the person represented. Along these lines, Odysseus speaks to the "image" of his mother. Plato in the *Sophist* 236 a-c, refers to the artist who produces images (*eidola*), and that images are seen in the mirror, while reflections are seen in water (239c - 240a). Thus, Homer's and Plato's *eidola* are visible, they show the original figure, but lack material substance of their own. Hence, image had an existence of its own. Following Homer's idea of *eidola*, that images are visible, Plato enhanced the concept by adding the physical objects and phenomena. He does, however, make the distinction between a likeness (*eidolon*) which is a copy of the original, and a semblance (*fantastiki*) far removed from the original. And in the *Timaeus* (52c) he says that the image is like the real thing, but its existence is separate.

One tradition in Greek art and religion was the clothing of the god's statue. It appears in several places in Greek literature (*Iliad* VI, 311), and in the Parthenon's frieze of the great Panathenea procession. The Greek Orthodox parallelism to this is the Saint's clothing used as protection against evil. Another classical Greek religious tradition that was carried over to Christianity was the bathing of the god's statue. Plutarch informs us that the statue of Athena was bathed on the special days of *Plynteria*.[8] We learn from Pausanias that Aphrodite's statue was bathed in Sykion. We see the god's image being treated as if it were a living being, and the statues treated as animated. The Greek believer couldn't tell his god apart from the image (statue) he saw in the temple. As Barasch says: "Dion Chrisostomus, in the 12th Olympic Oration, takes it as a matter of course that we imagine the gods in the shape of the cult images we see around us . . . the artist determines how we will imagine the gods in our minds."[9] Thus, the statues and images were reminders of the gods, very much in the way that sensual objects are the copies and reminders of the Platonic Forms. The Platonic notion of "participation" therefore prevailed in the theory of images: the image "participates" in the figure it portrays. As known, the Platonic notion of "participation" (*methexis*) is used to describe the relationship between *eide* and sensible particulars (Phaedo 100d, Parme. 130c-131a). Later on, Proclus, in his "Elements of Theology," used the *methexis* metaphor in the Platonic sense.

The Platonic notion of *methexis* was also used as a defensive argument by the Iconophiles, maintaining the icon's *methexis* in the original Christ. On the other hand, the Iconoclasts saw "participation" solely as a metaphysical problem which was outside of sensual experience. For them, the viewing of an icon was not similar to seeing the original. Apart from the notion of "participation," when works of art, a sculpture for example, were involved in Greek religion, the idea of beauty was the most important standard, for it brought about the viewer's inspiration, guiding it towards religious and aesthetic contemplation. Thus aesthetic contemplation goes hand in hand with religious feeling. The sense of beauty that was deeply planted in Greek culture was therefore used as a means to inspire people with religious feelings. This deeply Greek-rooted tradition continued throughout the centuries and can even be experienced in the Byzantine icons of the Greek Orthodox church.

Naturally, a number of serious questions were raised by the Iconoclasts. Their criticism focused on the god and its image, stressing the impossibility of creating an image of god because God, they say, is imageless. But what does this mean? Does it mean that God cannot be seen, or that God doesn't have a human form? They also pointed to the issue of idol worship, as well as the material origin of the gods' statues, meaning that from the same material the artist can create other objects, making the image of the god a material (physical) object.

It is interesting to note that some of the classical era's criticisms of statues are similar to that of the Byzantine era. I tend to agree with L.W. Barnard that the Christian tradition was united with paganism and that Byzantium became "the bridge linking the Graeco-Roman world to the Europe of the Middle Ages."[10] There was no sharp distinction between the two worlds. The Christian Orthodox followers did not have to relinquish their classical learnings. Consequently, Iconoclasm was a challenge to this sense of continuity with the Graeco-Roman past. But did the worshippers of the pagan world think of the statues and images as being the gods themselves? To this question, an answer that represents the world of that time was given by the Emperor Julian who apostacised from Christianity and inaugurated the fourth century pagan revival: "...when we look at the images of the gods, let us not indeed think that they are stones or wood, but neither let us think that they are gods themselves...world."[11] The Christian Iconophiles' idea that the divine is present in the material image, and therefore the material nature is penetrated by the divine, is a belief supported in the use of icons.

Actually, this is an ancient idea found in Plutarch and Pythagoras,[12] and continued by Plotinus and the Neoplatonists. In fact, the Neoplatonist Iamblichus attributed to statues a miraculous origin, while for Proclus the statues were fit to receive divine illumination like gods.[13] Images (icons) were extensively used during the early centuries of Christendom, particularly in Constantinople. The images of Christ and of the Virgin were used to instill courage in the troops during a battle. Also, images of Christ and the Virgin were carried around the walls of the city. Like the goddess Athena for the Athenians, the image of the Virgin Mary acquired a special position in Constantinople. As the city of classical Athens had become the center of culture and beauty, Constantinople was "the eye of the faith of the Christians."[14] Just as the Greeks believed in Athena's intervention for winning a particular war, so did the Greek Orthodox salvation from the Slavs, Persians, Arabs, and other invaders come from the icon of the Virgin. The Virgin's presence became magical in material objects and the icons were holy. Just like with Athena, "the icon became the visible expression of the invisible bond that linked the community with the intercession of its patron saint..."[15]

P.L.R. Brown's explanation of the rise of image culture on the basis of social and psychological reasons, in my opinion, is incomplete.[16] It leaves out the theological and aesthetic points of view. Brown points out that Iconoclastic debates did not happen for the sake of aesthetic experience or clarification of theological concepts. Rather, he says, they occurred because of political and social orders between radicals and conservatives.[17] While this may be true, one cannot ignore the classical Greek culture's influence, that is, the influence of the classical ancestors of Greek Christians. As mentioned, and as Hegel points out, the Greeks' religion was "a religion of beauty." Additionally, the notion of mimesis that Plato introduced was continued by Plotinus and the Neoplatonist Christians. In classical Greek culture it was important that objects, artistic or not, were rendered with an "aesthetic" approach, for they were conscious of the influence of beauty on the beholder, and consequently, beauty enhanced their religious belief through the making of the gods' statues. This Greek-rooted tradition is reflected in all Greek works of art, particularly in those of the fifth century B.C. idealistic sculptures. It is an "aesthetic" tradition that was inherited by the Byzantine Christians and was applied on the icon – making, thereby creating the aesthetic experience of icons. This means that certain qualities, or elements that make up the form (shape) of the image, have been used and painted in a certain way or style, so that they determine the character of the aesthetic experience. Some of these qualities are lines, shapes, colors, symmetry, harmony, and rhythm.

If one interprets aesthetic experience as a pure contemplation that leads nowhere beyond itself, then that kind of contemplation would not have influenced the icon viewer. Barasch notes that in the aesthetic approach the work of art must be considered in isolation from anything else and all by itself; this is called the "autonomy of art" and it follows that "to ask what essential features the work of art has in common with what is outside it is to undermine its autonomy."[18] However true this may be, it does not affect the icon's impact on the spectator or believer, especially the person who could not read or write, but who could be inspired from a beautifully painted icon of the Virgin or Christ. It is certain aesthetic qualities within the design that will enhance the viewer's religious feeling. To the question of how does communication between the image and the worshipper take place, it has been suggested that this is done through "affinity."[19] The idea of "affinity" was explored by Plotinus in his treatise on "Problems of the Soul," but was first introduced by Plato's *Cratylus*. A "perfect" picture, Socrates says, will produce good communication. According to Plato, in contemplation there always exists an affinity to visual experience. This idea was enhanced by Neoplatonism, and visual experience was seen in a new light, and images were considered "the main roads to cognition." Affinity also explains the establishment of shrines and images. On this, Plotinus says:

> ...the wise men of old, who made temples and statues in the wish that the gods should be present to them, looking to the nature of the All, had in mind that the nature of soul is everywhere easy to attract, but that if someone were to construct something sympathetic to it and able to receive a part of it, it would of all things receive soul most easily. That which is sympathetic to it is what imitates it in some way, like a mirror able to catch [the reflection of] a form. ...For it was certainly not possible for the thing made to be without a share in the god, not again for the god to come down to the thing made.[20]

Plotinus therefore suggests visual similarity, *i.e.*, resemblance between the prototype and the copy. His followers believed that it was the statue's similarity to the god that makes the god inhabit it, and the god in turn animates the image, thereby building the affinity between the god and the artistic image. But affinity for Plotinus depends on the artist's giving a "sympathetic" feeling to the god's form. "Sympathy" is therefore Plotinus' answer to the god's dwelling in the image. We see then that for Plotinus, in order for a statue to fit the attraction of God, it must be a *good semblance*. Naturally, what is meant by a good semblance is also a beautiful semblance for gods were visualized as such. For Plotinus, human beings feel the need to be close to the god, and they achieve this through the creation of the divine image. This tradition of course continued in the making of icons in Byzantium.

Plotinus' use of many metaphors and images in his *Enneads* leads him to use the term *icon* (image) repeatedly whenever he refers to a work of art. He distinguishes between mental images (dwell in soul) and a work of art, although both share common characteristics. [21] Images, he says, manifest "the non-discursiveness of the intelligible world."[22] We first think in images, and then we develop discursive thinking and knowledge. As a result, Plotinus perceives the chain of being or emanations as a chain of images. Thus the image of the Soul is Matter (*hyle*),[23] and the image of Intelligible Matter is Sensible matter. This "fusion" of god and its image into one form suggests that they are one. One feels close to god when one is near its image. Iamblichus, later followed Plotinus' teachings and added that images of gods can be filled with divine power and perform miracles. Images and names of gods share their "symbolic resemblance" to the gods;[24] icon, is a "likeness" or "reflection" of the god and the name and icon of the god are united in an "ineffable way" with the god itself. This concept of *eidolon* must have influenced the Greek artists in the carving and painting of their gods.

Since images were of concern to Plotinus, the aesthetic appearance of those images was also important to him. He spends a great deal of time on the notion of beauty in the universe, the soul, and of objects. He begins his *Ennead* 1.6 on *Beauty* by saying: "Beauty is mostly in sight, but it is to be found too in things we hear, in combinations of words and also in music..." Thus, we learn, contrary to Plato, that Plotinus appreciates the sense of sight. It is through sight that human beings come to appreciate the material universe which, for him, is good, beautiful, and was made by a divine power. The reason the world of sense is good and beautiful is because it is "a clear and noble image of the intelligible gods." And he adds:

> But it is false to say that the image is unlike the original for an image of soul would have no sort of use for darkness or matter, but when it had come into being, if it did come into being, would correspond to its maker remain in close connection with it.[25]

Plotinus emphasizes that those who despise and hate the beauty of this world cannot know and love the beauty of the intelligible beauty.

While Plotinus recognizes, in a Platonic fashion, the inferiority of human arts' process against the divine, he, however says:

> But if anyone despises the arts because they produce their works by imitating nature...natural things are imitations too. Then we must know that the arts do

> not simply imitate what they see, but they run backup to the forming principles
> from where nature derives and since, they possess beauty, they make up what is
> defective in things."[26]

This Plotinian approach to art and imitation is reflected in the Christian making of the icon, for as mentioned, for Plotinus the material nature is penetrated
and transformed by the divine in the images of gods.[27] Plotinus filled the gap
between the celestial and terrestrial worlds with emanations, or the overflowing of light from the celestial source to the terrestrial through hierarchy. This
opened the road for the Neoplatonists. Among the early defenders of the icons
was the Neoplatonist John Damascus, whose defense was based on a theological formation combined with his interest in the arts. He defined *image*, icon, as
grasped in reaction to its prototype. Image, he says,

> is of like character with its prototype but with a certain difference. It is not like
> the archetype in every way... the original is the thing imaged from which the
> copy is made.[28]

And like a real Plotinian follower, he held that the image "is a likeness, or a
model, or a figure of something, showing in itself what it depicts."[29]

The ancient view that the icon is identical to the prototype in form but not
in substance was also inherited by the Greek church Fathers. In his book
"Against the Arians" St Athanasius says:

> If we use the example of the emperor's image we will find this (the deity of the
> Son who resembles the Father) easier to understand. This image bears his form
> and appearance...[30]

Like Damascus, and according to the Greek tradition, Athanasius' quotation
implies the detachment of form from the matter into which it is imprinted.
This of course is consistent with Plotinus saying: "The more matter loses its
form, the closer it resembles its original model, the idea..." The image therefore imitates the prototype, and the essence of the icon is the portrayal of the
prototype. Like Plato, Damascus suggests that the reality of the image is less
authentic than the prototype. Consequently, Athanasius' image is the equivalent of the Platonic "appearance." [31]

All three (Plato, Plotinus and Damascus) stress the image's lack of reality and the notion of image as a copy, and this is consistent with the making of
Byzantine icons. Damascus' denial of the image's full reality is of course a

reflection of Plato's theory of *mimesis*. The image (icon) created by the artist is an illusion and an appearance of the object devoid of the prototype's physical reality. Hence, the image for Damascus possesses less reality than what it portrays. His statement that "an image is a likeness showing in itself what it depicts," has occupied several scholars' minds. Did he mean that the image is an autonomous object? He knew that the model preceded the image and therefore it could not be autonomous. But as has been pointed out by Barash, "in the process of our grasping what is represented in the image, the image comes to enjoy an autonomy of sorts." In other words, in order for the viewer to understand what the image shows, he does not have to rely on something else, for the picture shows that "in itself." This is what we call in the 20th century "aesthetic experience" that is, the viewer's pure contemplation and absorption by the image. However, in the case of icons, contemplation is achieved through the *form* of the image which points to the prototype: the spiritual *form*. The icon therefore resembles the prototype in terms of *form* only.

Since the distinction between *icon* and *prototype* could lead to idolatry, Damascus insisted on this and said: "For the image is one thing and the thing depicted is another. One can always notice differences between them, since one is not the other, and vice versa."[32] Naturally, crucial questions of an ontological nature are involved here though they are beyond the scope of this paper.

As mentioned earlier, while Damascus and Athanasius' theories reflect Plato's theory of Forms they are also consistent with the ideas involved in the making of fifth century classical sculptures such as the Zeus of Artemision and the Charioteer of Delphi. These works represent idealized beauty and perfection of *form* (shape), reflecting its inner understanding and contemplation through elements such as shapes, lines, rhythm, harmony, symmetry, and a sense of grandeur.

According to Damascus, the image (icon) "reaches farther than the perception of the human eye in natural experience, it shows what lies beyond the realm of visual experience."[33] The icon reveals more than what can be seen in nature; it makes us "see" the invisible. And since it represents the invisible, its purpose is to attain this goal: "...when the Invisible One becomes visible to flesh, you may then draw a likeness of its form..."[34] Naturally, this involves the worshiper and the icon's impact on him or her, and this formed one of Plato's bases for rejecting art works. Consequently, while Damascus follows Plato on the definition of image, he simultaneously accepts divine images for the same reason that Plato rejects them: for while the imitation of the prototype, is an unnecessary act for Plato, for Damascus, and the Orthodox Fathers, it was absolutely necessary. And while icons in the eastern church were accepted for their effects on the worshiper, the western church rejected them on the claim that icons do not have an autonomous value. The Orthodox fathers held steadfastly that icons attain value because of their effect on the believers. These effects seem to be primarily aesthetic. The aesthetic effects were the result of the way the "form" was treated; particular lines, shapes, color, and a detached, aloof expression suggesting immateriality and "otherness." Even the sixth century Pope Gregory the Great's notion of icons as didactic implements must have some aesthetic qualities in order to be able to function as such, that is, to teach people something through the inspiration of their aesthetic qualities.

It has been pointed out that the concept of images as embellishments of sacred objects is absent from Damascus, and that although he defended painted images, he had no appreciation for artistic imagination and workmanship.[35] In my opinion, the fact that Damascus did not use images as an embellishment of sacred objects, does not necessarily mean or support the claim that he had no appreciation for artistic imagination and workmanship. Let us not forget the political danger involved in this issue. Moreover, just because in his *Hymn to the Icon*, he does not mention any aspect or feature of the icon or make a reference to workmanship, does not necessarily support the claim that he was not interested in the icon from the artistic point of view. In his *Hymn* he says:

> The icon is a hymn to triumph, a manifestation, a memorial inscribed for those who have fought and conquered, humbing the demons and putting them to flight.[36]

The absence of a reference by Damascus to any artistic (aesthetic) qualities is not in disagreement with his saying that the icon is "a hymn of triumph." Such a hymn does not have to necessarily state any particular aesthetic qualities; but does this mean their exclusion? It is important to remember that Damascus made the distinction between an idol and an icon. Confusion of the two would have led to accusations of idolatry. Finally, Damascus' defense of the icon was based on the incarnation of Christ. Even though he asks questions that remind us of the physical portrayal of the Infinite, he supports the idea of icon and never answers these questions.[37]

Whether Damascus admitted that the artistic (aesthetic) component of the icon strengthened the believers' faith is up to his readers to decide. There may have been political, theological, and or social reasons for not doing so, but as we saw, his emphasis was on the icon's impression and influence on the worshiper. There are other theologians, not to mention Photius, who were also openly defending the icon's artistic influence on the believers. One such was Theodore of Stoudion. Consistent with the Greek tradition, Theodore, like Damascus, used Homeric and Platonic terms such as *eidos* meaning "appearance," implying *eidos* is not an idea in the artist's imagination, but a completed visible image. Another term he uses is *morphe*, meaning "form."[38] The Platonic *schema* appears again in Theodore's discussion of images as well as the term "character" referring to the icon as being a faithful rendering of the prototype. On this he says: "Is not every image a kind of seal and impression bearing itself the proper appearance of that after which it is named?"[39]

On the basis of the above, the icon and the prototype can be said to have several real elements in common. One of these is "form." According to Theodore, and the Iconophiles generally, "form" is present in both the mental image and the painted icon. For Theodore, the distinction between these two was the separation between "pure form" and a work of vision; that is, the shape, form, has an ideal existence only. Shape can be materialized by being painted or carved. Hence, the existence of "pure form" detached from any specific matter. Like Plotinus, Aristotle,[40] and Damascus, Theodore emphasizes the importance of the sense of sight. Even the Patriarch of Constantinople Nicephorus held that sight is above all other senses.

To sum up, the Greeks' 'religion of beauty, and supurb understanding of the "aesthetic"rooted back in the archaic period (sixth century B.C.), and reaching its peak in the first quarter of the fifth century idealized classical period, continued its tradition through Plotinus and the Neoplatonists in the Greek Orthodox church of Byzantium. The icons convey the Lord's message just like bells convey it with sound. The more aesthetically the icon is rendered, the stronger its impact on the believer (spectator). And, again, as Plotinus said: "...the arts...run back to the forming principles...they possess beauty..." (*Enn.* IV.3.11).

Notes

1.   Moshe Barash, *Icon* (N.Y. Univ. Press, 1992), 29.
2.   Quintilian, *Instituto Oratorica XII,* trans. by J.Watson, 10, 7-9.
3.   Barash, 70.
4.   *Ibid.*, 51. See Burkett, *Greek Religion.*
5.   *Ibid., 54.*
6.   Arnobius Adversus Gentes, XIX, trans. by H. Bryce & H. Cambell (Ante-Nicene Christian Library; Edinburgh, 1871), 288.
7.   Barash, 25.
8.   Pollux, Onomasti, 3.
9.   Barash, 41.
10.   L. W. Barnard, *The Graeco-Roman And Oriental Background of the Iconoclastic Controversy* (Leiden E. J. Brill, 1974), 80.
11.   N. H. Baynes, *Byzantine Studies and Other Essays* (London, 1955), 130.
12.   De Pyth. Orac. 8. On statue: alla peplhsqai panta qeothtoV.
13.   Barnard, 85.
14.   L. Sternbach, *Analecta, Anarica* in the Rozprawy of the Academy of Cracow (1900), 304.15.
15.   Barnard, 62.
16.   P. L. R. Brown, A Dark Age Crisis: Aspects of the Iconoclastic Controversy, *English History Review,* 346 (1973), 1-34.
17.   *Ibid., 4.*
18.   Barash, 3.
19.   *Ibid., 42.*
20.   *Ennead,* IV.3.11.
21.   *Ennead,* V.8.5, 19.
22.   *Ennead,* V.8.6.
23.   *Ennead,* V.2.1., III.9.3.
24.   Armstrong, 83.
25.   *Ennead,* II.9.11, 16-19.
26.   *Ibid.*
27.   *Ennead,* IV.3.11.
28.   *Apologies,* I,9; 19.
29.   *Ibid.,* III, 16.
30.   Barash, 198.
31.   *Republic.* "By *eikonas* I mean, first, shadows, and then reflections in water and on surfaces of dense, smooth and bright texture..." And in *Theatetus* 239: "...we mean the images (*eidola*) in water and in mirrors, and those in painting, too, and sculptures, and ..."
32.   *Apologies* III, 16; 73.

33. Barasch, 219 (See John Damascus, *On the Divine Images: Three Apologies Against Those Who Attack The Divine Images,,* trans. by David Anderson).

34. St. John Damascene on Holy Images, by Mary H. Allies (London, Thomas Baker, 1898).

35. Barasch, 203.

36. *Apologies* II, 12; 19.

37. *Apologies* I, 8; 18 "...How can the invisible be depicted? How does one picture the incinceivable? How can one draw what is limitless, immesurable, infinite?..."

38. Scholars disagree on the meaning of this term.

39. On the Holy Icons I, 9; 29, by St Theodore the Stradite, trans. by Catherine P. Roth (Crestwood, N.Y., 1981).

40. *Meta.* I, i; 980a 24ff.

The Neoplatonic Tradition
in the Art of El Greco

Robert Meredith Helm

Dominikos Theotokopoulos was a native of Candia, the capital of the island of Crete, which since 1204 had been a possession of the Serene Republic of Venice and which accommodated a substantial number of Venetians among its inhabitants. Virtually nothing is known of his early years, and even the date of his birth, probably in the year 1542, is uncertain. From the apparent depth and scope of his education, it appears that he was a member of a family of some standing, but the earliest documented reference to him that survived is an instrument signed before a notary public in 1561 by Maistro Menegos Theotokopoulos Sgourafos (Toledo Museum 15). Toward the end of that year, he offered one of his paintings for sale in a lottery. This sketchy information is all we know of his life in his native Crete.

We next hear of him in Venice, where there was a sizeable colony of Cretans. On August 18, 1658, he was making arrangements to dispatch drawings to a Candian cartographer. Two years later, he had moved on southward. A letter from John Clovis, a miniaturist, to Alessandro Farnese, written on November 15, 1570, says, "There has arrived in Rome a young man from Candia, a pupil of Titian, who, I think, is a painter of rare talent. ... He has painted a portrait of himself which is admired by all the painters in Rome. I should like him to be under the patronage of your reverend lordship without any other contribution towards his living than a room in the Farnese Palace" (*Encyclopaedia Britannica*, v. 22, 69).

Venice was a cultural link between East and West, and the art of that city at the time of the young Greek's residence there incorporated something of the spirit that would characterize the Greek's developing style. Titian, at that time in his nineties, and the grand old man of Venetian art, was a principal source of the style of painting that Theotokopoulos was to follow throughout the years of his residence in Italy. He was also strongly influenced by Tintoretto, Veronese, and Giacopo Bassano.

Non-Venetian sources of his Italian style are evident as well. Raphael's The Healing of the Lame Man in the Temple, also known as Peter and John at the Beautiful Gate, clearly provided some material for Theotokopoulos' small painting, The Purification of the Temple. Executed in tempera and staged in an architectural setting representing a hodgepodge of the tricks of perspective popular at that time, it shows Raphael's influence on some of the figures in the young Greek's painting, notably those of a woman and a little naked boy bringing their offering to the temple.

More significant for an understanding of El Greco is the fact that his works of the Venetian and Roman period, conforming in many respects to the prevailing Italian Renaissance style, nevertheless give hints of an earlier influence one that was later to reassert itself powerfully in the masterpieces that would establish the unique place he occupies in the history of art.

At about the age of thirty, having already attained some fame as an artist, Theotokopoulos left Rome. The reasons for his departure are somewhat obscure, but a story told by a seventeenth-century writer, G. Mancini, may shed some light on the matter. According to Mancini, the Greek was given the opportunity of becoming the breeches maker for the figures that Pope Pius considered indecent in Michelangelo's Last Judgment in the Sistine Chapel. Theotokopoulos suggested that it might have been better if the whole painting had been cast to the ground so that he himself might have done it with sincerity, decency, and artistic integrity. There seems little reason to doubt that such an insult to the foremost artist of the age may have raised the temperature of Rome to a point where he thought it advisable to find another place to live and practice his art.

Why he chose Spain is not known. It may have been because Philip II was building the Escorial and looking for artists to decorate it. At any rate, his choice turned out to be a felicitous one. He was obviously struck by the stark Spanish landscapes and he promptly began to incorporate in his paintings the clean and dramatic colors he found there, which must have reminded him more of those of his native Crete than of the lasher hues of Italy.

We find him in Toledo in 1577, completing a set of paintings for the rebuilt Church of Santo Domingo el Antiguo. Those works enhanced his already great reputation, and he was commissioned by the Chapter of Toledo

Cathedral to paint a picture for the Sacristy. The result was The Stripping of Christ before the Crucifixion, in which the essential elements of the altered style that would ultimately be dominant in his work were clearly evident.

Controversy about certain aspects of the painting and a dispute over his compensation entangled him for some time after its completion, but it must have impressed King Philip, for he asked Theotokopoulos to paint an altarpiece for his church in the Escorial.

El Greco, to use the name by which he must have been generally known by that time, responded to the monarch's request with the painting of St. Maurice and the Theban Legion, depicting the mass martyrdom of a body of third-century Roman soldiers who refused to obey orders to persecute their fellow Christians. He portrayed the event, not in the expected Spanish mode, with emphasis on the horror of the beheading, but in a way that demonstrated that he was not entirely hostile to the style known as *Maniera*, or High Mannerism, based on the paintings of Raphael and Michelangelo, but emphasizing artistic form over dramatic content. El Greco chose to place at the center of his painting an elegant Maurice, with members of his staff and a little armor-bearer, conferring courteously with an official about their impending execution and that of their comrades of the legion, who are seen in the distance lining up to have their heads cut off, a procedure which is already under way in matter-of-fact fashion, with no indication of ill feeling on either side. Meanwhile, the heavens above are an integral part of the scene, filled with a host of celestial beings preparing a reception for the prospective arrivals. Despite the religious propriety of the theme, the style so irritated Philip that he refused to have the painting installed over the altar, though it remained at the Escorial.

Quite undeterred by royal disapproval, the Greek went on with his painting, gradually developing a mode of artistic expression that eschewed earthly realism in favor of an embodiment of a philosophical and religious outlook that regarded the material world not as something ultimate in its own right, but rather as an expression of a transcendent spiritual reality.

The juxtaposition of the earthly and the heavenly became a frequent theme in El Greco's paintings. His colors, were borrowed less and less from the Venetian and Roman masters, taking on colder blues, greens, and steely grays, with accents of white, yellow, green, and wine red. All the time, his figures were becoming increasingly more sinuous and elongated, possibly owing something to such Italian painters as Tintoretto and Parmigianino, but clearly expressing something so significant for El Greco that it subordinated the influence of painterly convention to religious and philosophical influences more important to him than the more mundane concerns money, high living, romance, controversy, and the like that had their place in the other side of the balance of his complex nature. Those more spiritual and scholarly aspects of his character were fueled by a way of life marked by a thirst for books and an appreciation of good conversation with the *intelligentsia* of Toledo, with whom he was on the best of terms. One of those companions wrote of him, He was a great philosopher (Byron and Rice 183).

A thoroughly typical expression of the sort of art that ultimately became such a powerful vehicle for his philosophy is the Opening of the Fifth Seal, one of three works executed late in the artist's life for the Tavera Hospital in Toledo. The work was inspired by a passage in the Apocalypse of St. John:

> And when he had opened the fifth seal, I saw under the altar the souls of them that were slain for the word of God, and for the testimony which they held: And they cried with a loud voice, saying, How long, O Lord, holy and true, dost thou not judge and avenge our blood on them that dwell on the earth? And white robes were given unto every one of them: and it was said unto them that they should rest yet for a little season, until their fellow-servants also and their brethren, that should be killed as they were, should be fulfilled (*Revelation*, 6: 9-11).

Other painters of the High Renaissance had put on canvas their vision of heaven and earth, with descending angels, aspiring souls, and rejected sinners. They too had bathed their scenes in a celestial brightness that endowed the vivid, earth-based colors they employed a radiance that spoke of the presence of God in nature.

But these colors are different. They hardly seem to derive from earthly substances at all. The areas of red and yellow are muted and completely dominated by the cool and curiously other-worldly hues of the remainder of the painting. The gigantic figure of St. John on the left is enveloped in a gray-blue robe highlighted by a pure white light that must have its source in the celestial realm glimpsed behind the swirling clouds that seem to move in a line parallel to the saint's outstretched arm and of the body of the little angel floating at the upper right of the painting.

That same radiance robs the naked figures of the risen dead of any semblance of the human flesh tones with which Michelangelo in some degree and Memling in an even greater measure endowed their resuscitated saints and sinners in their depictions of the Last Judgment. In El Greco's space, the highlighted portions of the bodies gleam with the pure white illumination that streams through breaks in the dark storm clouds overhead, and the shadowed area tend toward the violet end of the spectrum.

And what are we to make of the figures themselves? Painted with consummate skill, they nevertheless defy the unwritten canon that set boundaries for even the most radical Italian masters who taught the Greek his craft. To be sure, it was not uncommon for Renaissance painters to make heads less long and bodies longer than they are generally seen in real life. Denys of Fourna, in his *Guide to Painting*, had written, Learn O my pupil that the body of a man is nine heads in height (Byron and Rice 94). This exaggerated proportion is especially evident in Michelangelo's frescoes on the ceiling of the Sistine Chapel. But El Greco's sinuous and elongated figures of his later Spanish period are quite unlike Michelangelo's idealized human forms. They are attenuated, fluid, unearthly, hardly seeming to be bodies at all.

How are we to account for this astounding climactic development in Renaissance art? A great deal of insightful criticism and a fair amount of nonsense have been written about El Greco in attempts to explain the characteristics that set his paintings apart from others of the era. He has been seen as a Mannerist, a reviver of Byzantine art, a madman, a proto-modernist, and, most curiously, a painter whose distinctive style can be attributed to astigmatism.

This latter theory, which enjoyed surprising popularity during the early years of the twentieth century, was presented as a plausible explanation for the figures that fill the Greek's later paintings. It is difficult to understand why it was not apparent to the critics who espoused the ophthalmic hypothesis that even if El Greco had indeed suffered from such a condition, he himself would inevitably have seen his exaggerated figures as abnormal in comparison with those who served as his models. The real explanation must lie elsewhere, and if we want to divine the reason, we must attend less to some possible visual pathology or to personal eccentricity than to the intellectual orientation that governed his artistic activity during the last years of his career.This latter theory, which enjoyed surprising popularity during the early years of the twentieth century, was presented as a plausible explanation for the figures that fill the Greek's later paintings. It is difficult to understand why it was not apparent to the critics who espoused the ophthalmic hypothesis that even if El Greco had indeed suffered from such a condition, he himself would inevitably have seen his exaggerated figures as abnormal in comparison with those who served as his models.

It is astonishing that even the modern critics who defended El Greco against the charge of visual aberration were for the most part oblivious to a ground of art in which his roots were so deeply embedded. Meier-Graefe, who, unswayed by a turn-of-the-century characterization of the Greek as a painter of horrors, asked, Where does he come from? replied simply, We do not know (Byron and Rice, 6).

That same critic, to be sure, later found a clue to some of the mystery of El Greco's art in the mosaics of Daphne near Athens. He was not the first of the modern commentators to see Greek and Byzantine influence in Theotokopoulos paintings, but the organic continuity between Byzantine painting and the art of El Greco was clearly recognized only when critics began to discover an affinity between Byzantine and modern art and it became apparent to some of them that El Greco was a sort of missing link. The painting and sculpture that had emerged in the Eastern empire as a consequence of its struggles against iconoclasm turned away from the naturalism of earlier centuries in favor of a mystical aspiration to express in finite works the mysteries of the eternal and immutable. The felicitous result was the great tradition of Byzantine iconography, coexisting with the sort of Aristotelian philosophy espoused by St. John Damascene, whose writings were later to have a profound influence on Eastern Scholastics (Byron and Rice, 91). In the ninth century, the Patriarch Photius sparked a revival of Platonism in Byzantium (Byron and Rice, 17). Though it did not result in a revival of the naturalistic Greek and Hellenistic art, it did humanize the iconographic representation of the Byzantine painters and breathed into the art of Christendom a spirit that would ultimately move westward and transform European art.

Two centuries after Photius, Michael Psellos, a fundamentally Neoplatonic scholar, put an indelible stamp on Byzantine culture. Psellos had an encyclopedic range of knowledge, combined with a Platonic rational mysticism. One result of his enormous influence was a form of art characterized by a warmer sort of representation of the divine, which, without sacrificing anything of the mystery, nevertheless brought a still more humanistic element to iconographic art and produced its full flowering.

In a very real sense, Psellos may be considered the progenitor not only of a revitalized Byzantine and Greek culture, but of the Italian Renaissance, though centuries were to elapse after his death before the Neoplatonic spirit of humanistic mysticism would come into full flower in the West.

The relation of that spirit to art is no accident. An understanding of the relationship between philosophy and the arts permeates the *Enneads* of Plotinus in a somewhat less ambiguous fashion than is the case with Plato's writings. Works of art, Plotinus said, go back to the Reason-Principles from which Nature derives and ... are holders of beauty and add where nature is lacking (Plotinus *Enneads* IV. 8. 1. McKenna 422-423).

There is a real sense in which the World Soul is for the Neoplatonists an artist, acting on the bare potentiality of matter to express something of the ineffable beauty shining through *Nous* from the One. Human bodies are expressions of soul, and the individual soul shares in the nature of the ultimately real. It too can shape its own nature as an artist shapes his work.

> Withdraw into yourself and look. And if you do not find yourself beautiful yet, act as does the creator of a statue that is to be make beautiful: he cuts away here, he smoothes there, he makes this line lighter, this other purer, until a lovely face has grown upon his work. So do you also: cut away all that is excessive, straighten all that is crooked, bring light to all that is overcast, labour to make all one glow of beauty until there shall shine out on you from it the godlike splendour of virtue, until you shall see the perfect goodness established in the stainless shrine (Plotinus, *Enneads* I.6.9. MacKenna 63).

None of this is to deny that not only has the Platonic tradition in is entirety been a fountainhead of inspiration for great art, but that Plato himself was not insensitive to the proper role of the arts in human life. It is true that in the *Republic* he expressed doubts not only about drama but about *all* works of representative art as simulations twice removed from reality faulty copies of particular objects that are themselves flawed reproductions of Ideas.

His criticism of the arts, however, was far less sweeping than his *penchant* for hyperbole would make it appear, for he never condemned them on the grounds of their impotence, but rather on his conviction that they are too powerful to be trusted in the hands of those not versed in philosophy. He proposed to harness that power for good by challenging the artists to prove that they could elevate their work to a sufficient height to convey to those who contemplated it the essence of the truths that lie behind the world of phenomena. This is precisely the role that Plotinus assigned to works of art. We do not so much contemplate *them* as employ them as focusing glasses through which we see with greater understanding the more real world of *Noeta*.

In the Byzantine world, the victors in the war against the iconoclasts claimed a precisely similar function for art. This was the chief iconodule contention, art historians Byron and Rice say, that pictures, like statues to Plotinus, were an effective means of communication with the extra-terrestrial universe.

This was the way iconographic painting was viewed in Crete when young

Domenikos Theokotopoulos was a boy there. The spirit of those vivid representations of spiritual truths followed him to Venice, where it was again alive in an uniquely Adriatic mode, and then to Rome, where it had found expression in the colossal work of Michelangelo, whom the boy from Crete first studied and then emulated and at last rejected. Michelangelo was a good man, he was later to remark, but he could not paint (Byron and Rice 78).

It was not until he got to Spain and became El Greco that he gradually became able to to draw his nourishment from the very roots of that spirit, incorporating in his work all the skills he had learned from the Italian masters, but purifying and spiritualizing his art from sources that sprang from the rich soil of the Eastern Platonic and Neoplatonic tradition. This is not to say that at some point he discovered that he was a Platonist or Neoplatonist and decided to paint according to the canon. He was, to be sure, interested in philosophy and enjoyed talking with philosophers. He had a substantial library, though it is not known whether he ever read the writings of Plato or Plotinus. He never lectured or wrote essays on metaphysics.

Rather, his philosophy, as an expression of his soul, is in his paintings, and it is clear that he intended them to be his way of stating his profoundest convictions about the world. Like Plotinus and the Christian Neoplatonists, he saw the natural world not as inert matter, but as animate and fluid. Material objects are created and sustained by soul, and even a relatively horizontal city, in his View of Toledo seems to be straining upward, seeking to regain its identity with some celestial city from which it derives its nature.

As for human bodies, they are unlike even the most spiritually inspiring bodies of the Italian painters. Whatever incarnation of *Nous* and Soul is celebrated in the figures of El Greco's later works is an incarnation that has passed the point at which the Word initially becomes Flesh and revels in bone and muscle and sinew. The bodies of his saints and sometimes even of the infant Jesus are bathed in a white radiance that seems to draw them upward toward the One. Reality that typically makes its presence known only through rifts in the storm clouds that must be penetrated before the aspiring souls can achieve the destiny that awaits them in the celestial realm. That realm, as seen through El Greco's painting, has a reality that transcends that of the ephemeral world beneath it, imparts to it whatever life it is capable of receiving, and draws it back toward itself. Even souls in danger of damnation in these paintings never wholly lose that touch of derivative radiance, suggesting Plotinus conviction that in the very nature of a soul, it can never be entirely lost.

In 1577, the year El Greco moved to Toledo, St. John of the Cross was imprisoned there. Whether or not he and El Greco ever knew each other is uncertain, but much of St. John's poetry embodies the qualities that the Greek achieved in his painting, as evidenced in these lines about the ascent of the soul:

> The dreadful force of dazzling light
>> Blinded me as aloft I flew,
>> The greatest gain that ere I knew
>> Was made in blackness of the night.
>> But love it was that won the day,
>> Blindly, obscurely did I fly;
>> I soared aloft and soared so high
>> That in the end I reached my prey (Myers and Copplestone 85).

The recognition of El Greco as a painter whose works embody a whole philosophy is well expressed by Byron and Price:

> ... for us, and in relation to us, he is always relevant and always great, great not only as a painter but as a man, one to whom the vision of his World's reality was vouchsafed and who pursued it independently of mental fashion, a cosmic figure, sustained in his own life by a profound conviction of his own magnitude. On his canvasses, the whole gamut of emotions provoked by landscape, allegory, or sitter, are co-ordinated in the expression of a grand philosophy, of the intrinsic, mystical seed of perfection contained in all terrestrial phenomena and the artist's debt thereto in his communing (Byron and Rice 3).

The grand philosophy that invested the paintings of the Greek with their enduring power to move and inspire us can have been none other in essence than the philosophy of Plotinus and the Christian Neoplatonists.

References

Robert and Rice Byron, David Talbot. *The Birth of Western Painting*. (New York: Hacker Art Books, 1968).

Encyclopaedia Britannica. (Chicago, William Benton, 1958).

Bernard S. and Copplestone Myers, Trewin, eds. *Art Treasures in* Spain. (New York: McGraw-Hill, 1969).

Plotinus. *The Enneads*. Trans. Stephen McKenna, third ed. (London: Faber, 1962).

Revelation. Holy Bible. Authorized King James Version. (Nashville: Thomas Nelson, 1976).

Giorgio Vasari's *The Toilet of Venus:* Neoplatonic Notion of Female Beauty

Liana De Girolami Cheney

In *Emblematum libellus cum commentarii*, Andrea Alciato states that "the universe is a forest of symbols," that is to say, "things that are visible are the mirror of those things which are invisible (and) all the world objects have a signification." His theory of the emblem conveys a Neoplatonic view concerning the meaning of an idea or conceit (*concetto*) which was eloquently explained by Marsilio Ficino in *De vita celitus comparanda*. In this book he discusses the use and the magic potency of images by deliberating on the virtue of imagery, what power pertains to the figure in the sky and on earth, which of the heavenly configurations were impressed on images by the ancients, and how the images were employed in antiquity.

Giorgio Vasari's understanding of Neoplatonic philosophy and interest in and use of emblemata derived, as he recounts in his autobiography, from his education in the classics with Pollastra, his tutoring with the mythographer Piero Valeriano during his formative years, and his contact with the emblemist Andrea Alciato in Bologna in 1530s. Vasari assimilated specific meanings from emblem books such as Andrea Alciato's *Emblematum libellus cum commentarii* (1536), Piero Valeriano's *Hieroglyphicae* (1556), and Vincenzo Cartari's *Imagine de I Dei degli Antichi* (1547), to name but a few. These sources provided him with an extensive repertoire of images which he collected and used in the iconography for his paintings.

Under these humanistic influences, Giorgio Vasari (1511-1574) considered himself to be not merely a painter but an aesthetician as well.[1] His ambitions culminated in his writing of *The Lives of the Most Excellent Painters,*

Sculptors, and Architects (Le vite dei più eccellenti pittori, scultori e architetti), the first edition of which appeared in 1550; a second, enlarged and revised, containing woodcut portraits of the artists, appeared in 1568.[2] Vasari's *Lives* consists of two components: biographies and prefaces. In writing the biographies, Vasari discusses stylistic qualities and techniques of art.[3] In the Prefaces *(Proemi)* he establishes not only the historical scheme for his writing of the biographies but also his aesthetics by defining the criteria by which he selects the "most excellent" artists and the standards by which their works were judged (Preface I, 7).

Vasari's criteria for assessing art accorded with conventional standards in sixteenth-century Neoplatonic philosophy. He embodies the aesthetic judgment of his time in the criteria he uses to evaluate individual works of art. Qualities he applauded were: technical proficiency especially in drawing; good composition; imitation of nature; variety and invention; and adherence to the classical art of ancient Rome. He felt that such qualities must be attained with beauty and grace of style, which meant that the work must appear to have been executed with masterful ease. He emphasized that a magical, godlike quality (genius) is the essential quality of great art. He assumed that artists individual achievements were essentially manifestations of their own peculiar genius. But genius itself - and with it, major changes in style and technique - could be explained only by invoking of the intervention of divine forces: "To save us from such great errors...the Most Benign Ruler of Heaven turned his eyes clemently to earth...and consented to send down a Spirit..."[4] Vasari's theory of genius or divine intervention to explain the execution of works of exemplary merit can be seen particularly applies to the artist's perception of feminine beauty and its function in the integrity of artistic expression.

Within this framework, this study considers the following: Vasari's concept of beauty as advanced in the Prefaces of the *Lives*; its Renaissance literary and philosophical sources for his concept of beauty; and its artistic embodiment in his painting *The Toilet of Venus* of 1558 (Fig. 1; Staatsgalerie, Stuttgart, Germany) and the pendant painting of *The Bacchanal* of 1558 (Fig. 2; Radiscev Museum of Fine Arts, Saratov, Russia).[5]

In his Third Preface of the *Lives*, Vasari defines his theory of beauty in terms of the laws of design as consisting of *"regola, ordine, misura, disegno e maniera"* (rule, order, proportion, design, and manner).[6] He further states:

> Design is the imitation of the most beautiful things in nature, used for the creation of all figures whether in sculpture or painting; and this quality depends

Fig. 2.   Giorgio Vasari, *The Bacchanal*, 1558
Saratov, Russia, Radiscev Museum of Fine Arts

Fig. 1.   Giorgio Vasari, *The Toilet of Venus*, 1558
Stuttgart. Germany, Staatsgalerie

on the ability of the artist's hand and mind to reproduce what he sees with his eyes accurately and correctly onto paper or a panel or whatever flat surface he may be using. The same applies to works of relief in sculpture. And then the artist achieves the highest perfection of style or *maniera* by copying the most beautiful things in nature and combining the most perfect members, hands, head, torso, and legs, to produce the finest possible figure as a model for use in all his works; this is how he achieves what we know as fine style or *maniera*. (Preface III, 35).

Vasari's aesthetics (the word aesthetic derives from the Greek *aisthesis* - sensation) are concerned with the nature of the beautiful as it exists in art or in art and nature as well as with the physicality and spirituality of beauty.[7] For Vasari, physicality of beauty is perceived in the painted image and the spirituality of beauty is reflected in the evocation of the visual experience. His philosophy of art depends upon the philosophical and poetical tradition of the Renaissance, in short the Marsilio Ficino's restatement of Neoplatonism. In accordance with the Neoplatonic theory of beauty, Vasari understands beauty to be a divine creation," He (God) fashioned the first forms of painting and sculpture in the sublime grace of created things."[8] Consequently, he refers to beauty as the mirror of the human soul reflecting methaphysical light and associates the beautiful with Ficino's light of the sole principle of the universe (*De Amore*) and with Plotinus's concept of "heavenly Aphrodite"(*kalon* and *kaloni*) radiance or splendor, an element that results from the quality of unity inherent in the object (*Enneads*, 5- 8, 13).[9] Correspondingly, Vasari absorbs from Ficino's *Commentary on Plato's "Symposium" about Love,* the ancient Greek philosopher's definition of beauty "as the splendor of *divine goodness* present everywhere, personal beauty expresses an interior moral goodness," as well as, Ficino's explanation of beauty as "a process of ascent from sensual cognition of earthly beauty to the apprehension of the immortal ideal of beauty itself."[10] By appropriating from Ficino the interconnection between love and beauty, Vasari also embraces his notion on the essence of beauty that consists in proportion, that is, the ancient doctrine of symmetric and pleasant relationship of individual parts. According to Vasari, the origin of beauty derives from order and proportion (la bellezza nasce da ordine e proporzione), and at times he relates the concept of beauty with goodness (bellezza e bontà).[11] Obviously, Vasari is following Marsilio Ficino; in the *Symposium*, Ficino discusses how many things are required to create a beautifyul body, such as arrangement (means the distance between parts), proportion (means quantity), and aspect (means shape and color). He further analyzes how the proportioning of the parts have their natural position: "that the ears be in their place, and the eyes and nose, etc., and that the eyes be at equal distances near the nose...proportion of the parts...preserve the proper portion of the whole body."[12]

For Vasari, when artists returned to consider nature, in imitation or emulation of their ancient forbears, a rebirth occurred in the arts. Renaissance artists first imitated nature, then equalizing nature, and finally surpassed nature. Fidelity to nature meant artists mastering "naturalism" in the rational representation of perspective, foreshortening, chiaroscuro, and the knowledge of anatomy," pleasing both the eye and the mind, creating a beautiful form."[13]

By improving on nature, Vasari suggests, Italian Renaissance artists corrected nature's imperfections by working with the canons of proportion, by selecting the best aspects of nature, and, by achieving graceful or idealized beauty. When artists surpassed nature, according to Vasari, they responded to their *concetto* (conceit), an idea, or image of beauty, partly innate in the mind of the artist art (*invenzione*) and partly derived from previous study of nature and art (*imitazione*). Therefore, Vasari's concept of beauty derives from two principles: the ideational, a *concetto* to create an image of beauty, and the realistic, a current idea about how an image of beauty can be conceived Vasari's *The Toilet of Venus* visually represents his theory of beauty.[14]

Furthermore, Renaissance poets such as Baldesar Castiglione, Angelo Poliziano and Pietro Bembo adhere to Petrarch's and Dante's models of female beauty, such as Laura and Beatrice, and assimilated the poets' Neoplatonic aesthetics.[15] For them, a beautiful female image reflected a "celestial beauty which leads the poet or philosopher upward to the experience of divine or heavenly beauty."[16] Correspondingly, Agnolo Firenzuola, in his book on *On the Beauty of Women* (1548) declares:

> A beautiful woman, is the most beautiful object one can admire, and beauty is the greatest gift God bestowed on His human creatures. And so, through her virtue we direct our souls to contemplation, and through contemplation to the desire for heavenly things.[17]

Thus, Vasari's aesthetics derives from the philosophical and poetical Renaissance Neoplatonic notion of spiritual beauty. For Vasari Neoplatonic spiritual beauty meant the manifestation of vivacity, radiance, and grace in the image perceived through reason and sight in order to move the human soul and delight the spirit, as illustrated in his *Toilette of Venus* (1558; Fig. 1).[18]

Moreover, Vasari deliberately selects the image of Venus as the manifestation of his theory of beauty following not only the Neoplatonic philosophy but also the literary tradition of sixteenth- century treatises on love and beauty such as Mario Equicola in *Libro di natura d'amore* (Venice, 1525), Leone Ebreo in *Dialoghi d'amore* (Rome, 1535), Benedetto Varchi in *Lezioni sull'Amore* (1540), and Agostino Nifo in *Del bello. Il bello è nella natura* (Lugduni, 1549). These Cinquecento treatises on love were inspired, in turn, on the philosophical discourse on love by Marsilio Ficino, such as his *De amore* or *Sopra l'amore* (On Love, 1474) and *Commentary on Plato's Symposium on Love.* [19]

Fascinated with the subject of beauty and love embodied in the image of Venus, Vasari depicted her in the theme of the Toilet of Venus in several media: in a large cartoon, in a stained glass window, and in three paintings. The large cartoon is presently lost but an elaborate description of its imagery is recorded in a letter from Vasari to Nicolo Vespucci:

> A seated, nude Venus surrounded by the Three Graces: one while kneeling holds a mirror; the other with artistry braids her hair with pearls and corals in order to beautify Venus, another pours, with an emerald crystal vase, perfumed clear water in a mother-of-pearl conch for her bath. Eros, holding a bow and arrows, sleeps, reclining on Venus' garment. Other Cupids encircle the group while covering them and the landscape with roses and flowers. The ground is filled with stones; through their cracks flow water. Doves and swans taste this water. Hidden in the trees and bushes a satyr contemplates the beautiful Venus with the three Graces. His lascivious attitude, expressed by his open, wild eyes, and implied lust gesture was highly praised by Pope Clement who suggested that I paint a picture based on this drawing.[20]

The stained glass window was executed by Gaultieri d'Anversa in 1558 probably after Vasari's cartoon design for the Study Room in the Chamber of Caliope at the Palazzo Vecchio in Florence. The paintings were commissioned by Cardinal Ippolito de Medici (1532), by Jacopo Capponi (1559, both paintings are now lost) and by Luca Torrigiani (1558, Staatsgalerie in Stuttgart, Germany, Fig. 1)[21] (The stained glass window has a similar composition to the Luca Torrigiani's painting, probably because both versions draw from the cartoon design).

In Torrigiani's painting of *The Toilet of Venus,* Vasari portrays Venus being dressed and adorned by the Three Graces (*Charites* in Greek or *Gratiae* in

Latin) with numerous attributes of roses, myrtle, and a pair of doves, alluding to spiritual as well as erotic love.[22]

By selecting and depicting the classical subject of Venus beautifying herself, admiring herself in the mirror, and posing for the viewer's gaze and arousal, Vasari has addressed the physicality of an image embodying his aesthetic of female beauty. By suggesting she personifies both Love and Lust he alludes to astrological traditions and by including emblematic references to both Vanity and Prudence he adds Christian qualities.[23] Thus he manifests his assimilation of Renaissance Neoplatonism - the Christianization of pagan myths or the secularization of Christian religion.

Since antiquity the image of Venus has been defined in terms of physical beauty. In ancient Latin, the word Venus (*phosphorous*) means *the luminous one*. This appellation alludes to Venus as both planet and a goddess.[24] Therefore, the classical representations depict her holding a mirror (*speculum*) for reflecting her beauty, alluding to Venus magically linked to her reflection or life source, as in the Roman mosaic of third century, AD. at the Musée National du Bardo in Tunisia.

For the Platonist philosophers (Plato, Plotinus and Ficino) the planetary gods and goddesses represented poetic analogies of celestial and psychological functions. They described the operational principles of action, heart, and mind, that is to say, the psyche in which emotions, instincts and thought orbit the luminaries of the self and ego. Therefore, as a female symbol, Venus assumes the female planetary aspects associated with Luna (Moon), sensualism. For example, Venus as a planet or sphere expresses the active instinctual desire for pleasure and love, because "Love was born on the birthday of Venus."[25] It rules the arts, as illustrated in the *De Sphaera*, an Italian illuminated manuscript of the fifteenth-century, at the Biblioteca Estense in Modena, where Venus is depicted holding a mirror, nude, with flowers and jewelry; controlling the heavens with the zodiac signs of Libra and Taurus, and ruling on earth the aspects related to the arts and love.[26] Vasari endows his Venus in *The Toilet of Venus* with these ancient cosmological, philosophical and psychological implications.

In Vasari's *The Toilet of Venus*, the accompaniment of the Three Graces, as handmaiden to Venus, accords with the writings of Horace, *Odes*, I, 3 and Seneca, *De beneficiis*, I.3. Accordingly, for Horace, The Graces are usually depicted as semi-clothed because they are "free of deceit," and for Seneca, the Graces were partially clothed with exposed breasts because "benefits want to be seen." The Graces's dual character is associated with Venus's cosmic nature - planet and goddess - and derives from their personification in antiquity. In the Greek period the Charities personified grace, charm and beauty and were named Aglaia (meaning Splendor), Euphrosynem (Mirth), and Thalia (Abundance) and during the Roman era the Gratiae were a symbol of gratitude - Castitas (Chastity), Voluptas (Pleasure), and Pulchritudo (Beauty). Vasari's inclusion of the Graces adds yet another dimension to the symbolism of Venus, providing a moral basis for her actions such as decorum.

In Vasari's painting Venus gazes at her reflection in the mirror. The mirror, for Christian symbolism, represents the conventional attribute for truth and is traditionally carried by a personification of Prudence. Venus' action takes place at the same time as one of the Graces pours water, an action alluding to another virtue, the personification of Temperance. The other two Graces who assist Venus in her beautification, connote through their actions yet another virtue - Charity, which is inherent in their name "Charites." Thus the visual bond that exists between Venus and the Graces in the painting alludes and reinforces the spiritual aspects of Christian or Neoplatonic "sacred love." For Vasari, then, the Graces represent Beauty, Love, Pleasure as well as Giving, Receiving, and Requiting.

In acknowledging the complex signification of the image of Venus, one realizes that Vasari's rendition of Venus does not adhere to a specific meaning. The Vasarian goddess may be viewed as a cosmological power such as the pagan planetary Venus or as a natural element such as one of the five senses, Venus might symbolize Sight. Another Vasarian's interpretation can be associated with Christian personifications of virtue such as Chaste Love, Truth (*Veritas*) or Prudence (*Prudentia*) or vice such as Vanitas or Luxuria. Futhermore, Vasari's *oeuvre* may also aesthetic reflect his eclectic nature in perceiving and conceiving art; therefore, even though paradoxically, Vasari's conceit for the image of Venus combines a mixture of significations alluding to symbols of virtue as well as vice. In addition, the use of the mirror as an attribute of the sense of Sight can imply two perceptions: the viewer's perception of Venus as young and beautiful, and Venus's intimation of her future age and ugliness reflected in the mirror. The eye of the viewer becomes the mirror of present life whereas Venus's mirror becomes the mirror of her past. Although viewers see in the painting the present beauty and future ugliness of Venus, they are seduced by the now, the narcissistic exhibition of her body (*Luxuria* and *Vanitas*). Conversely, Venus is reminded by the mirror's reflection of the the transience of life and truth of her nature: "I am who I am" (Exodus 3:14). Vasari elaborates on the signification of vanitas in depicting a narcistic action of the part of the sacred birds of Venus–the doves–who are fascinated with viewing their image in the basin of water placed at the feet of Venus. Purposefully, Vasari creates with a diagonal movement for the viewer a symbolic and visual connection between the dove's water reflection and Venus' mirror image.

With the recent discovery of *The Bacchanal* (Fig 2), the pendant painting to *The Toilet of Venus* (Fig. 1), a voyeuristic interpretation maybe further suggested. For the Luca Torrigiani commission, perhaps, Vasari decided to represent two paintings based on his cartoon designes - *The Toilet of Venus* and *The Bacchanal*. In the drawing studies for the Bacchanal painting and in the painting itself, the "lascivious" satyr is included, assisting the intoxicated Silenus or stealing grapes and libations for himself. In the painting of *The Bacchanal*, the Three Graces, who attended and completed the toilet of Venus, can be seen, now, as Maenads dancing at the music performed with tambourines and recorders by the nymphs, fauns, and satyrs in the Dionysiac forest. Unlike Venus's beautiful attendants, Bacchus's escorts can be seen as wild beasts from the forest, such as wild horses, lions, tigers, or panthers, rams, and as symbols of fertility, since they were held sacred to him. Bacchus's companions and worshippers, intoxicated with the nectar of grapes provided by Bacchus during a drinking contest, crown and decorate their god with wreaths of laurel, ivy, and grape leaves.

The young, effeminate, idealized body of Bacchus contrasts with the aging, coarse and muscular body of Silenus and the satyrs. Vasari in representing Bacchus as an image of male beauty relies on Pliny and Vitruvius' theory of human proportions[27] as well as on Ficino's description *On a painting of Love* according to the poet Agathon where Love is personified by a young, tender, agile, well-proportionate and glowing man.[28] From Vasari's perspective, then, the beautiful depiction of Bacchus expands his theory of beauty to include the male body as well as the female body (Venus) and both images of beauty reflect a conceit of love.

These pendant paintings portray parallelism of poses, gestures, coloration, and movement. However, although Venus and Bacchus are facing each other, they do not gaze at each other: they are both self-absorbed with their individual preparation for their thirst, as Venus actively adorns herself and Bacchus passively indulges in his revelry.[29] Familiar with the legend of the liaison between Venus and Bacchus, which resulted in Priapus, Vasari creates with these two paintings a theatrical scene where the viewer, with humor, visually connects their actions and with pleasure anticipates a passionate conclusion.

In contrast to the cartoon's description, the painting of *The Toilet of Venus* excludes the voyeuristic satyr; however, Vasari has cleverly replaced him with the pendant painting or the viewer. This maniera conceit or teasing technique fits in well with the maniera spirit of joviality and self-absorption. On the one level the gazing action may appear to be fortuitous and puerile, with the viewer or satyr ogling the beautiful naked woman; or, on another level, the narcissistic behavior of Venus regarding herself in the mirror can be seen as an allusion to her vanity, thereby manifesting the temporal world. Obviously, the reflected image in the mirror ought to be of a beautiful, voluptuous, and ageless woman. However, on careful observation, the reflection reveals an aging and sexless woman. Is Vasari tantalizing the viewer again? Is he conveying the paradox of the Neoplatonic aesthetic, as well as his own? Does he as the Renaissance Neoplatonists attempt the reconciliation of pagan myths and attitudes reinforced by Christian religion and beliefs? Can feminine beauty be both sensual and spiritual? Vasari, again, allows the viewer to speculate and adjudicate!

Mannerist painters such as Vasari chooses the image of Venus because she symbolizes both intellectual and physical powers. As a planet she rules the arts. In turn he, Vasari, as an artist and creator is ruled by her planetary force. As a female the goddess displays her beauty, and the artist, as man, is bewitched by her physical beauty.

Notes

*.   I want to expresses my gratitude to Professors Aphrodite Alexandrakis of Barry University, Florida, Christopher Evangeliou of Towson University, John Anton of University of South Florida, and architect John Hendrix of Cornell University, for their stimulating comments. A version of this study was presented at the Neoplatonism and Western Aesthetics Conference, University of Crete, August, 1998.

1.   Patricia Rubin, *Giorgio Vasari* (London: Yale University Press, 1996) and Liana De Girolami Cheney, ed. *Readings in Italian Mannerism* (New York/London: Peter Lang Publisher, 1997), for an historical discussion of Mannerism and Maniera.

2.   I have used the Italian version of Giorgio Vasari, *Le vite dei piu eccelenti pittori, scultori et architettori* ed. by Gaetano Milanesi (Florence: G. C. Sansoni, 1970-74, here noted as Vasari-Milanesi) and an English version on Giorgio Vasari, *The Lives of the Most Excellent Painters, Sculptors, and Architects,* modern translation by George Bull (Baltimore: Penguin Books, 1965 and revised edition 1971).

3.   For studies and excellent bibliographies on Vasari and his technique of art, see Louis S. Maclehose, *Vasari on Technique* (New York: Dover Publications, Inc., 1960); Roberto Panichi, *La Tecnica dell'Arte negli Scritti di Giorgio Vasari* (Florence: Alinea Editrice, 1991); and, Roland LeMollé, *Georges Vasari et le vocabulaire de la critique d'art dans les "Vite"* (Grenoble: Ellug, 1988).

4.   Cochrane, E. *Historians and Historiography in The Italian Renaissance* (Chicago: University of Chicago Press, 1985), 402, and Vasari-Milanesi, Preface, I, 7.

5.   See catalogue entry of G. Ewald, "La Toeletta di Venere," in *Giorgio Vasari: Principi, letterati e artisti nelle carte di Giorgio Vasari,* ed. by Laura Corti, et. al (Florence: Edam, 1981), 74-75, and Vittoria Markova, "Un Baccante ritrovato di Giorgio Vasari, proveniente dalla Galleria Gerini," *Kunst des Cinquecento in der Toskana,* 1994, 21-30. The Gerini collection was recorded in the drawings of Ranieri Allegranti and subsequently in the engravings of Lorenzo Lorenzi and Ferdinando Gregori in 1786, included in the engravings were these two paintings by Vasari. (See Plates III and IV in Corti, *Giorgio Vasari*), Catherine Monbeig-Goguel has located several preparatory drawings for these paintings at the Louvre and Uffizi. See Catherine Monbeig-Goguel, *Vasari et son temps, Dessins Italiens du Musèe du Louvre* (Paris: Éditions des Musées Nationaux, 1972), 172-73, Plate 222 and Uffizi drawings No. 620 F and 641 F.

6.   See Vasari-Milanesi, Preface, III, 35, for a definition of these terms, and James V. Mirollo, *Mannerism and Renaissance Poetry* (New Haven: Yale University Press, 1984), 10-14. Obviously, Vasari is following Marsilio Ficino, see Sears Jayne, ed. and trans. *Marsilio Ficino: Commentary on Plato's Symposium on Love* (Dallas: Spring Publications, Inc., 1985), 93-95 and Laura Vestra, "Love and

Beauty in Ficino and Plotinus," in Konrad Eisenbichler and Olga Zorzi Pugliese, ed. *Ficino and Renaissance Neoplatonism* (Toronto: Dovehouse Editions, 1986), 178.

7.   Philip P. Wiener, ed. *Dictionary of the History of Ideas* (New York: Scribner's Sons, 1974), Vol. III, 510-12; Jayne, *Marsilio Ficino,* 89-91; and Laura Vestra, "Love and Beauty in Ficino and Plotinus," 179-80.

8.   Vasari-Milanesi, Preface I, 93.

9.   Christos Evangeliou, "Koros Kalos: Plotinus on Cosmic Beauty and Other Beauties," paper read at the Neoplatonism and Western Aesthetics, University of Crete, August, 1998, and John Anton, "Plotinus' Conception of the Functions of the Artist," *Journal of Aesthetic and Art Criticism,* XXVI (Fall 1967), 91-101.

10.   Jayne, *Marsilio Ficino,* 90. Ficino explains how Beauty is the splendor of the divine countenance, 89-91; Vestra, "Love and Beauty in Ficino and Plotinus," 185, and Liana De Girolami Cheney, *Botticelli's Neoplatonic Images* (Potomac, MD: Scripta Humanistica, 1993), 32-34.

11.   Vasari-Milanesi, VII, 710 and V, 386.

12.   Jayne, *Marsilio Ficino,* 93-95.

13.   Vasari-Milanesi, Preface, III, 8.

14.   Erwin Panofsky, *Idea: A Concept in Art Theory* (Columbia, SC: University of South Carolina Press, 1968), 71-79. For a clear study on Vasari's concept of nature and an extensive bibliography on this subject see Mirollo, *Mannerism and Renaissance Poetry,* 8, and Liana De Girolami Cheney, "Vasari's Interpretation of Female Beauty," in *Concepts of Beauty in Renaissance Art* (London: Ashgate, 1998), 179-190.

15.   See Baldesar Castiglione, *Il Cortegiano,* Chapters XXVI and XXVIII of Book I in Barocchi, "Bellezza e Grazia," 1609-1708;. Luigi Baldacci, "*Gli Asolani* del Bembo e Venere celeste," *Il petrarchismo italiano nel '500* (Milan-Naples: Riccardi, 1957), 107-110; Olga Zorzi Pugliese, "Varianos on Ficino's *De amore*: The Hymns to Love by Benivieni and Castiglone," in *Ficino and Renaissance Neoplatonism* , 113-121; and, Mary Rogers, "The Decorum of Women's Beauty: Trissino, Firenzuola, Luigini and the Representation of Women in Sixteenth-Century Painting," *Renaissance Studies,* 2, 1988, 47-87.

16.   Wiener, *Dictionary of the History of Ideas,* Vol. III, 508.

17.   For the theory of female beauty in Italian Renaissance art, see, Elizabeth Cropper, "On Beautiful Women: Parmigianino, Petrarchismo and the Vernacular Style," *Art Bulletin,* 58, 1976, 374-94; Elizabeth Cropper, The Beauty of Woman: Problems in the Rhetoric of Renaissance Portraiture," in *Rewriting the Renaissance: The Discourses of Sexual Differences in Early Modern Europe,* ed. Margaret Ferguson, Maureen Quilligan and Nancy Vickers (Chicago: University of Chicago Press, 1986), 175-90; Elizabeth Cropper, "The Place of Beauty in the High Renaissance and its Displacement in the History of Art," in *Place and*

Displacement in the Renaissance, ed. Albin Vos. (Bimington, NY, 1994), 159-205; Mary Rogers, "The Decorum of Women's Beauty," 47-87; and, Agnolo Firenzuola, *On the Beauty of Women, 1548,* trans. and ed. by Konrad Eisenbichler and Jacqueline Murray (Philadelphia: University of Pennsylvania Press, 1992).

18.   Erwin Panofsky, *Idea: A Concept in Art Theory* (Columbia, SC: University of South Carolina Press, 1968), 129-41.

19.   Paolo Lorenzetti, *La bellezza e l'amore nei trattari del cinquecento* (Pisa: Scuola Normale, 1922), John Nelson, *The Renaissance Theory of Love* (Florence, 1933) and Cynthia M. Pyle, "Il neoplatonismo e le favole mitologiche," in *Milan and Lombardy in the Renaissance: Essays in Cultural History* (Rome: La Fenice, 1997), 151-182.

20.   Karl Frey, *Der Literarische Nachlass Giorgio Vasaris* (Munich: George Müller, 1923), I, 2, 3, and 8.

21.   See n. 4.

22.   For illustrations representing the Three Graces in art, see Jane Davidson Reid, ed. *The Oxford Guide to Classical Mythology in the Arts: 1300-1990s* (New York: Oxford University Press, 1993), 475-80; for The Toilet of Venus. 13-44.

23.   In representing the ambiguity of Vanity and Prudence, who both traditionally are shown looking into a mirror, Vasari may have referred to Michelangelo's drawing on the *Allegory of Prudence* at the British Museum in London. See Paul Barolsky, *The Faun in the Garden* (University Park, PA: The Pennsylvania State University Press, 1994), p 10. Fig. 5.

24.   Jayne *Marsilio Ficino,* 116-17.

25.   *Ibid.*, 120. Ficino goes on elaborating on the nature of love as well as passions stating: "Love follows and worships Venus and is seized by a desire for the beautiful, since Venus herself is very beautiful. "

26.   Solange de Mailley Nesle, *Astrology: History, Symbols, and Signs* (Rochester, VT: Inner Traditions International, 1985), 134-35.

27.   Vitruvius, III, I, 3 ed. and trans. by Morris Hicky Morgan, *Vitruvius: the Ten Books on Architecture* (New York: Dover, 1960) and Pliny, VII, 77, ed. and trans. by Jex-Blake Sellers, *The Elder Pliny's Chapters on The History of Art* (Chicago: Ares Publishers, Inc., 1976). See also Erwin Panofsky, "The History of the Theory of Human Proportions as a Reflection of The History of Styles," in *The Meaning of the Visual Arts* (New York: Doubleday, 1955), 89-99.

28.   Jayne *Marsilio Ficino,* 95-96. See Aline Rousselle, *Porneia: On Desire and The Body in Antiquity* (Oxford: Blackwell, 1993), 5-23, for a discussion on the bodies of men, and 24-46, on the bodies of women.

29.   Walter F. Otto, *Dionysus: Myth and Cult* (Dallas, Spring Publications, 1986), 176, for a discussion on the sensual affair between Aphrodite (Venus) and Dionysus (Bacchus).

Neoplatonism in the Design of Baroque Architecture

John Hendrix

Certain elements of seventeenth-century Roman Baroque architecture, especially in the work of Pietro da Cortona and Francesco Borromini, can be shown to be an enactment and representation of conceptual systems and epistemic structures of Neoplatonic philosophy. Neoplatonism played a role in the expression of Renaissance architects such as Leon Battista Alberti and Andrea Palladio. Neoplatonic writings by Plotinus, Pseudo-Dionysius, Nicolas Cusanus, Marcilio Ficino and Giovanni Pico della Mirandola were available to architects in seventeenth-century Rome in libraries such as the Biblioteca Casanatense, Angelica, Vallicelliana, and the Accademia dei Lincei. The ideas of those writers were also expressed in archaeological and scientific treatises by Athanasius Kircher, Giuseppe Rosaccio, Alessandro Piccolomini, Giovanni Agucchi and Ristoro d'Arezzo, and artistic treatises by Gian Lomazzo, Federico Zuccaro, and Pietro da Cortona. The writings were known by the architects and collected by their patrons. They contributed to a climate in seventeenth-century Rome which combined philosophical development, artistic theory, scientific discovery and theological tenets into a unique intellectual culture which was expressed and reflected by the architecture along with the other arts of painting, sculpture, music and drama.

The most significant elements of Neoplatonic philosophy which were translated into architectural form were the representation of the structure of the cosmos; the relationship between the universe as macrocosm and man as microcosm; the hierarchy of being, including corporeal, mental, and spiritual levels, or nature, mind and God; and the passage from multiplicity to unity.

Artistic theory addressed the imperative to connect the human mind with the mystery of the natural world in the visual arts, involving the Neoplatonic Idea, which connected the creative process of the artist with the process of creation in nature. Neoplatonic conceptual formulations were borrowed by architects and translated into architectural designs. The formulations provided the architects with a way of thinking, a way of seeing the world which they applied to the architecture. Architecture became a visual model of philosophical systems that had been developed in the Neoplatonic tradition, a tradition combining Platonism and Aristotelianism, and philosophy and theology. Elements of Baroque architecture can be shown to be an artistic expression of those systems, and a culmination of the conceptual development from the early Middle Ages through the Renaissance. Such intentions would be inherited in the late Baroque architecture of Guarino Guarini and Bernardo Vittone in Piedmont.

The Structure of the Cosmos

In Book IX of *On Architecture*, Vitruvius described the universe as an architectural design, and the laws of architecture were identical to the laws of the cosmos. God was seen as *deus architectus mundi,* or architect of the world, and the architect was seen as *architectus secundus deus*, a second God.[1] In *La Sfera del Mondo*, published in 1566 in Venice, Alessandro Piccolomini wrote: "We must first know that this huge machine which we call our world was made by an extremely wise and powerful architect."[2] In reconstructions of the Vitruvian theater, Giovanni Giocondo and Cesare Cesariano, among others, inscribed four equilateral triangles in a circle to create twelve points along the circumference of the theater, to "define the twelve locations of the zodiac described by astrologers as harmonious music derived from computations based on the stars."[3] Giulio Camillo wrote of his *theatro*, where information was categorized by location in the plan of a theater to aid memory, published in *Tutte le opere* in 1552: "When these signs have been gathered together according to an organic order and impressed on the memory by their images and symbols, the mind can move away from this middle celestial world...towards the supercelestial world of the Ideas...in harmony with astral influences."[4] The links between levels of reality in the *theatro*, between the signs and what they signified, are occult forces and astral influences.

The purpose of the *theatro* was to allow the soul to be harmonized with the celestial machine of the universe through the symbols. Frances Yates has written, "The theater is a vision of the world and of the nature of things seen from a height, from the stars and the super-celestial founts of wisdom." Renaissance cosmology was the meeting ground between the rational and mathematic order of Greek science and the mythology and magic of the East.[5] In the Pythagorian musical theory revived by Nicolas Cusanus and the Florentine Platonic Academy, music is divided between the inner (*humana*) and the cosmic (*mundana*).[6] The *musica humana* was seen as the movement of the macrocosm, the planetary rhythms, reflected in the soul. Similar intervals would be found between musical tones as between planets, and between aspects of thought and aspects of external reality. As Ficino wrote in the *Commentary*, "In all these things the internal perfection produces the external."[7] Pythagorian ratios of numeric harmony were enacted by Alberti in the facade of Santa Maria Novella.[8]

In seventeenth-century Rome, Pietro da Cortona's painting *Allegoria del Tempio della Sapienza*, and his preliminary design for the church of the Accademia di San Luca, Santi Luca e Martina, can be read as "allegorical representations of a cosmological idea."[9] Numerology and symbolic geometry were incorporated into the design of many Renaissance and Baroque churches. In *Allegoria del Tempio della Sapienza*, the *Sapienza Minerva, Magna mater* and also allegory of Rome, appears seated in a temple surrounded by columns in a circle, with a statue of Mercury in a niche. The Allegories of Virtue stand between the columns, while female figures representing the cosmological sciences enter the temple carrying a globe with stars, a model of the planets, and geographical maps. The architect, with a table on which the orders of columns are depicted, gestures to the cosmological sciences as the origin of the orders.[10] In the plan for Santi Luca e Martina, circles of columns, twelve on the exterior and eight on the interior, are references to a cosmological system, as is a circle inscribed in a square. The twelve columns on the circumference of the round plan refer to the twelve locations of the zodiac; the number eight is a universal symbol of resurrection, combining pagan numerical symbolism and Christian theology. In *The Celestial Hierarchies*, in the sixth century, Pseudo-Dionysius ascribed angelic hierarchies to the zodiac. Cortona's circle represents God as well, while the square represents the squaring of the four elements of the physical world - earth, air, water, and fire - from Plato, and the conception of man, from Neoplatonism. In the *Teatro del Cielo e della terra*, a book owned by Cortona,[11] Giuseppe Rosaccio stated that the elementary or incorruptible part of the cosmos is divided into the four elements,[12] an idea derived from Alessandro Piccolomini's *La Sfera del Mondo*.

The circle inscribed in the square can be read as both a Platonic symbol of universal harmony and the *Christos-Logos* of Christ.[13] In Neoplatonism the symbolic representation of cosmic harmony and the intellectual "Idea of the Beautiful" are combined with Christian theology. As described by Plotinus in *The Enneads*, "One who has attained to the vision of the Intellectual beauty and grasped the beauty of the Authentic Intellect will be able also to come to understand the Father and Transcendent of that Divine Being."[14] A papal brief issued by Gregory XV in 1623 and owned by Cortona read "No faculty can compete with the three arts from antiquity (architecture, sculpture and painting), as God himself participated in the construction of the world...where he was an admirable painter drawing the perspective of the earth and an amazing sculptor shaping clay with his hands in the creation of man, and he was the greatest architect in the great construction of the universe."[15] God, who had created Man in his image, consented to allow man to form a new intelligible cosmos through the work of art, a second cosmos as a reflection of the original divine creation. From the *Enneads*, "Artists do not simply reproduce the visible, but they go back to the principles in which nature itself had found its origin."[16] Such an intention can be related to Alberti's conception of *concinnitas*, where Pythagorean ratios of numeric harmony, or eurhythmia, were enacted with the intention to represent the laws by which nature produces works so as to transfer them to architecture, in order that architecture embody the ideational formation of an abstract beauty according to those laws, as at Santa Maria Novella.[17] In such a way the structure of the universe and the structure of the mind are enacted and related simultaneously.

In the treatises on the Vitruvian theater by Giocondo and Cesariano, an exterior semi-circle is inscribed in a square to form the proscenium area of the theater, and a square is placed on the interior. In Renaissance art, the square is associated with the Four Virtues, and the four personifications of the arts. A catafalque constructed for Michelangelo in the church of San Lorenzo in Florence includes paintings representing the Four Virtues as Spirit, Mercy, Knowledge, and Industriousness,[18] and the four personifications of the arts, Architecture, Painting, Sculpture and Poetry. In Neoplatonic thought, the square represents the earth as a manifestation of God. It also corresponds to human form, and the materialization of the Idea, or the design in the mind of the Creator.[19] From Ficino, "The form of all things conceived in the celestial Mind are the Ideas."[20]

Cortona described the relation between intuition and cosmic structures in the *Tratatto della pittura, e scultura*:

One benefits from [intellectual] delight, while in images the soul knows through discourse the reason of various things, without apprehension and sensual knowledge: as in a painting of a serene and nocturnal sky, the intellect understands the great speed of celestial motion, the many revolutions of the heavens, and the motions of the planets, which indicate the magnitude of the sun, the moon, and the stars; with this knowledge intellectual delight is received.[21]

The mind is connected with the mysteries of the cosmos through the visual arts. Images communicate intellectual ideas, which are signs of God in nature. "Divine and eternal Ideas are images made by God...of the entire machine of the universe."[22] In his *Discourse* of 1611, Giovanni Agucchi, with the help of Galileo Galilei, developed a metaphorical system of the universe in which the central immobile motor is the seat of the eternal and divine Idea, the seat of absolute unity, goodness, and beauty. The center is the divine sun, "which as the beginning brings back and unites all things." It is the source of all beauty and "true form and idea," the beginning and end of all movement, and the center of the revolving cosmos.[23] Agucchi said that this theory "conformed to Christian truth."[24] Gian Paolo Lomazzo, in his *Idea del Tempio della Pittura* of 1590, which was inventoried in the library of the Accademia di San Luca in 1624,[25] sought to apply the "order, measure and appearance"[26] of the mathematical system of the structural harmony of the cosmos to the design arts. Ristoro d'Arezzo wrote in *Composizione del mondo* that the cosmos is "a well organized house, or a solemn temple, with a sky with points of stars like a historiated stained-glass window with holy images, which bears the sign of God which rises from a chorus of angels."[27] The role of the artist was to observe nature in order to discover "the forces which agitate the conscience of beings and spirits which circulate in the middle of things,"[28] and then to read and represent them. In a design for the Villa Pamphili, Borromini intended to construct an architecture based on the observation of celestial movements, as he wrote in a letter preserved in the Vatican Library.

In Neoplatonic philosophy, the human being is a microcosm of the universe, interior relations and movements are connected to cosmic relations and movements, and the individual soul participates in the Divine mind. Ficino described man as a microcosm organized and functioning according to the same principles as the macrocosm of the universe, given coherence by the "dynamic principle of Platonic love, so that the soul in its own way will become the whole universe."[29] For Cusanus, "Human nature contains in itself the intellectual and the sensible natures, and therefore, embracing within itself all things, has been called the microcosm or world in miniature."[30] Renaissance architects saw the church as being a microcosmic recreation of the universe as temple of God, as for Palladio "The little temples we make ought to resemble this very great one, which, by his immense goodness was perfectly completed."[31] Alberti expressed an intention to impart the presence of God in the architecture of the church: "I would deck it out in every part so that anyone who entered it would start with awe for his admiration at all the noble things, and could scarcely restrain himself from exclaiming that what he saw was a place undoubtedly worthy of God."[32]

The Hierarchy of Being

In the design of many Renaissance and Baroque churches, the ascension of forms from the ground floor to the cupola and lantern can be read as a passage which the worshipper experiences from the corporeal world to the world of God, represented by the pure light shining through the lantern. The light shining through the oculus at the end of the nave of Alberti's Sant'Andrea can be read as the attainment of the absolute oneness of God, resulting from a passage through a multiplicity of forms in the elevations of the nave, where geometrical shapes and architectural elements appear in a complex variety of sizes, positions, and inter-relationships. "Relations among the multiplicity of forms manifest the one Final Cause of Harmony,"[33] creating the impression of unity through diversity and harmony through multiplicity, as a microcosm of the order of the universe, as the singularity of the soul relates to the universality of the cosmos in Neoplatonic thought. The interior of the church in seventeenth-century Rome often accommodates the procession down a long barrel-vaulted nave of a Latin Cross plan, lined with columns and architraves representing classical temple fronts, toward a vanishing point which is the altar and the sight of transubstantiation, the culmination of the spiritual journey represented by the procession. Such a construction can be seen in designs for apparatus for church festivals, combining church interior and stage construction, such as Cortona's design for the *Quarantore in San Lorenzo e Damaso* in 1633. The finite representation of the infinite is acheived through the mechanism of perspectival construction.

As Alberti expressed his intention to impart the presence of the ineffable God through architecture, so that "anyone who entered it would start with awe for his admiration at all the noble things," the incitement of such awe would be accomplished through *concinnitas*, involving the composition of "parts that are quite separate from each other by their nature, according to some precise rule, so that they correspond to one another in appearance,"[34] in the attainment of the absolute through the multiple, enacting the relationship of the human mind to the external world through underlying principles unknowable to reason or sensual experience alone, as enacted at Santa Maria Novella. Alberti's conception of *concinnitas* can be related to Marsilio Ficino's ideal of a mystical property as an organizing element. As for Alberti, where *concinnitas* is an ideational object beyond sense experience, "conjoined to the spirit and reason,"[35] so for Ficino in the Commentary,

> Since the single parts of the soul have been reorganized into one mind, the soul is now made a single whole out of many...when the soul has been made one which is in itself the very nature and essence of soul, it remains that immediately it recovers itself into the One which is above essence, that is, God.[36]

Concinnitas is for Alberti the law of that ideational One which is above essence. For both Ficino and Alberti, God is both exterior to and producing the finite universe, and identical with the infinite universe, reconciling Platonism and Aristotelianism, as in Neoplatonism.[37]

In seventeenth-century Rome, Francesco Borromini inherited certain intentions to relate architectural structure to philosophical ideas, interweaving theological traditions, Platonic hierarchies of being and Aristotelian development into his architecture. Aspects of Neoplatonism which can be read in Borromini's architecture, especially the church of San Carlo alle Quattro Fontane, were a syncretic coincidence or reconciliation of opposites, a structuring of the conceptual process as a microcosm of the order of the universe, the representation of the absolute being inaccessible to reason, the transition from multiplicity to singularity, and the hybridization of form.

Cusanus wrote, "In the providence of God contradictions are reconciled."[38] The design of San Carlo contains the reconciliation of contradictions: alternating balustrades, convex and concave elevations enclosing a space, and simultaneous enclosure and expansion through the illusion of extended barrel vaults from the central space. The building may have been conceived as a conceptual microcosm, a metaphysical system, based in the hierarchies of Neoplatonic philosophy. Borromini may have been associated with Athanasius Kircher, who taught Neoplatonic philosophy at the Università dei Marmorari, which met at the church of Santi Quatro Coronati al Celio in Rome in the early Seventeenth

Century. Borromini is recorded as having been a student there at the same time in the Book of the Carmelengo in the *Archivio dell'Università*.[39] He was a friend of Virgilio Spada and was employed at the Palazzo Spada. His uncle and mentor, Carlo Maderno, was a member of the Accademia di San Luca.

San Carlo can be read, like many Italian Renaissance and Baroque churches, as an analogue to an ascending movement throught levels of being in the structure of the universe, where the ascension through the forms of the interior space to the cupola and to the lantern corresponded to Neoplatonic elements of the corporeal, mental, and spiritual levels of being. In the *Platonic Theology* and the *Commentary on Plato's Symposium*, Ficino classified the elements in the hierarchy of being in ascending order as Body, Nature, Soul, and Mind, corresponding to the four elements of the physical world. "Just as a single ray of the sun lights up four bodies, fire, air, water, and earth, so a single ray of God illuminates the Mind, the Soul, Nature, and Matter."[40] Those elements were characteristics of both man and the universe, so that the building as structural conception of being was a microcosm of the universe. Mind is the first level emanating from God, "turned toward God, illuminated by his ray...God, who is omnipotent, imprints on the Mind, reaching out toward him, the natures of all things which are to be created. On the Angelic Mind are painted all the things which we perceive in these bodies."[41] The lower level of Mind is the Soul, self-moving, originating from chaos and receiving forms from the Mind. "Although the World Soul is at first formless and a chaos, when it is directed by love toward the mind, having received from it the forms, it becomes a world."[42] The soul is divided into higher and lower, or reason and perception. The Higher Soul is divided into two faculties, Reason and Mind, Reason being directed toward corporeal perception, while Mind is directed toward the *intellectus divinus*, or contemplation. The Lower Soul is biologically predetermined, by fate. It is composed of functions relating to physiology, external perception and internal perception. The physiological functions are propagation, nourishment and growth. "If we say that man procreates, grows, and nourishes, then the soul, as father and creator of the body, begets, feeds, and nourishes."[43] External perception incorporates the five senses while interior perception is an imaginative faculty which translates physical signals into mental images. "Men possess both reason and sensation. Reason by itself grasps the incorporeal Reasons of all things. Sensation, through the five instruments of its body, perceives the images and qualities of bodies."[44]

The design of San Carlo contains the use of three basic geometries, the octagon, cross, and circle or oval, repeated in different combinations in the plan and elevations of the worship space, and the cupola and lantern.[45] The interwoven, inter-penetrating geometries which define the plan and elevations correspond to the sublunary, corporeal world of nature and the body, the realm of procreation and growth, where divine light has become corrupted and diffused, resulting in imperfect beauty and obscured knowledge in the world of images. The ordering and juxtaposition of the geometries in the pattern of the cupola correspond to the Soul or Intellect, the lower part of the Mind, mediating between the corporeal and spiritual, rationalizing the forms found in the chaotic realm of matter. The resolution of the same geometries in the emblem in the lantern, as they became a single unified image, expresses the absolute, unified and pure form of the Divine spirit and Mind, the source and point of emanation of light and form, illuminating the congregational space. The forms of the lantern are uncorrupted and inaccessible, "containing the prototypes of all that which exists in the lower zone."[46] The church can be seen as a representation of the Neoplatonic *circuitus spiritualis* of the universe where the static ideas of the Cosmic Mind are converted into "dynamic causes moving and fertilizing the sublunary world," in the words of Erwin Panofsky.

The interweaving of the three geometries, the circle, cross and octagon, in the plan of San Carlo is an elaboration of the Pythagorean juxtapositions begun by Alberti. It is a geometric construction based in numeric proportions. For Nicolas Cusanus, the transmutation of geometries was the transcendence of boundaries of thought, and thought was defined as the imperceptible movement from the universal to the particular.[47] A logical geometric progression, a transmutation of geometries by Borromini, is disguised in the unrecognizable form of the plan of San Carlo, an inexplicable "lozenge" shape, as the underlying reason of nature is unrecognizable in its forms, as resulting from *concinnitas*, in the projection of logic onto nature. In the tradition of medieval guilds and occult knowledge, the hidden or secret, the underlying geometry of the architecture was not to be revealed.

The conception of the structure of thought in the hierarchies of Ficino's *Teologica Platonica*, or *Platonic Theology*, the architectonic, can be characterized as a combination of hierarchy and motion, or dynamic passage, as a microcosm of the structure of the universe, as elaborated in *Five Questions Concerning the Mind*:

> First, whether or not the motion of the mind is directed toward some definite end; second, whether the end of this motion of the mind is motion or rest; third, whether this end is something particular or universal; fourth, whether the mind

is ever able to attain its desired end; fifth, whether, after it has obtained the end, it ever loses it...We cannot reach the highest summit of things unless, first, taking less account of the inferior parts of the soul, we ascend to the highest part, the mind. If we have concentrated our powers in this most fruitful part of the soul, then without doubt by means of the highest part itself, that is, by means of mind, we shall ourselves have the power of creating mind...The motion of each of all the natural species proceeds according to a certain principle...the limits of motion are two, namely, that from which it flows and that to which it flows. From these limits motion obtains its order.[48]

The power of the creating mind is enacted in the architecture of the Baroque church, by an ascension through the soul to its highest part, the mind. Each of the five questions is in turn enacted: the teleology of the ascension, the juxtaposition and interweaving of movement and repose in architectural forms, and of particular and universal, the possibility or impossibility of absolute knowledge, and the teleology of that knowledge. Movement is directed both towards and away from the divine source of emanation, the light from the lantern, so it can be inferred that the teleology of the ascension and of the absolute knowledge are the same. From the *Commentary*, "As they flow from Him so they flow back to Him...Mind, Soul, Nature, and Matter, proceeding from God, strive to return to the same."[49] In the tradition of Cusanus, the architectonic is constructed on the knowledge rather than the existence of God or universal intelligence. Such would be a structural analogy between the conceptual process and the structure of the universe, imaged in terms of structure and motion, generation, procreation, fragmentation and dissemination in both thought and physical reality. Erwin Panofsky described the motion of the hierarchies in Ficino's *Teologica Platonica*:

> This whole universe is a *divinum animal*; it is enlivened and its various hierarchies are interconnected with each other by a "divine influence emanating from God, penetrating the heavens, descending through the elements, and coming to an end in matter." An uninterrupted current of supernatural energy flows from above to below and reverts from below to above, thus forming a *circuitus spiritualis*, to quote Ficino's favorite expression. The Cosmic Mind continually contemplates and loves God, while at the same time caring for the Cosmic Soul beneath it. The Cosmic Soul in turn converts the static ideas and intelligences comprised in the Cosmic Mind into dynamic causes moving and fertilizing the sublunary world, and thus stimulates nature to produce visible things...With all its corruptibility the sublunary world participates in the eter-

nal life and beauty of God imparted to it by the "divine influence." But on its way through the celestial realm the "splendor of divine goodness," as beauty is defined by the Neoplatonists, has been broken up into as many rays as there are spheres or heavens. There is therefore no perfect beauty on earth.[50]

Such is the aesthetic of the Baroque, the contrast between the purity of the ineffable Cosmic Mind as "that which is denied to words," and the signification of the "dynamic causes moving and fertilizing the sublunary world," an "infinite materiality of images and bodies"[51] in architectural forms which "proliferate beyond everything signified, placing language in excess of corporeality." The proliferation and fragmentation of rays is best represented in Bernini's *Ecstasy of Saint Theresa* and *Chair of Saint Peter* in Rome.

The dynamic passage through the hierarchy of being, interwoven physical matter and proliferation of bodies, toward a resolution of forms in the purity and transcendent light of the lantern displayed in the structure of San Carlo can be read as well in ceiling frescoes in Baroque Rome such as the *Glorification of the Reign of Urban VIII* by Pietro da Cortona in the Gran Salone of the Palazzo Barberini, and the *Missionary Work of the Jesuits* by Andrea Pozzo in the church of Sant' Ignazio and the *Triumph of the Sacred Name of Jesus* by Baciccio in the church of Il Gesù at the end of the century. In the Renaissance, the passage could be read in the *Assumption of the Virgin* in the Cathedral of Parma by Correggio from 1526, where entangled, gesturing bodies encircle and give way to a blinding ineffable light, the light of the sun and Divine wisdom. For Ficino "God is the center of all things, completely single, simple, and motionless. But all things produced from Him are many, composite, and in some way movable."[52]

The void at the center of a circle is an element of Neoplatonic thought and Dionysian Negative Theology, where God is unknowable and inaccessible. Cusanus's version of negative theology is the *via negativa*, where God can only be perceived in His absence and cognitive knowledge is rejected to achieve mystical union in the 'cloud of unknowing', later manifest as the Baroque *stupefazione*. The circle is the perfect manifestation of God, and at the same time absolute unknowing, or learned ignorance. In Renaissance treatises on theater design, Alberti described the stage of the theater as the void at the center,[53] and Cesariano wrote that "the formation of a theater begins with the base perimeter circling around the central void in a rotating line.[54] In the void at the center of Roman Baroque ceiling frescoes, the blank space of a blinding divine light can be understood to represent the inaccessible and unknowable God, as can the source of light in the lantern of the Baroque church.

Late Baroque Architecture

Intentions to represent philosophical systems in architecture, including Neoplatonic ones, were inherited by Guarino Guarini and Bernardo Vittone in Piedmont. The exterior of Vittone's Cappella della Visitazione in Vallinotto, for example, reveals a three-tiered hierarchy of the worship space, cupola and lantern, as at San Carlo. Vittone wrote about the church in his *Istruzioni diverse*, that "The visitor's glance travels through the spaces created by the vaults and enjoys, supported by the concealed light, the variety of the hierarchy which gradually increases."[55] Vittone's architecture incorporates conceptual systems, as can be seen in the architecture and passages from his *Istruzioni elementari*, published in Lugano in 1760. The laws of nature continue to inform the laws of architecture for Vittone. Mathematics and geometry, the keys to the universe, as in the *visio intellectualis*, are related to movement and variation in time and continuums, and drawn from celestial observations, as knowledge was given for Lomazzo and Cortona. Guarini described geometry as the "mirror of the world." Vittone wrote in *Istruzioni elementari*, "If a glance is raised to the sky, one watches to see in its movements the order of the many luminous bodies, constant and exact in correct division, and inalterable measure in time...demonstrating according to the science of numbers revolutions around variable centers, and the value of force."[56]

The law of numbers and proportion, translated and displayed in architecture, is innate in organic bodies and natural phenomena, as in *concinnitas*. "Were not the rays of the sun demonstrated to be reflections, refractions and influences with immutable orders of numbers, with changing and well-regulated vicissitudes, and with intervals of space and divisions of musical grades?"[57] All mathematical and numerological relations and proportions found in the natural universe are manifestations of the instrument of God, of the universal and divine intellect. "God created in the Holy Spirit, which was seen, counted and measured...This among the human sciences is that in which God wishes, in a singular manner more than in any other, to deposit and conceal its mysteries."[58]

Conclusion

There is ample evidence to indicate that Neoplatonic philosophy played a role in the conception of the design of seventeenth-century Roman Baroque architecture, and that there is a philosophical or conceptual basis underlying Baroque architectural forms. The forms of the architecture can be understood in relation to their cultural context - the epistemological structures, philosophical and scientific beliefs, and artistic theories of the seventeenth century. This architecture can be seen to express and reflect the complexity of the epistemology of the culture, the foundations of its knowledge, unique in its combination of theological tenets, philosophical understanding and scientific knowledge and practice. Architecture can enact the relation between thought and physical reality. As Ficino wrote in the *Commentary*, "If anyone asked in what way the form of the body can be like the Form and Reason of the Soul and Mind, let them consider the building of the architect."[59]

References

Leon Battista Alberti, *On the Art of Building*, Cambridge, MA: MIT Press, 1988.

Assemblage 28, Cambridge, MA: MIT Press, 1995.

Ksenija Atanasijevic, *The Metaphysical and Geometrical Doctrine of Giordano Bruno in His Work* De Triplici Minimo, St. Louis: Warren Green, 1972.

Giordano Bruno, *Opera omnia*, Bari: Lateranza, 1907.

Christine Buci-Glucksmann, *Baroque Reason: The Aesthetics of Modernity*, London: Sage Publications, 1994.

Ernst Cassirer, *The Individual and the Cosmos in Renaissance Philosophy*, New York: Harper & Row, 1963.

Ernst Cassirer, *The Renaissance Philosophy of Man*, Chicago:University of Chicago Press, 1948.

Nicolas Cusanus, *Of Learned Ignorance*, Westport: Hyperion Press, 1979.

Marsilio Ficino, *Commentary on Plato's Symposium*, Dallas: Spring Publications, 1985.

Joan Gadol, *Leon Battista Alberti: Universal Man of the Early Renaissance*, Chicago: University of Chicago Press, 1969.

Eugenic Garin, *Astrology in the Renaissance: The Zodiac of Life*, London: Routledge & Kegan Paul, 1983.

Donald Kelly, *Renaissance Humanism*, Boston: Twayne Publishers, 1991.

Robert Kinsman, ed., *The Darker Vision of the Renaissance*, Berkeley: University of California Press, 1974.

Hanno-Walter Kruft, *A History of Architectural Theory: From Vitruvius to the Present*, New York: Princeton Architectural Press, 1994.

Rosemary Ann Lees, *The Negative Language of the Dionysian School of Mystical Theology: An Approach to the Cloud of Unknowing*, Salzburg: Universität Salzburg, 1983.

Gian Paolo Lomazzo, *Scritti sulle arti*, Firenze: Marchi e Bertolli, 1973.

Ferruccio Marotti, *Storia documentaria del teatro italiano, Lo spettacolo dall'Umanesimo al Manierismo, Teoria e tecnica*, Milano: Feltrinelli Editore, 1974.

Bernard McGinn, *The Foundations of Mysticism*, New York: Crossroad, 1995.

Thomas Moore, *The Planets Within*, London: Associated University Presses, 1982.

Lionello Neppi, *Palazzo Spada*, Roma: Editalia, 1975.

Karl Noehles, *La Chiesa dei SS Luca e Martina nell'opera di Pietro da Cortona*, Roma: Ugo Bozzi Editore, 1970.

Giovanni Ottonelli e Pietro da Cortona, *Trattato della pittura, e scultura, uso et abuso loro*, Fiorenza: Antonio Bonardi, 1652.

Erwin Panofsky, *Idea: A Concept in Art Theory*, Columbia: University of South Carolina Press, 1968.

Erwin Panofsky, *Studies in Iconology: Humanistic Themes in the Art of the Renaissance*, New York: Harper & Row, 1962.

Dino Pastine, *La nascita dell'idolatria, L'Oriente religioso di Athanasius Kircher,* Firenze: La Nuova Italia Editrice, 1978.

Alessandro Piccolomini, *La Sfera del Mondo,* Venetia, 1566.

Leros Pittoni, *Francesco Borromini, L'Iniziato,* Roma: Edizioni De Luca, 1995.

Plotinus, *The Six Enneads,* Chicago: Encyclopedia Brittanica, Inc., 1952.

Giuseppe Rosaccio, *Teatro del Cielo e della Terra,* Fiorenza: Scalee di Badia, 1594.

Giuseppe A Spadaro, *Il "Caso" Borromini, ricostruito per identificazione,* Roma: Edizioni Mediterranee, 1992.

Leo Steinberg, *Borromini's San Carlo alle Quattro Fontane, A Study in Multiple Form and Architectural Symbolism,* New York: Garland Publishing, 1977.

Vitruvius, *On Architecture,* Cambridge, MA: Harvard University Press, 1931.

Bernardo Vittone e la Disputa fra classicismo e barocco nel Settecento, Torino: Accademia delle Scienze, 1972.

Zygmunt Wazbinski, *L'Accademia Medicea del Disegno a Firenze nel Cinquecento,* Idea e Istituzione, Firenze: Leo S. Olschki Editore, 1987.

Rudolf Wittkower, *Architectural Principles in the Age of Humanism,* London: Alec Tiranti, 1962.

Rudolf Wittkower, *Art and Architecture in Italy,* 1600-1750, New York: Penguin Books, 1983.

Notes

1. Hanno-Walter Kruft, *Architectural Theory from Vitruvius to the Present* (New York: Princeton Architectural Press, 1994), 24.

2. Alessandro Piccolomini, *La Sfera del Mondo* (Venetia, 1566), 29: *"Doviamo primieramente sapere, che questa gran machina, di cui parliamo, e che noi Mondo chiamiano, fu da quel sapientissimo, e potentissimo Architetto."*

3. Ferruccio Marotti, *Storia documentaria del teatro italiano, Lo spettacolo dall'Umanesimo al Manierismo, teoria e tecnica* (Milano: Feltrinelli Editore, 1974), 97: *"quibus etiam in duodecim signorum coelestium descriptione astrologi ex musica convientia astrorum ratioinantur."*

4. Eugenio Garin, *Astrology in the Renaissance: The Zodiac of Life* (London: Routledge & Kegan Paul, 1983), 109.

5. *Ibid.,* xi.

6. Marc Bensiman, "Modes of Perception of Reality in the Renaissance," in Robert Kinsman, ed., *The Darker Vision of the Renaissance* (Berkeley: University of California Press, 1974), 236.

7. Ficino, *Commentary,* 84.

8. See Rudolf Wittkower, *Architectural Principles in the Age of Humanism* (London: Alec Tiranti, 1962).

9. Karl Noehles, *La Chiesa dei SS Luca e Martina* (Roma: Ugo Bozzi Editore, 1970), 6: *"...concepito quale rappresentazione allegorica di un 'idea' cosmologica."*

10. *Ibid.*: "...*la Sapienza-Minerva (contemporaneamente Magna Mater e allegoria di Roma) vi appare seduta in un tempietto circolare a colonne; dietro si vede in una nicchia la statua di Mercurio...Tra le colonne stanno le allegorie delle virtù, mentre entrano nel tempio le figure femminili che rappresentano le scienze cosmologiche e recano in mano il globo delle stelle, il modello dei pianeti, e alcune carte geografiche; alle scienze cosmologiche segne l'artista, caratterizzato come architetto da una tavola su cui è raffigurato un ordine di colonne...*"

11. *Ibid.*, 12, doc. 17, Accademia di San Luca, 1624.

12. Giuseppe Rosaccio, *Teatro del Cielo e della Terra* (Fiorenza: Scalee di Badia, 1594), 7: "*per dir prima della corruttibile, e divisa ne quattro elementi, cioè, Fuoco, Aria, Acqua, Terra.*"

13. Noehles, *La Chiesa dei SS Luca e Martina*, 174: "*Essi avrebbero saputo interpretare da sè sia il rapporto cosmologico tra cerchio e quadrato...come il simbolo platonico a X dell'armonia universale (Timeo 36 a-d), sia la particolare forma della croce greca come il Logosnimbus di Cristo...*"

14. Plotinus, *The Six Enneads* (Chicago: Encyclopedia Brittanica, Inc., 1952), 239.

15. Noehles, *La Chiesa dei SS Luca e Martina*, 176: "*niuna facoltà può gareggiare d'antichità in concorrenza delle tre dette arti (architettura, scultura e pittura), imperciocchè furono esercitate da Dio stesso nella fabbrica del mondo, ove egli fu pittore mirabile...nella prospettiva della terra e fu scultore sorprendente configurando colle sue mani la creta nella creazione dell'uomo: e fu sommo Architetto nella gran fabbrica dell'Universo.*"

16. Translated in Erwin Panofsky, *Idea: A Concept in Art Theory* (Columbia: University of South Carolina Press, 1968), 26.

17. See Rudolf Wittkower, *Architectural Principles in the Age of Humanism* (London: Alec Tiranti, 1962).

18. Zygmunt Wazbinski, *L'Accademia Medicea del Disegno a Firenze nel Cinquecento, Idea e Istituzione* (Firenze: Leo S Olschki Editore, 1987), 168: "*il Genio che soggioga l'Ignoranza, la Misericordia che combatte il Vizio, la Saggezza che sconfigge l'Invidia, la Laboriosità che vince Pigrizia.*"

19. Leros Pittone, *Francesco Borromini, L'Iniziato* (Roma: Edizioni de Luca, 1995), 39: "*Il quadrato rappresenta la terra, è simbolo della manifestazione di Dio. Per i platonici si riferisce alla materializzazione dell'Idea. Il quadrato, inoltre, corrisponde all forma dell'uomo.*"

20. Ficino, *Commentary on Plato's Symposium* (Dallas: Spring Publications, 1985), 38.

21. Giovanni Ottonelli e Pietro da Cortona, *Trattato della pittura e scultura* (Fiorenza: Antonio Bonardi, 1652), 59: "*E tal diletto si gode, mentre nell'immagini l'animo conosce col discorso della ragione varie cose, alle quali non giunge con l'apprensione, e cognition del senso: come nella pittura d'un ciel notturno, e*

sereno l'intelletto discorre, e intende, che grande è la velocità del moto celeste, che molti sono i giri de' cieli, e i moti de' pianeti, che segnalata è la grandezza del Sole, della Luna, e delle Stelle; e con questa cognitione riceve diletto intellettivo..."

22. Quoted in Noehles, *La Chiesa dei SS Luca e Martina*, 5: "*Le divine, et eterne Idee sono immagini fatte da Dio...che tutta la macchina del mondo dir si puo."*

23. Noehles, *La Chiesa dei SS Luca e Martina*, 172: "*A tale fine l'Agucchi svillupa metaforicamente un sistema dell'universo il cui immobile centro motare è sede delle Idee eterne e divine, e dell'assoluta 'unita', 'bonta' e 'bellezza'. Tale centro ¡e il sole, fonte di ogni bellezza e che "altro no può essere che Iddio, che come principio aggroppa e unisce tutte le cose'. Esso è pricipio e fine di ogni movimento e centro del cosmo rotante."*

24. *Ibid.*, 173: "*...si conforme alla christiana verità."*

25. *Ibid.*, 175, doc. 17, Accademia di San Luca 1624.

26. Gian Paolo Lomazzo, *Scritti sulle arti* (Firenze: Marchi e Bertolli, 1973), 33: "*...ordo, modus et species..."*

27. Quoted in Noehles, *La Chiesa dei SS Luca e Martina*, 48: "*...una casa benordinata, anzi un tempio solenne, ove il cielo con i suoi nodi di stelle è come una vetrata istoriata di immagini sante, che recano il segno di un Dio che si leva fra cori d'Angeli."*

28. *Ibid.*: "*...le forze che agitano l'intimo degli esseri e gli spiriti che si aggirano in mezzo alle cose..."*

29. Quoted in Donald Kelly, *Renaissance Humanism* (Boston: Twayne Publishers, 1991), 42.

30. Cusanus, *Of Learned Ignorance* (Westport: Hyperion Press, 1979), 135.

31. Translated in Joan Gadol, *Leon Battista Alberti: Universal Man of the Early Renaissance* (Chicago: University of Chicago Press, 1969), 135.

32. Leon Battista Alberti, *On the Art of Building* (Cambridge, MA: MIT Press, 1988), 194.

33. Gadol, *Leon Battista Alberti*, 138.

34. Alberti, *On the Art of Building*, 302.

35. Gadol, *Leon Battista Alberti*, 106.

36. Translated in Thomas Moore, *The Planets Within* (London: Associated University Presses, 1982), 106, 110.

37. See Panofsky, *Studies in Iconology*, 131.

38. Cusanus, *Of Learned Ignorance*, 49.

39. Leros Pittoni, *Francesco Borromini, L'Iniziato* (Roma: Edizioni de Luca, 1995), 37 (no inventory citation).

40. Ficino, *Commentary*, 51.

41. *Ibid.*, 38.

42. *Ibid.*, 40.

43.   *Ibid.*, 74.

44.   *Ibid.*, 84.

45.   See Leo Steinberg, *Borromini's San Carlo alle Quattro Fontane: A Study in Multiple Form and Architectural Symbolism* (New York: Garland Publishing, 1977).

46.   Panofsky, *Studies in Iconology*, 132.

47.   Bensiman, "Modes of Perception of Reality in the Renaissance," in Robert Kinsman, ed., *The Darker Vision of the Renaissance*, 227-228.

48.   Translated in Ernst Cassirer, *The Renaissance Philosophy of Man* (Chicago: University of Chicago Press, 1948), 193.

49.   Ficino, *Commentary*, 47.

50.   Panofsky, *Studies in Iconology*, 132.

51.   Christine Buci-Glucksmann, *Baroque Reason: The Aesthetics of Modernity* (London: Sage Publications, 1994), 58.

52.   Ficino, *Commentary*, 47.

53.   Marotti, *Storia documentaria del teatro italiano*, 70: "*Baptista de Alberti scriva ch'el theatro...ha la area mediana vacua di pulpiti scenici.*"

54.   *Ibid.*, 113: "*lo medio centro collocato sia circumacta in circuito una linea de rotundazione.*"

55.   Translated in Rudolf Wittkower, *Art and Architecture in Italy* (New York: Penguin Books, 1958), 427.

56.   Quoted in Marcello Fagiolo, "L'Universo della luce nell'idea de architettura del Vittone" in *Bernardo Vittone e la Disputa fra classiciso e barocco nel Settecento* (Torino: Accademia delle Scienze, 1972), 131: "*Se al cielo alzando lo sguardo, si regolare ci si fa vedere ne' suoi movimenti l'ordine di que' tanti luminosi corpi, si costante, ed esatto nel ripartire con giusta, ed inalterabile misura il tempo...si in somma rispettose dimostrarsi verso la scienza de' numeri le rivoluzioni di quelli attorno i loro volubili centri, e forza e commendare della scienza de' numeri l'ammirabile forza e valore.*"

57.   *Ibid.*: "*Non ha egli dimostrato farsi d'essi raggi le riflessioni, refrazioni, ed inflessioni con ordine immutabile di numeri, con alterne e ben regolate vicissitudini, ed a intervalli di spazio con musicale grado divisi?*"

58.   *Ibid.*, 132: "*Deus creavit illam in Spiritu Sancto, et videt, et dinumeravit, et mensus est (Ecclesiastico, I, 9)...Questa insomma fra le umane scienze è quella in cui volle Iddio in un modo tutto singolare piu che in ogn'altra depositare e nascondere i suoi Arcani.*"

59.   Ficino, *Commentary*, 92.

Poetic Hierarchies in the Works
of Nikos Kazantzakis

John P. Anton

1. Introduction

Much has been written on the varieties of hierarchies of values and beings. The model *par excellence* that has influenced art and literature, in particular, is Plato's *Symposium*. The topic of my paper takes me back to the Platonic ladder of Eros and the Plotinian ascent to the One as models for poetic hierarchies, including Kazantzakis' own, but for one difference, as I hope to show, namely that Kazantzakis' concept of the ladder is closer to the Neoplatonic vision of ontic hypostases and the religious deontology of the Byzantine philosophers and theologians than it is to Plato. It was Plotinus who for the first time assigned to the poet and the artist in general the task of stratifying the ontic values of the emanations of the One in accordance with their degree of beauty and goodness. He showed the way to the Christian theologians on how to adjust their salvational teachings to their alternative systems of religious virtues. The ensuing movement, reflected in the writings of Pseudo-Dionysius, reached its apex in the deontic hierarchies of Ioannis of Klimakos in the sixth century.

As far as I know no one of Kazantzakis' commentators has referred to a possible connection to Plotinus or Ioannis of Klimakos, probably on account of the absence of conspicuous signs indicating direct influence. Nevertheless, his indebtedness to Plotinus' aesthetics is there. The Renaissance and modern formulations of the role of the artist have their origins in the Neoplatonic philosophy of art, despite what the manifestoes of modern art say about the nature of that role after turning away from all ties to Platonic and Plotinian ontologies, with much help from the rising tide of subjectivism and of psychoanalysis.

Kazantzakis, as creative artist, is part new and part old. In his reflections on the role and mission of the artist-poet he still uses the idea of the ladder though not that of Eros in Plato's *Symposium* or of the hierarchy of the Plotinian hypostases, but with an important difference. As I mentioned before, he replaces their conceptions of duty with a deontology of his own hierarchies, that is, a ladder of duties in accordance with his special understanding of religious consciousness. As a result, the artistic act takes on the character of a new type of *hubris*, one that heralds the salvation of God. In fact, the act stems from a duty to be performed by the estranged human being who must span the abyss of human existence between birth and death. To make this point clear, I must first discuss briefly the Platonic and Plotinian models.

2. Diotima's message and the Ladder of Eros.

When Socrates' turn came in the *Symposium* to praise Eros on the evening of the celebration of Agathon's victory in 416 B.C., instead of following the pattern of the previous speakers, he proved faithful to his avowal of ignorance and limited his peroration to the lessons he learned from the priestess Diotima.

I will not try to offer yet another account of the Platonic grading of the desirable erotic objects. My remarks address only the main points. To begin with, eros is the desire for fulfillment, and more precisely, for immortal things, the "everlasting goods." There is more to be said about the identity of eros as "the desire for the perpetual possession of the good" (206a). Diotima taught Socrates the mysteries of eros but not without some doubt whether he could grasp the perfect revelation. It was right after this admission that Socrates proceeded with the narrative about the path the pilgrim must follow to climb the ladder of eros, the upward way of the *anabathmoi*: (1) falling in love with one beautiful person and together beget noble thoughts; (2) loving all beautiful bodies and learning how to control the passion for the one person; (3) loving the soul as more worthy and of greater honor than the beauty of the body, content "to make the young people better;" (4) loving the beauty that exists in actions, institutions and the laws; (5) loving and preparing to turn to the beauty of the sciences and especially the science of beauty once the person has matured and become inexhaustible in spirit; (6) finally, at the end of the journey, when loving is for beauty itself, marvelous, perfect, unique and eternal. And at the opening of her summary Diotima states:

This is the right way of approaching or being initiated into the mysteries of love, to begin with examples of beauty in this world, and using them as steps to ascend continually with that absolute beauty as one's aim, from one instance of physical beauty to two and from two to all, then from physical beauty to moral beauty, and from moral beauty to the beauty of knowledge, until from knowledge of various kinds one arrives at the supreme knowledge whose sole object is that absolute beauty, and know at last what absolute beauty is.[1]

The person who reaches the heights of the last rung of eros, she concludes,

will be able to bring forth not mere reflected images of goodness but true goodness, because he will be in contact not with a reflection but with the truth. And having brought forth and nurtured true goodness will have the privilege of being beloved of God, and becoming, if ever a man can, immortal himself."[2]

The levels of beautiful objects in the Platonic hierarchy of Eros, forming as they do, an ascending order, have exerted a long and interesting influence in the history of Western aesthetics and poetry. As a model of hierarchies it found a special place in the philosophies of the Neoplatonists. Two things stand out here: (1) the priority assigned to beauty in the unfolding of Eros, and (b) the pursuit of virtue as an imperative to quicken the awakening of Eros.

The ascending order of the objects of eros, forming an unbreakable continuum of aesthetic, ethical and epistemic values, eventually was absorbed into the doctrines of subsequent philosophical speculations. Many of the systems that assimilated the Platonic hierarchy of love, although themselves different in structure and objectives, e.g. the various Neoplatonist schools, did so to bolster their ontologies or enrich their ethical and religious visions. What interests us mainly is the influence the Platonic model exerted by assigning to Beauty the highest place in the erotic pyramid of values.

Speaking of influences, it is interesting to note that Kazantzakis published an article titled "The Sickness of the Century" in 1906, when he was only twenty-four years of age, and stated the following: "I never get tired of reading Plato's *Symposium*. In my view it is the great, the holy revelation of the Hellenic world."[3] The fervor subsided as he grew older and he found other mentors and new teachers with different messages and novel concerns. I will return to this side of his development later in my paper. I must now move on to Neoplatonism to show how its conception of the role of the artist-poet anticipates and resembles closely certain modern views of the artistic self-image, including that of Kazantzakis.

3. Beauty and the Ontic Hierarchies in Plotinus

Plotinus' views on the role of the artist-poet are surprisingly close to certain dominant currents and concepts regarding the modern artistic self.[4] I will limit my comments only to those aspects that pertain to the hierarchy of duties in Kazantzakis's *Spiritual Exercises* (*Salvatores Dei*), specifically to Plotinus' views on the origin of Beauty, artistic creativity, and the role of the artist in the pursuit of the union with the absolute One.

For Plotinus, absolute Beauty is of divine origin. Being one of the eternal Ideas, it resides in the hypostasis of *Nous*. In lesser grades it is also present in descending order in the hypostases of the World Soul and Nature. The human soul, although it partakes of the higher hypostases, never ceases to desire the unity with the source of its being. Thus Eros for Plotinus has a cosmic mission, to bend the human will to its ultimate purpose while following the course on the path of Beauty. If so, the model for a fulfilled life is not rooted in social, not even in religious experiences, but in the universe itself, the origin of which is the One, the highest good and ultimate purpose of the soul. The absolute One is therefore the womb of all values and the target of the soul's voyage, the Return. Human life is an Odyssey with a transcendent Ithaka: the One.

The ascending path guides the traveler through the Ideas of *Nous*: the Forms of Truth and Beauty and of the Good. There remains then only the ultimate move, the last step beyond all beings: the mystical union with the absolute One. On the way to pursuing this end, the soul discovers how the Beauty of art converges with the truth of philosophy to attain the Good of the ethical life.

Artistic creation, when aiming at Beauty, is at once ethical and cognitive action. Art, for Plotinus, is both imitation and creation. It must imitate only the Idea of Beauty and create things that cannot be found in the sensible world. As imitation, genuine art is not beholding for content to themes that lie lower than the soul's own essence, and therefore it neither copies nor describes the sensible objects in nature, plants and animals, not even the passions and sufferings of human beings. Art as imitation must pursue the higher values residing in the World Soul and in the Ideas of *Nous*. From its own stance, art treats the world as a symbol of the ideal. To succeed in his mission the artist must assign a new role to the imagination: to create symbols representative of the higher realms of Beauty. The initial duty of the artist is to save the beauty of nature and at the same time transcend it. Whereas nature makes beautiful things unconsciously, the human agent as authentic artist adds to the natural matter of the sensible entities the beauty of the spirit.

Hence, the true artist can only turn within the soul to elevate nature to spiritual heights. In consequence, the value of art works flows only from the artist's soul, not from any moral, political or religious beliefs. Such is the tradition that forms much of the background of Kazantzakis as an artist-poet. Thus, since Beauty pervades nature in all its variety, the artist's duty is to save the divine through acts of superior creativity.

According to Plotinus, the two creative agencies, nature and the human soul, are also causal principles and both have a common ultimate source: the absolute One: "Every prime cause must be, within itself, more powerful than its effect can be: the musical does not derive from an unmusical source but from music" (*Enn.* V.5.1, 30-31). None of the artist's creations expresses the Prime Cause fully. Even the best works of art fall short of the Idea of Beauty that resides in the soul, or rather in the mind (*nous*) of the poet who has attained knowledge of the higher hypostases. For Plotinus, the artist expresses the beauty that resides in the imagination exclusively with the aid of symbols and the imaginative imitation of the higher grade of being. The artist has the ability and the duty to reveal or decipher the ideal face of aesthetic perfection and can do so only through the return to the hypostasis of *Nous*. The artist hence saves and humanizes nature. The aesthetic worth of his creations results from his own assertive act, not from external customs, rules, beliefs.

The theory that art springs mainly from the aesthetic wealth of the cognizing imagination is found in Plotinus its first defender. In his ontology of Beauty, art, despite its divine origin, does not embody the highest good. Beyond art lies the wisdom that is needed to train the human soul to master the method of the hierarchical ascendancy to Being. More importantly, wisdom alone can foreshadow the vision that accompanies the last leap. Only thus can the soul gain full understanding of its descent and ascent, its fall from and return to the One:

> If one goes on from oneself, as image to original, one has reached 'the end of the journey'. And when one falls from the vision, he wakes again the virtue in himself, and considering himself set in order and beautiful by these virtues he will again be lightened and come through virtue to Intellect and wisdom and through wisdom to that Good. This is the life of gods and of godlike and blessed men, deliverance from the things of this world, a life which takes no delight in

the things of this world, escape in solitude to the solitary." (*Enn.* VI. 9. 11, tr. A. H. Armstrong, in Loeb).

4. Kazantzakis and the Hierarchies of Action

By the time the Neoplatonic tradition reached Kazantzakis, the cosmic hierarchies had withered but not the role of the artist. The duty to respond to the inner beauty of the soul had lost none of its force. It called for new and different hierarchies.

Early in his career as poet-artist, Kazantzakis was responding to a world he believed had lost faith in the eternal vigilance of the living God and had shifted its attention to a culture without permanent values. In a world where God is dead, the human spirit has a duty to save the divine. Such is the motif of Kazantzakis's *Spiritual Exercises* and his *Odyssey*. Both works, the first as theoretical vision, the second as epic action, stress the command that man in despair must heed the call to resurrect the divine. Both works herald the new imperative: Man must save God. Since God can no longer save man, creative action must follow a new chain of duties, a new deontological hierarchy. The rungs on the poetic ladder of duty become clear as soon as the imperative is put into action. But what is the meaning of the imperative and how can man save God if God does not exist?

Substituting the term 'religion' for the term 'God' makes it easier to understand how Kazantzakis follows a Nietzschean model to enlist art in the service of a revitalized sense of religiosity beyond and above the Christian salvational goal. But preserving the initial expression engenders a thorny problem. The term 'divine' in its traditional sense and if no longer in force could be taken to elicit the projection of exaltation or generate deep fears and submission to the emptiness that the rejection of a supreme power creates. If so, insistence on a substitute sense of 'God' as such signifies nothing specific except perhaps the great nothing, lacking the power its original referent once had to serve as savior of man. To fill the vacuum in religion, given that Kazantzakis is himself profoundly religious, the idea of God had to be transformed. The poet's new responsibility became a mission to assign meaning to "Nothing," to humanize it and grant it a place in a new poetic hierarchy of values on the ladder of duty.

For Kazantzakis, the poetic gradations of duty emerge through the struggle of creativity but only after the requisite theoretical work has done its part. And now comes the question: What precisely does Kazantzakis, working in the hierarchic manner of the Neoplatonic tradition, hope to save through the process of the new pursuit? The arrow of the Plotinian voyage is targeted to the hypostases of Being, whereas Kazantzakis' own is meant to show the way to the gradations of the soul's discoverable objects: Ego, Ancestor, Humanity, Earth, Universe, and finally God. Throughout the voyage, man and God engage in mutual salvation. Since the concept of God, as Prevelakis once remarked, "implies a new ethic," Kazantzakis came to believe that man conquers death through death and that immortality, properly redefined, requires a different view of God.

The *Spiritual Exercises* opens with a counter-Plotinian statement: "We come from a dark abyss, we end in a dark abyss, and we call the luminous interval life. As we are born the return begins."[5] And further down comes the quasi Platonic note: "Because of this many have cried out: The goal of ephemeral life is immortality."[6]

The salvational process in pursuit of immortality demands climbing the ladder of duty. The first step is for ruling Reason to recognize its limitations, since all it can grasp is ephemeral things, never things of essence. The supreme virtue of Reason is Discipline. Next comes the second duty: to renounce the limits of Reason and accept the ensuing agony. The Heart must do what Reason cannot and heed the duty "to bend down and dig!" The third duty commands the ship of soul to sail towards the abyss. Next comes the gradation of the voyage: Ego, Ancestor, Humanity, Earth. The preparation is now complete for the vision of the divine to follow. Expectedly, the needed virtue is Courage. With the vision of the divine attained, the time is ripe for *praxis*. The action required for the Return is threefold: human to human, human to nature, human to God. *The Spiritual Exercises* (*Salvatores Dei*), ends on a shrill note of two cries and several incantations, the last of which is a blessing: "thrice blessed be those who bear on their shoulders and do not buckle under the great, sublime and terrifying secret that even this ["Lord, you and I are one"] does not exist."

Even if God does not exist, it is man's duty to discover, encounter, reveal and save God through the creative actions conceived as the poetic hierarchies of duty as outlined. The vision was given a poetic form of action in his epic *Odyssey: a Modern Sequel*. At the end of the voyage Odysseus dies on the iceberg alone in the absolute silence of nothingness. Suddenly, all hierarchies of action vanish in the abyss of inaction. Why, then, the voyage?

5. Possible Neoplatonic sources?

The ideas and list of duties in *Spiritual Exercises* are rooted partly in Nietzsche and partly in the socialist messianic vision. However, the undercurrents that feed and support the gradation of values in Kazantzakis' literary text and express his *credo* as a religious poet, have another origin, very old and with a career of its own: Hellenic, Hellenistic, Byzantine. The flight of steps on the Platonic ladder of Eros, the ontological hypostases of Plotinus and the other Neoplatonists, were eventually transformed and selectively assimilated into the body of Christian dogma and given a place in the canon of monastic virtues. They are part of the intellectual background of Ioannis of Klimakos and the thirty-one rungs of his conception of religious duties, if we include the "Logos of the Shepherd," the last rung that links together the dominant virtues of the trinity of faith, hope, and *agape*. There is a similarity between Kazantzakis and Ioannis of Klimakos regarding a negative feature, namely that both share the subordinate role of the logical faculty in the ascending process to the higher hierarchies.

There is no direct evidence that Kazantzakis was intimately acquainted with the moral theology of Ioannis of Klimakos. Additional research will be needed before any questions of influence can be settled. Nevertheless there are certain unmistakable signs of familiarity in the similarities of their corresponding hierarchical conceptions. Both think in terms of religion; Kazantzakis moves in the direction of a ladder of duties while Ioannis of Klimakos has his eyes set on the ascending order of virtues. In Kazantzakis the *askesis* reverses the goal of the Christian saint and instead of the salvation of man the goal becomes the salvation of the divine. Hence the only positive correlation between the two ladders can be seen as a common interest in the religious deontology of stratifying a mixture of duties and virtues. It is no accident that the structure of the *Spiritual Exercises* makes one think of Ioannis of Klimakos, especially the duty that runs through the thirty-one rungs of virtue in the agonistic process of religious devotion. It is well known that Kazantzakis had shown a strong, even apostolic, interest in a revitalized religious life. His *Spiritual Exercises* testifies to his engaged use of literature combining poetic sensitivity with missionary intensity. While being swept by the currents of his visionary mission to save the world, he wrote to his friend the Rev. Manolis Papastephanou, in Boston, a letter that foreshadows the idea behind the *Spiritual Exercises*. In the letter, dated September 5, 1922, he stated the following:

> The world is rot...We must plant a new one. Never before was the earth more painfully ploughed as it is today. Everything is ready. What is missing? The seed! I feel that I hold the Seed in my hands as though a hand-grenade. Oh, that I could, by jumping over the barrier of logic, throw it on the human fields.[7]

Many readers have found Kazantzakis' poetic inspiration attractive as it shoots its arrow skyward and marks the trail of the hierarchy of duties. Its aesthetic quality remains unalloyed but the substance it contains owes its force to the religious bent of its deontology. And it is so intense, so engaged, that it bears no resemblance to the features of the Platonic Eros; and, if anything, it creates the suspicion that it intentionally runs counter to Ioannis of Klimakos and his virtues of obedience, repentance, memory, death and the joy of mourning. By way of education and early studies Kazantzakis became quite familiar with the literature of Christian ethics. His messianic religiosity shows him determined later to deliver the new gospel of salvation and move the world beyond the horizons of Hellenism and Christianity.

The path that led Kazantzakis to the deontology of the *Spiritual Exercises* winds through many signposts, particularly the ones the Neoplatonists left behind, from Ammonius Sakkas, Plotinus, the Apologetic Fathers, the Athenian School of Proclus down to the theologizing philosophers of Byzantium and all the others who sifted the teachings of the Ancients in order to build the new virtues of Christianity and promote asceticism as the true model of life. At one point the path makes a stop at the doorstep of Ioannis of Klimakos. It takes no leap of the imagination to understand why centuries later Kazantzakis chose the word *askētikē* as the title for his text and projected it as the symbol for his *credo*. It is intended to convey the meaning of a new and different spiritual exercise. Suddenly the teleological theory of virtue the Greeks held in high esteem is pushed aside and replaced with a new deontology demanding the salvation of the divine, where 'God,' to use Kazantzakis expressions, stands for a *diffused, muted, yet omnipresent* divine, awaiting its fulfillment to come as the product of the agonistic human will.

Admittedly, the signs of any direct presence of Neoplatonic ideas in Kazantzakis are not readily detectable; the same holds for Ioannis of Klimakos. This feature makes the tracing of parallel influences in their writings an arduous if not tenuous task. Regardless of these difficulties and the meandering course of the successive phases of Neoplatonism through the centuries, by the time we come to Kazantzakis' gradations of duties, the issue of influence is hardly less inviting. Comparably, in the case of Ioannis of Klimakos the difficulties remain but not to the point of making us reject all possible historical affinities.[8] It seems rather unlikely that Ioannis of Klimakos' moral theology was not affected by the Neoplatonic religious currents still in force during the sixth century. The language and the terminology alone would suffice to alert us to the conceptual continuities from the Apologetic writers down to the era of monastic theology, i.e., from Alexandria to Mt. Sina. It is a tradition that became firmly established and remained unbroken in the affairs of the Eastern Church. That Kazantzakis was exposed to the monastic ideals and teachings early in his life, just like all Greek intellectuals of the period, makes it feasible to surmise that this is the tradition of religious asceticism with which he was destined to work. As such, it is a tradition that inevitably and quietly touched anyone who tried to fuse together a moral deontology and a vision of poetic gradations, as is the case of Kazantzakis' *Spiritual Exercises*.

While we should not exclude an affinity with the tradition of religious deontology of Ioannis of Klimakos, we must also look elsewhere to explain the originality of Kazantzakis' *Spiritual Exercises*. More specifically, it could be found in the restless mind of modern Europe that had already read into the Greek marbles a questionable purity and disputed the ontic foundations of religious orthodoxy. It is there, in the same modern trends that we must look for the starting point of the other, the novel branch of Neoplatonism that reached Kazantzakis as a radical and worldly poet. The critic who will try to unravel the strands in Kazantzakis' works that have their roots in the diverse shapes that modern Neoplatonism took in the hands of German idealists from Hegel to Nietzsche, and from the latter to Bergson's creative evolution, faces a formidable and complex, though not impossible task.

The paradox of the two paths, as it weaves its way into Kazantzakis' works, allows one to read his texts as contemporary intimations of Plotinus' "flight of the alone to the alone." With this in mind, the interested reader of Kazantzakis' *Report to Greco* (1965) might wish to pay closer attention to two special chapters, both covering an early phase of his life, when he was visiting Mt. Athos and Mt. Sina. Notably, in chapter 18 (on Mt. Athos) Kazantzakis recalls a conversation he once had with a certain Father Ignatius and ended with a question and a query. The question was: "What conclusion must we draw, Father, now that it seems that both [Reason and Heart] are right?" And the query followed: "I was talking and thinking to myself but didn't say it: New Ten Commandments! New Commandments! But how would this new decalogue arrange the virtues and the vices, I could not think. I would only say and repeat to myself: New decalogue. Great need! Who will give it to us?" Did Kazantzakis, one may ask, ever read carefully and seek the answer in the texts of Ioannis of Klimakos? Is it possible that the theme of the *Spiritual Exercises* was conceived during his stay at Mt. Sina? One can only guess.

I should like to end this address with a comment on the confluence of the two currents of Neoplatonism. By the time the currents reached him as a modern European poet and messianic Cretan there was little left in them to remind him of the Platonic Eros. Beauty as the end of the journey was replaced with the Nothing of the Abyss. Whether unwillingly or acting in innocence of the tradition, Kazantzakis pushed the European consciousness to the edge of the abyss of nihilism, where Nietzsche himself did not dare to look, forcing it to face the implications of the new *hubris*. It took the sharpness of the Cretan Glance, itself hubristic, to indict before the court of Europe's intelligentsia the impasse to which Western Civilization had come: its nihilism. He understood the futility of the modern salvational schemes, including the grandiose promise of Marxism. Absorbed as he was in his cultural and aesthetic stratagem, he turned his back to the prospect of learning from Diotima the duty that Eros had recommended.

The *hubris* is noticeably prevalent and, in a more general way, beyond the refusal to return to the erotic rungs on Diotima's ladder. If the highest duty is to meet the challenge that the spiritual confusion of our times imposes in the face of a multi-faceted cultural impasse and to find a way to end the contemporary crisis, it would be sheer folly to overlook the possibility that the creative renascence of the Hellenic heritage, the life of reason, might provide a desired starting point. But adopting such a stance would call for more than yet another deontology of an apostolic vision. It would also demand the critical assessment of the Neoplatonic elements that have survived under the guise of poetic hierarchies and gradations projected as salvational devices designed to help humanity overcome the crisis of nihilism. Only thus we may be able to decide whether, in trying to find a solution to the persisting crisis, the Platonic model of Eros or something like it still holds the key to restoring cultural sanity.

Notes

1. *Symposium* at 211c, tr. Walter Hamilton (Penguin Books 1951), 94.

2. *Symp.* 212a, *ibid.*, 95.

3. Quoted in Lily Zografou, Νικος Καζαντζάκης. Ενας τραγικός. (Αθήνα: Αλεξάνδρεια 1976), 73-4. Translation mine.

4. I have discussed this topic in my "Plotinus' Conception of the Role of the Artist," *Journal of Aesthetics and Art Criticism, XXVI* (Fall 1967), 91-101; also in my "The One and the Many: the Changing Roles of the Artist," *The Minnesota Review*, V (May/July 1965), 170-82.

5. N. Kazantzakis, *The Saviors of God: Spiritual Exercises*, tr. Kimon Friar (New York: Simon and Schuster, 1969), 43.

6. Ibid. 43.

7. The text in L. Zographou, *op. cit.*, p. 191. Translation mine. Ο κόσμος σάπισε... Πρέπει καινούργιο να φυτέψουμε. Ποτέ η γής δεν ήταν πιο οδυνηρά οργωμένη όπως σήμερα. Ολα έτοιμα. Τί λείπει; Ο σπόρος! Νοιώθω στα χέρια μου να κρατώ το Σπόρο έτσι σα χειροβομβίδα. Αχ να μπορούσα πηδώντας το φράχτη της λογικής να τόνε ρίξω στ' ανθρώπινα χωράφια.

8. In his article on Ioannis of Klimakos, published in the 'Εγκυκλοπαίδεια ~Ηλιος, vol. 'Ελλάς, K. Georgoulis has argued that there is no conceivable connection between Neoplatonic ideas and the moral theology of Ioannis of Klimakos.

Neoplatonic Elements in the Spiritual Life

John Lachs

At a time when the history of philosophy receives less than respectful and conscientious attention from those who consider themselves constructive philosophers, it is good to remember that some of the great thinkers of the past were also masters of the great thoughts or systems of others. George Santayana, in particular, spent countless hours studying the classical works of philosophy.

He studied Plato in exquisite detail and was an avid reader of Aristotle, all of course in Greek. Story has it that, late in his life, an earnest priest tried to bring him back to the Catholic faith of his youth. The priest attempted to quote St. Thomas to show Santayana the error of his ways, but did not quite get the passage right. Santayana helped him out by giving a precise rendition of the text in Latin.

Santayana was no less familiar with the works of the moderns. He read everyone from Descartes to Hegel in the original language of the author and his library contained annotated copies of the works of Bergson, Heidegger and Bertrand Russell, among many others.[1] He read Plotinus and was thoroughly familiar with both major and minor figures in the Neoplatonic tradition. Similarities between his thought and selected elements of Neoplatonism are due not to historical accident but to elective affinity on his part.

I must add at once that, though it is important to see Santayana as in some central respects a Neoplatonic thinker, we cannot rightly say that his complex philosophical views come simply to a repetition of some prior position. In *Platonism and the Spiritual Life*, his most explicit discussion of Plotinus and Plotinian themes in contemporary thought, he specifically limits the scope of his agreement with Neoplatonism. He has two fundamental quarrels with the tradition. He is deeply suspicious of metaphysics, particularly a metaphysics that operates with such dialectical ideas as those of Being, the One, and Mind.

And he charges that the Neoplatonic conception of spirituality is not spiritual enough. I shall discuss the first disagreement immediately, the second only near the end of this essay.

In one sense, of course, Santayana has a metaphysics, or at least an ontology, himself. But his is a characteristically modern, almost postmodern, ironic metaphysics—one that does not claim access to the hidden structures of reality. He thinks that metaphysics of the traditional sort cannot yield results. The nature of reality is best explored by science; philosophy has no alternative to offer to careful empirical investigation. Instead of engaging in metaphysical speculations, he wishes to concentrate on explicating the view of the world tacitly contained in the active life, in the undeniable fact that we act in a multi-centered cosmos deployed in space and time.

He views his ontology as nothing more than a systematic account of the beliefs implicated in what he calls "animal faith," the confidence of the human animal in the independent existence of enduring but manipulable objects. Philosophy can do no more, he thinks, than follow the outlines of common sense. Speculations beyond that amount to "dialectical physics," which is the attempt to gain insight into the real or into what matters by means of the play of words. I wish more of our postmodern colleagues shared his caution about such an enterprise.

Here is the way he puts it himself. "Metaphysics, in the proper sense of the word, is dialectical physics, or an attempt to determine matters of fact by means of logical or moral or rhetorical constructions."[2] Such an enterprise is "neither physical speculation nor pure logic nor honest literature, but...a hybrid of the three, materialising ideal entities, turning harmonies into forces, and dissolving natural things into terms of discourse."[3]

By contrast, Santayana views his own ontology as consisting of categories that capture the features of the world he finds "conspicuously different and worth distinguishing." The ontology is modest, constituting his attempt "to think straight in such terms as are offered to me," in order "to obviate occasions for sophistry by giving to everyday beliefs a more accurate and circumspect form."[4] It is, therefore, nothing new: as "a feast of what everybody knows,"[5] it expresses "a certain shrewd orthodoxy which the sentiment and practice of laymen maintain everywhere."[6]

This means that in adopting and adapting the insights of the Neoplatonic tradition, Santayana strips them of their straightforward metaphysical bearing. He takes Plotinus' account of cascading emanations to be a story pointing to potential salvation for humans, rather than as a description of the structure of existence. But even if the story reveals no facts, it discloses profoundly significant aspects of the human condition, especially the condition of the human spirit or consciousness in a moving and dying world.

In *Platonism and the Spiritual Life*,[7] he criticizes the Neoplatonist William Ralph Inge, Dean of St. Paul's, by arguing that, if we take it literally, Plotinus' view of our distance from the source is severely misleading. Yet he also demonstrates that the same idea, used as a symbol, offers deep insights into our spiritual condition. The rejection of literal and the embrace of symbolic truth is typical of Santayana's approach to the work of philosophy.

We need to distinguish two distinct moments in the development of Santayana's aesthetics. His reflections on the technical problems of aesthetics are contained in his first book, entitled *The Sense of Beauty*.[8] Although Hobbes and other British empiricists lurk in the background, the primary influence on this work is German philosophy. Santayana draws on Schopenhauer's aesthetics and responds to Kant's view of the nature of beauty. A thorough search of the text could perhaps reveal some connections to Neoplatonic sources, but it would be difficult to see these as more than incidental.

His later, ontologically explicit work, which began to see the light of day in 1923 with the publication of *Scepticism and Animal Faith* and continued to develop until the appearance of the fourth volume of *Realms of Being* in 1941,[9] presents an altogether different picture of aesthetics. *The Sense of Beauty* dealt with aesthetics as a set of philosophical problems; the system articulated in *Realms of Being*, by contrast, incorporates the disinterested intuition of beauty as a structuring feature of ultimately satisfying human lives.

That system depicts aesthetic immediacy as the central character of what Santayana calls "the spiritual life," and establishes spirituality as the only way of escaping the concerns, pains and tragedies of the world of change. At this stage of Santayana's work, Neoplatonic influence is ubiquitous. This is the aesthetics I shall discuss.

There is no better place to begin the study of anything Neoplatonic than the contrast between the temporal and the eternal. Santayana finds himself in wholehearted agreement with drawing a sharp distinction between the two and assigns important prerogatives to the eternal. The temporal world, of course, is our home as human animals. Santayana is uncompromising in viewing biological existence as the foundation of all life, including the spirituality that in a special and limited sense takes us beyond it.

Existence as an animal, however, is fraught with frustration and danger; not even momentary victory lifts fear and worry from organisms that must fight to survive. The insecurity of existence permeates all aspects of life, and the imperfection of time, doling out only passing moments of satisfaction, makes it impossible for us to rest. No animal can thus elude disappointment, aging, and eventual death. None of us, as he puts it, is "too good for extinction," [10] and in the meantime none can experience more than momentary joy.

Morality cannot help us overcome the structural inadequacy of the processes of life. Good and evil are categories attaching to things and actions as a result of the interest our living psyches, which are physical organisms, take in them. Such assessments are the outcome of caring, and caring is an expression of the vulnerability of animals. "The whole psyche is a burden to herself, a terrible inner compulsion to care, to watch, to pursue, and to possess."[11] Frustration and death are the certain fate of a creature as much in need as this.

So no repose or ultimate satisfaction can come from the tortured life of pursuing the good. Our only hope is to transcend the world of means, of unmeaning processes, and embrace something timeless and perfect. Yet actual transcendence, implying departure from our ambushed bodies, is impossible. Since taking leave of our spatial and temporal stations would mean instant death, not eternal life, we must find the moment of peace within the one life we have been granted.

Transcendence of animal life within the confines of that life is made possible by Santayana's Platonism. Organisms fighting one another in a treacherous world are endowed with consciousness. This sentience, "the total inner difference between being asleep and awake,"[12] serves as an indispensable condition of knowledge.

Santayana adopts Plato's idea that the objects of mind are eternal forms; these forms, which he calls "essences," constitute the realm that appears to consciousness. Each moment of awareness reveals an essence or set of essences and thereby opens immediate access to the eternal. The eternal thus surrounds us, or at least stretches in all directions before the mind, in such a fashion that we can partake of it without effort. We sink into the eternal simply by waking up or by focusing our minds.

Santayana's view of universals differs in three centrally important ways from Plato's. First, although they are objects of thought, essences do not function, for Santayana, as objects of knowledge. Cognition connects the animal to its world, making it possible for it to identify the forces that affect its life.

Knowledge, therefore, is discovery of realities that bear hidden potential, that is, true belief about what exists in the flux. It is "belief in a world of events, and especially of those parts of it which are near the self, tempting or threatening it."[13] Awareness, by contrast, presents crystalline pictures of eternal actualities that lack potential. The object of knowledge is the dynamic substance of the world, the object of mind is essence in its lifeless and hence indestructible eternity. Santayana summarizes this point by his oft-repeated motto that "nothing given exists," which amounts to the claim that only inexistent forms can be present to consciousness.

Second, essences are, for Santayana, forms of definiteness unlimited in number. Plato found it difficult to decide whether or not hair and dirt had forms corresponding to them. Santayana, by contrast, maintains that every identifiable specificity is an essence. He holds that numbers, the generic forms that define natural kinds, such moral ideas as goodness and justice, all colors and relationships, and even the forms of events are essences.[14] This makes the realm of essence a nested infinity, that is, an infinity consisting of such infinities as the number of numbers and the number and diversity of motions that have, will have and could have taken place during the unending history of the world.

The infinity of essences strips them of power. In its native element, no form has sufficient claim on existence to instantiate itself. In the great Western tradition, the ontological proof of God's reality was supposed to have identified the one and only essence that required or entailed its own existence. As usual, Spinoza held a stronger view, maintaining that all essences containing no contradiction automatically exist.

Santayana rejects the ontological proof and notes that Spinoza can sustain his belief only by refusing to allow the distinction between essence and existence, or by denying that in the final analysis anything touched by time is real at all. In sharp contrast, Santayana thinks that the temporal world is the only existent reality; the realm of essence serves only as an infinite reservoir of passive forms or, as he puts it in a striking image, a costumer's gallery of the clothes in which existence may garb itself.[15]

Third, the infinity of essences removes their moral prerogatives. No essence is any better than another and hence the realm does not constitute a hierarchy cascading down from the Good or the One. The value of essences is extraneous to them, as is their meaning. They are characterized by the principle of self-identity and consist of all and only the features they display.[16]

The essence of a black lab that includes the character of friendliness or trustworthiness is not a better, only a different, essence from that of the same dog characterized by viciousness. Since we can focus on them, there are such essences as Being, the Good, and the One, but there is nothing special about them, except perhaps their excessive emptiness or generality. Trees create their own structure and animals generate other animals, but generic essences do not construct themselves or beget specific beings. In Santayana's language, they do not belong to "the generative order" of nature.

A consciousness confronted with an infinity of essences has no basis on which to choose among them. Choice is a hallmark of animal life: love and revulsion express the values of organisms. This leads to the shocking, and redeeming, realization that selectivity is of no significance to essence or to pure consciousness. Since essences are inactive, eternal forms, nothing matters to them. And consciousness, or "spirit" as Santayana calls it, is "an impartial readiness"[17] to intuit any universal; it is as happy to contemplate one form as another.

This consideration reveals that inexistent essence and spirit in its purity are for each other; they constitute a natural pair. When essence is instantiated, it becomes a part of the physical world and acquires significance to the struggling animal. And so long as spirit is harnessed to the service of the organism, it cannot take joy in all that comes its way; it suffers the loves and pains of the organic psyche that gives it birth. But spirit set free from servitude to the demands of the body can delight in whatever form it finds. When spirit is permitted to be spiritual and intuition to be pure intuition, the concerns of animality fall away and we taste the peace that passes all understanding. The reward is eternal joy.

This joy is eternal but not everlasting.[18] Animal life is limited: the moment passes and soon we are no more. But eternity is not a quantity to measure. It is activity (energeia) in Aristotle's sense, requiring no duration in time.[19] How long the bliss lasts is thus irrelevant. Only its quality matters, and that is unsullied so long as consciousness remains unperturbed by care and retains a clear view of its object. What counts is the moment in which, as Santayana puts it, the ultimate becomes immediate[20] and we rest, if not in the bosom of Abraham, at least in the Elysian fields of transcendent delight.

Spirituality becomes, in this way, the aesthetics of blessedness. The relation between spirit and its objects is clearly aesthetic. It is immediate apprehension that carries joy in the beautiful. The mind leaves its cares behind as it focuses attention on the play of forms. The joy experienced is, as Kant correctly believed, disinterested: as means to nothing further, contemplation and enjoyment constitute an ethereal song.

Since consciousness is involved and forms are apprehended, such moments display a cognitive, or what Santayana sometimes calls a "synthetic" element. But they do not constitute knowledge in the full sense of the word. They have no external objects and they are not intelligently adaptive to surrounding substances or facts. On the contrary, what makes them special is that they are freed from the demand to adapt to anything—they are unconnected or superfluous to the needs of animal life.

Pure intuitions or moments of liberated, unconcerned consciousness move in this way beyond all preference and valuation. The distinction between good and evil and the drive for perfection express "the subterranean" activities of the animal psyche,[21] its desperate need to distinguish what fosters from what inhibits its life. There is, therefore, nothing spiritual about moral judgments. The latter constitute testimony of the work of selectivity essential for continued life; the former is the selfless—and, dare I say, indiscriminate—embrace of whatever essence may come our way. The latter wants victory over time; the former is content to disappear into the eternal.

This is the source of the second major criticism Santayana levels against the Neoplatonic tradition. In *Platonism and the Spiritual Life*, he repeatedly characterizes the Neoplatonic adherence to exalted values, including the value of spirituality, as "political." He says, for example:

> The friends of spirit, in their political capacity, will of course defend those forms of society in which, given their particular race and traditions, spirit may best exist: they will protect it in whatever organs and instruments it may already have appeared, and will take care that it pursues its contemplative life undisturbed in its ancient sanctuaries.[22]

This is an understandable interest in safeguarding what are normally seen as the conditions of spirituality. They are, however, moral and not spiritual concerns about the human good; they express the desires of our psyches to live long and to live well. Such "political zeal, even in the true friends of spirit is not spiritual,"[23] for much as the life of the spirit in us presupposes a flourishing or at least a relatively intact organism, it cannot adopt the aims of that animal without losing its soul.

Santayana's critique of the Neoplatonic tradition comes, then, to the claim that it presents an impure conception of spirituality, mixing true devotion to the eternal with the moral or political desire to protect its sources and to extend its dominion indefinitely into the future. The lesson Santayana wants to teach, instead, is that "spiritual life is not a worship of 'values'," but "a disintoxication from their influence."[24] This means that the pure intuitions constituting spirituality take no interest even in their own continuance; they are absorbed in a satisfaction that is "free from care, selfless, wholly actual and, in that inward sense, eternal."[25]

Evidently, Santayana does not wish to deny that, as living creatures, *we* can have a legitimate desire to extend our moments of spirituality for as long as possible. But from the standpoint of the spiritual life, such desires have no standing. Considered from the outside of such experiences, we may well wish for the moments of rapturous union to continue. But from the inside, that is, in those moments when we find ourselves absorbed in a landscape of eternal forms, no desire for anything temporal is possible or proper. If a desire arises, the magic of eternity is shattered; if, amazingly, the magic is sustained, the desire loses its urgency and becomes but another eternal object to contemplate.

We may characterize such all-encompassing absorption in the immediate in a variety of ways. We can speak of it in secular terms as joy in the beauty of all things. But we can also say that it involves the concentration of mind that constitutes the heart of prayer. Santayana refers to it as liberation, as well:[26] it gives us the feeling that we have been set free of the incubus of material existence so we may dwell in eternity.

In *Realm of Spirit*, Santayana also uses the language of union with God, with the One, with the Absolute and with Brahma.[27] Phenomenologically, absorption in the object feels like return to the source or reunification with primordial reality. The outcome is a profound sense of selflessness or a oneness whose vibrant reality cannot be expressed in words.

That the experience Santayana calls to our attention can be captured in the language of metaphysics, aesthetics, religion and poetry suggests that these disciplines converge on key elements in the life of spirit. For Santayana, at least, none of these discourses can be taken as literally true, though all of them constitute useful languages in which we can express vital insights, and remarkably the same ones, into the human condition.

Spirituality does not constitute a life that can serve as an alternative to the one requiring food and air. It does not liberate us in any permanent way from the burdens of existence, nor does it return us to Being or its Source. The experience may feel as though that were happening, and the languages we use to convey or explicate it are marvelous symbolic tools for fixating it. But when all is said and done, what happens is simply that in these moments of calm consciousness the mind touches the eternal. It does not embrace the One or achieve union with God, though saying so can be a splendid poetic way of describing the event.

These last few comments can be used to measure the true distance between Santayana and Neoplatonists. Although he is in full agreement with the great tradition of Neoplatonism concerning the central significance of eternity for achieving the measure of perfection possible for our finite frame, he cannot accept the metaphysics of Neoplatonism at face value.

Emanation schemes, talk of a unitary source of Being, hierarchical conceptions of reality and the idea that determination is negation strike him as dialectical moves out of touch with the physical reality in which we operate. When it comes to existence, he says again and again, all substance is material, meaning that it is "the physical substance...found in things or between them."[28] If we ever discover the structure of the real world, we will have physics and not metaphysics to thank.

This means that in Santayana's view Neoplatonism as a philosophy of existence or nature will always be wide of the mark. As a philosophy that points the way to salvation, however, it is right on the money. "The Greek naturalists," he says in one place, and in others specifically adds Plotinus,[29] "have been right on the chief issue, the relation of man and of his spirit to the universe."[30] And when we look past the heat of desire and the fierce partialities of animal life, that alone is what truly matters.

Accordingly, it is no small achievement to have developed an understanding of our relation to eternity. None but Plato and his followers were able to do this in the West. Even if we reject their metaphysics, we must accept its spiritual significance for the human race. The enduring worth of Neoplatonism resides not in what it says about the world, but in how it shows us the boundless play of eternity in our lives.

Notes

1. Daniel Cory, his literary executor, sold portions of Santayana's library to interested universities. A significant collection of his books may be found in Austin at the University of Texas Library.
2. George Santayana, *Scepticism and Animal Faith* (New York: Dover, 1955), vii. Hereafter *SAF*.
3. *Ibid.*
4. *Ibid.*, v, vi.
5. *Ibid.*, ix.
6. *Ibid.*, v.
7. George Santayana, *Platonism and the Spiritual Life*, in *Winds of Doctrine and Platonism and the Spiritual Life* (New York: Harper, 1957).
8. George Santayana, *The Sense of Beauty* (New York: Scribner's, 1896).
9. George Santayana, *Realms of Being* (New York: Cooper Square, 1972).
10. George Santayana, *Physical Order and Moral Liberty*, John and Shirley Lachs, eds. (Nashville: Vanderbilt University Press, 1969).
11. *Realms of Being*, 341.
12. *Ibid.*, 572.
13. *SAF*, 179.
14. *Ibid.*, 293.
15. *Ibid.*, 70-71.
16. George Santayana, "Some Meanings of the Word 'Is'," in *Obiter Scripta*, J. Buchler and B. Schwarz, eds. (New York: Scribner's, 1936).
17. *SAF*, 284.
18. Santayana presents a marvelous discussion of these and related terms on pages 270-271 of *SAF*.
19. *Ibid.*, 217. See also, *Realms of Being*, 816.
20. *Platonism*, 301.
21. *Realms of Being*, 335ff.
22. *Platonism*, 256.
23. *Ibid.*, 257.
24. *Ibid.*, 248.
25. *Ibid.*, 247.
26. *Realms*, 736ff.
27. *Ibid.*, 769.
28. *SAF*, 209.
29. *Platonism*, 288 and elsewhere.
30. *SAF*, viii.

Martin Heidegger on *Mimesis* in Plato and Platonism

Constantinos Proimos

> In recent decades we have often heard the complaint that the innumerable aesthetic considerations of and investigations into art and the beautiful have achieved nothing, that they have not helped anyone to gain access to art, that they have contributed virtually nothing to artistic creativity and to a sound appreciation of art. That is certainly true, especially with regard to the kind of thing bandied about today under the name "aesthetics."[1]

These provocative words by Martin Heidegger were pronounced between the years 1936-1940 during his university lectures on Nietzsche. Even today, more than fifty years later, they remind to many of us, similar experiences of complaints against aesthetics, particularly from the part of artists.

The task of this paper is to propose and analyze some of the reasons why Heidegger was prompted to such a fierce condemnation of aesthetics. Through his detailed, long and critical account of Nietzsche and under the shadows of Hegel and Kant, Heidegger attempts in his university lectures, a definite clearing of accounts with Plato and Platonism. This is certainly no small task. For he clearly sees Platonic philosophy as well as Platonism to be endemic to the entire history of Western philosophy. Even if one disagrees with Heidegger's rejection of aesthetics, there can hardly be any disagreement on the fact that Plato by his thought and via his many epigones has set the standards for all discussion of art.

However, Heidegger's problem with aesthetics does not merely reside in the fact that he wants to propose a different understanding of art, beyond the ones proposed by the history of aesthetics. Heidegger's problem is greater than this: it concerns Plato's basic assumptions about thinking and in particular about truth and its production. Therefore Heidegger's condemnation of aesthetics goes hand in hand with his criticism of truth as representation, whether this is understood as correspondence, ὁμοίωσις, imitation, μίμησις, or as adequation, *adequatio*. Understanding his problem with aesthetics provides the best access to one of the most fundamental tenets of Heidegger's thinking, namely his notion of truth.

For, according to Heidegger, truth is neither representation of something that exists outside thinking, nor correspondence of the concept to reality. Likewise, truth cannot be measured through adequation or ὁμοίωσις between the concept and the real. According to my interpretation of Heidegger, all these traditional models of truth which he rejects, and found in his days not only incorrect but also gravely misleading and ill-fated, depend on μίμησις. Μίμησις, this major Platonic notion that we may abusively translate as imitation or representation, has the key role in the Platonic theory of ideal forms. Schematically speaking and according to most of the traditional interpretations of Platonism, all reality in Plato and in Neoplatonism strives to imitate or represent the reality of the ideal forms, always unsuccesfully and yet always necessarily. Again schematically speaking, according to Platonism, only the reality of ideal forms is genuinely true, good and beautiful. Now translated to our modern times this thought means that through logic, ethics and aesthetics, humans strive to reach this reality and to imitate it, in the best way they can. Humans set the rules for this imitation via logic, ethics and aesthetics. According to Heidegger's interpretation of the history of metaphysics, logic is "knowledge of *logos,* that is the doctrine of assertion or judgement as the basic form of thought. Logic is knowledge of thinking, of the forms and rules of thought."[2] Ethics is "knowledge of *ethos,* of the inner character of man and of the way it determines his behavior."[3] Aesthetics is *episteme aisthetike*, "knowledge of human behavior with regard to sense, sensation, and feeling, and knowledge of how these are determined."[4] Now it is better understood what metaphysicians mean when they teach that humans strive to imitate the true, good and beautiful reality of ideal forms through logic, ethics and aesthetics. The knowledge which these domains of thinking produce, via their rules and standards, orients the action and comportment of humankind. According to Platonism however, this knowledge is ultimately and permanently determined by the ideal forms and this has of course numerous consequences for thinking and philosophy, which Heidegger attempts to analyze and criticize.

It is easy to infer from our presentation so far, that Heidegger's problem with aesthetics hides in fact a problem with Platonism, in general. For if Platonism accepts as the only valuable reality the reality of the ideal forms, most Platonists despise beings for what they are "on the basis of what (they) should or ought to be."[5] For if truth, goodness and beauty are ultimately placed in the supersensuous realm, all that is grounded in the sensuous is, in the final analysis, opposed or excluded. If art is affirmation of the sensuous[6] then it can be understood why art has traditionally been interpreted to have an inferior role in Plato's *Republic*, in his ideal state. It is also easy to understand why according to Heidegger, Nietzsche became Plato's most notorious and fierce opponent. As he famously put it himself, Nietzsche struggled to overturn Platonism by maintaining in his *Will to Power* that art which espouses the sensuous is worth more than truth which espouses the supersensuous. Nevertheless, overturning the tyranny of Platonism, is not such an easy task as it may seem. For by espousing the sensuous and declaring this reality in which we live as the only possible one, by celebrating the senses and art, we may easily end up in positivism, something of which Nietzsche also, was aware. Positivism, according to Heidegger, accepts as the only standard "what lies before us from the outset, what is constantly placed before us, the *positum*. The latter is what is given in sensation, the sensuous."[7] However, it would be at best naive to limit the scope of reality in what is given to sensation, in what is constantly placed before us. For in such a case, Heidegger argues, we develop a dangerous blindness to all that is nonsensuous, therefore to all tradition, culture and history, whose courses Platonism has so much contributed to shaping.

Thus, truth, according to Heidegger, is neither in Platonism, nor in positivism, at least in these crude versions of them, so far presented.

> What is needed is neither abolition of the sensuous nor abolition of the nonsensuous. On the contrary, what must be cast aside is the misinterpretation, the deprecation, of the sensuous, as well as the extravagant elevation of the supersensuous. A path must be cleared for a new interpretation of the sensuous on the basis of a new hierarchy of the sensuous and nonsensuous. The new hierarchy does not simply wish to reverse matters within the old structural order, now reverencing the sensuous and scorning the nonsensuous. It does not wish to put what was at the very bottom on the very top. A new hierarchy and new valuation mean that the ordering *structure* must be changed. To that extent, overturning Platonism must become a twisting free of it.[8]

Ironically, the path that Heidegger himself chooses, in order to twist free of Platonism is a reinterpretration of *mimesis* on the basis of Plato's book X of the *Republic* but also with reference to *Phaedrus* and the *Symposium*. For to twist free of Platonism does not at all mean the impossible and ill-fated wish to dispense with Platonist thinking, writing or heritage. Quite on the contrary, according to Heidegger, twisting free of Platonism means a strong reinterpretation of Platonism. The itinerary which leads Heidegger to this reinterpretation is too long and detailed to be presented here with justice. However, I shall attempt to sketch the main idea and present its results in the best way possible. Interpreting the Greek-Platonic concept of *mimesis*, Heidegger argues:

> What is decisive for the Greek-Platonic concept of *mimesis* or imitation is not reproduction or portraiture, not the fact that the painter provides us with the same thing once again; what is decisive is that this is precisely what he cannot do, that he is even less capable than the craftsman of duplicating the same thing. It is therefore wrongheaded to apply to *mimesis* notions of "naturalistic" or "primitivistic" copying and reproducing. Imitation is subordinate pro-duction.[9]

As it is well known from Plato's *Republic*, the craftsman of a bed creates it with a view both to the ideal form of the bed as well as with due consideration to the bed's use.[10] However, ultimately, the ideal form of bed remains unknown to him and this is the reason why we have many different constructions of beds, feather beds, water beds etc. Likewise, the painter who paints a bed or the poet who describes one is based on crafted beds. The form of the ideal bed is far from her or him. And we, users of beds, acquire our criteria of judgement when it comes to beds from craftsmen and painters. If moreover, we are well informed and researched we can imagine the form of the ideal bed. However, as long as we live we may come to the point of trying or knowing a bed that is far superior than anything we have tried or known up until then. Thus for us too, the ideal form of bed is ultimately unknown, for no matter how much out of our ways we go to purchase the most ideal bed, for sure there is always going to be a better one. The point here is that whatever access we have to the ideal form of things, this access is necessarily mediated by craftsmen as well as painters, by their subordinate and yet necessary production of things. And if we come across the most ideal form of bed we have ever imagined or tried, then we can infer that all the rest of our previous beds have been inferior to it and that this bed is indeed close to what the ideal bed must be. Then, the fact that we often proclaim "This is a real bed!," "This is truly a bed!," "This is a true bed!" means, first, that there is truth assigned to the thing, second, that truth pertains to actual things, in general and third, that some actual things, even of the same kind, can be truer than others. When we come across a good bed, at least a better than the one we already have, then something of the ideal form of bed is revealed to us. The better bed is disclosed as closer to the ideal bed and yet prudence and modesty about our possessions and perhaps a little bit of consumerist addiction, dictate that there must always be a better bed, closer to the ideal.

Likewise according to Heidegger truth belongs to things themselves. Or rather some of truth. For some things, even of the same kind are truer than others. Heidegger defines his notion of truth in an earlier essay than the Nietzsche lectures, with the title "Plato's Doctrine of Truth" from 1931/1932. There Heidegger defines truth as unhiddenness. "As unhiddenness truth is a fundamental trait of beings themselves."[11] To the extent that all beings show themselves to us, they emerge from hiddenness, and to this extent such beings are true.

> In Greek, unhiddenness is called αλήθεια, a word that we translate as "truth"...Originally for the Greeks hiddenness, as an act of self-hiding, permeated the essence of being and thus also determined beings in their presentness and accessibility ("truth"); and that is why the Greek word for what the Romans call "*veritas*" and for what we call "truth" was distinguished by the alpha-privative (ά-λήθεια). Truth originally means what has been wrested from hiddenness. Truth is thus a wresting away in each case, in the form of revealing. The hiddenness can be of various kinds: closing off, hiding away, disguising, covering over, masking, dissembling.[12]

To be sure, according to Heidegger, truth does not only belong to things themselves. At the same time that Heidegger discovers truth as αλήθεια he also acknowledges truth as ορθότης, the correctness of the gaze, which is equally being developed by the Platonic dialogues. Truth as ορθότης, is "the correctness in apprehending and asserting."[13] Truth as correctness of the gaze "becomes a characteristic of human comportment toward beings"[14] rather than a characteristic of beings themselves. Finally, truth as correctness of the gaze is the representational form of truth, as it concerns the correctness of representation and assertion. This truth which concerns human intellect, finally prevails in the history of metaphysics after Plato and Aristotle. Truth as correctness of representation recurs periodically as *adaequatio* in medieval Scholasticism, notably in the work of Thomas Aquinas, as *veritas* in Descartes' rules, as "the necessary error" in Nietzsche's *Will to Power*. Concomitantly, the essential ambiguity in the works of both Plato and Aristotle between truth as αληθεια and as ορθότης is subsequently to their works, lost.[15]

Heidegger aims to retrieve and use this Platonic ambiguity in the determination of the essence of truth in order to criticize and limit the scope of the mimetic model of truth, truth as correctness of representation. The main notion of truth through which he operates is that of ἀλήθεια, that truth which as unhiddenness pertains to things themselves and which is non representational. To the extent that unhiddenness becomes an operating principle of his thinking, Heidegger arrives at some peculiar sort of earth-bound Platonism which is however stripped from the constitutional and traditional roles ascribed to *mimesis* and to the supersensuous realm. Truth as unhiddeness has its opposite in hiddenness. Of course, Heidegger claims, things do not err. They only conceal themselves. Erring in this case belongs to the very constitution of humans and consists of humans turning away from the mystery of things "toward what is readily available, onward from one current thing to the next, passing the mystery by..."[16] Erring is therefore to accept things as they are hidden and not to expose oneself to their unhiddenness. The essence of truth according to Heidegger is freedom and freedom is letting things be. For Heidegger letting things be means engaging with things and caring for them.[17] To what extent this is some sort of Platonism or is a definitive twisting free of Platonism, remains an open question.

In any case, in Plato himself, Heidegger finds the seeds to twist free of Platonism. Twisting free of Platonism for him means to abandon the all dominant mimetic notion of truth, truth as correctness of representation and assertion, in favor of truth as αλήθεια, unhiddenness. Furthermore what this means is that Heidegger does not limit the scope of truth in all matters which have to do with intellect and representation. Truth is not solely pertinent to logic but also applies to the individual, social or historical comportment of humans and finally equally concerns their productive activities, the manner in which they create or fabricate things. Heidegger's Hegelianism resonates here. For the neat traditional separation of metaphysics among logic, ethics and aesthetics does not hold in Heidegger's views. Rather, his notion of truth as unhiddenness allows him to consider in an all-encompassing manner all the activities of humankind which were hitherto separated and distinguished.

Heidegger's non mimetic notion of truth has however a particular significance for all reflection on art nowadays. For the mimetic notion of truth which has been predominant in aesthetics blinds us to the significance of many art-works and artefacts, old and new. The temple of classical Greek antiquity, an example that Heidegger employs in "The Origin of the Work of Art," stands there without being a copy of anything. The historical, political and religious ideas and views it exemplifies do not have a direct formal resemblance with its forms and contours. Certainly the forms and contours of the temple mean historically, politically and religiously, in a way that crystallizes the views and the values of classical Greek antiquity. In fact, the construction of the temple is associated in our memory with everything that the ancient world of classical antiquity was for us. Its truth is one of our few remaining accesses to this world. But its truth depends on how in each historical era, this same temple emerges from hiddenness, how it is discovered and rediscovered and what special significance each historical people attaches to this discovery. Likewise, a crafted thing like a bed has a significance for us today which depends on the rich variety of beds which exist and are available in the market. However, contrary to Plato's assumption a bed's significance and value are not solely inferred from the rich variety of actual beds. For example, a non existent bed, the bed described by Homer during Ulysses's meeting with Penelope and the event of his recognition by her, directly or indirectly influences the way we see all beds and the special significance we attach to them as symbols of marital love and faith. Even as a subordinate literary production, according to the Platonic doctrine, this bed has an ineffable mark on our memory and may indeed more than any water or feather bed, stand in our imagination as that bed which is closest to the ideal. Furthermore, if we ever hope to get a clue of modern and contemporary art of the 19th and 20th centuries, it is imperative to extend our notion of truth beyond *mimesis*. For as it is broadly known a great deal of modern and contemporary art signifies without representing anything real. Modern and contemporary artworks are rather examples of things in the Heideggerian sense of the term. They have their own truth which relates with aspects of the world in which we live. They reveal this truth and emerge from hiddenness once we let ourselves be exposed to these aspects, once we research them and engage with them. Therefore, it is narrow-minded to restrict artworks to the domains of representation, aesthetics, feeling. Often their significance in terms of these domains is secondary when it is not non existent. Hence Heidegger's condemnation of aesthetics aims to direct our attention to an alternative non representational, non aesthetic understanding of art which of course stems from his alternative understanding of truth and how this pertains to all things.

Heidegger's non mimetic notion of truth is therefore of great value in order to get an insight in various historical developments of the different arts. Moreover, the insights that Heidegger's notion of truth allows us into the state of the arts are theoretical and political too, exactly in the same way as Plato's inquiry into art in the *Republic*. This is why Heidegger, like the Greeks, locates art between *techne* and *poiesis*. On the one hand, art as *techne* signifies "an ability in the sense of being well versed in something, of a thoroughgoing and therefore masterful *know-how*."[18] On the other hand, art as *poiesis* means "*what is brought forward in a process of bringing-forth*, what is produced in production, and the producing itself."[19] Finally art is not irrelevant, according to Heidegger to the Greek μελέτη and ἐπιμέλεια, carefulness of concern.[20] In all cases art for Heidegger is by no means restricted to *mimesis* but is well beyond and above it.

Of course, taking under consideration the dates during which Heidegger developed his thinking on art, truth, and politics during the tumultuous decade of nineteen thirties which also hosted his Nazi period, can be quite troublesome for anyone engaging with his understanding of art. This troublesome consideration of dates is what prompts Philippe Lacoue-Labarthe, one of the most important contemporary critics of Heidegger, to assert that despite the latter's rejection of aesthetics and criticism of *mimesis*, Heidegger falls prey to both of them. First, he falls prey to aesthetics to the extent that he equates art with thought and politics under the rubric of *techne* and thus consciously or unconsciously participates in the general reactionary tendency of the thirties towards the esthetization of politics. Second, Heidegger falls prey to *mimesis* to the extent that his thought offers no resistance to the German obsession during the thirties of restoring in Germany the glory of ancient Greece.[21] Whether one agrees or disagrees with Lacoue-Labarthe, his criticism must indeed be taken seriously but it is well beyond the scope of this paper to examine it in further detail. It is true that a certain degree of caution should always be applied towards the Heideggerian texts of the period which connect art, truth and politics so closely. However, it is also true that the Heideggerian notion of truth provides an important platform on the basis of which we can think constructively and pertinently about art, its ontological status and its theoreticopolitical significance. As it is the case with all great and controversial philosophers, one is free to employ this platform at one's own risk.

Now when it comes to Plato's epigones, Platonists and Neoplatonists, the popular belief prevailing among the historians of philosophy is that Platonists after Plato, lack the complexity and subtlety of the master. Pressing to the extreme such aspects of the Platonic theory as the distinction between sensuous and supersensuous, the verdict against many Platonists is that they rendered the Platonic philosophy rigid and repressive, much to the expense of its essential ambiguity. Typical example is Nietzsche's views on the matter, according to which the entire Christianity is characterized as "Platonism for the people."[22]

This popular and demeaning belief about Platonism and Neoplatonism should however in each case be carefully scrutinized. For Plotinus, the most celebrated Neoplatonist, it is certainly not the case. Rather on the contrary, the reader of Plotinus's views on beauty discovers aspects which resolve many of the Platonic difficulties in the account of the arts. Plotinus, for example, extends the scope of beauty in the very same way that Heidegger extends the scope of art. For, as it is known, beauty, according to Plotinus need not be restricted to the physical world but equally concerns matters of conduct and intellect.[23] Furthermore, beauty is neither exclusively founded upon the senses, nor does it uniquely depend on symmetry and proportion.[24] Again like Heidegger, Plotinus relates closely beauty and truth. For the latter in the fifth ennead eighth claims that: "We ourselves possess beauty when we are true to our own being; our ugliness is in going over to another order; our self-knowledge, that is to say, is our beauty; in self-ignorance we are ugly."[25] Even Heidegger's criticism of *mimesis* is first articulated in Plotinus' work.

> Still the arts are not to be slighted on the ground that they create by imitation of natural objects; for to begin with, these natural objects are themselves imitations; then, we must recognize that they give no bare reproduction of the thing seen but go back to the Reason-Principles from which Nature itself derives, and, furthermore, that much of their work is all their own; they are holders of beauty and add where nature is lacking. Thus Pheidias wrought the Zeus with no model among things of sense but by apprehending what form Zeus must take if he chose to become manifest to sight.[26]

Art therefore, according to Plotinus, is also appraised as a theoreticopolitical activity of a historical character and is endowed with bringing forth truth in the form of Reason-Principles. It is praised and esteemed more than nature, for through art the opportunity is given to behold and admire the idea, infer the intellectual principle from what is less to it and love and desire Being.[27] Contrary to Plato, art, according to Plotinus, is esteemed more than mere craftsmanship. But in this act of irreverence towards his master,

Plotinus is in the good company of Heidegger. The latter indicates his disagreement with Plato through an anecdote:

> A statement by Erasmus which has been handed down to us is supposed to characterize the art of the painter Albrecht Dürer. The statement expresses a thought that obviously grew out of a personal conversation which that learned man had with the artist. The statement runs: *ex situ rei unius, non unam speciem sese oculis offerentem exprimit*: by showing a particular thing from any given angle, he, Dürer the painter, brings to the fore not only the single isolated view which offers itself to the eye. Rather-we may complete the thought in the following way-by showing any given individual thing as this particular thing, in its singularity, he makes Being itself visible: in a particular hare, the Being of the hare; in a particular animal, the animality. It is clear that Erasmus here is speaking against Plato.[28]

So does Heidegger of course. Therefore both Plotinus and Heidegger conceive of art in a broad manner and in connection to truth, they deem it as the vehicle of truth or the vessel of whatever is highly esteemed in their thinking. Both Plotinus and Heidegger criticize *mimesis* and attempt to limit its scope. Finally, without straightforwardly rejecting *mimesis*, both Plotinus and Heidegger repeat Plato's essential ambiguity on it.

The connection between Heidegger and Plotinus that we attempted to establish a little bit too quickly and schematically, in relation to the great chronological distance separating the two thinkers, testifies to the fact that Platonism has been travelling a long way and surely will continue doing so, during the years to come. However, Platonism's travel itinerary is extremely mutational and in modern times has become increasingly less dependent on *mimesis*. Hence the startling differences of approach and interpretation by historians of philosophy to one and the same body of texts, those of Plato and his epigones. One differing in itself as Heraclitus would put it,[29] perhaps offers the best description of Platonism. The Heraclitean description also indicates something else: that in the times in which we live, longing for the right to difference and pluralism, Platonism which has steadily been the aim of our rage may become an ally of our passion, once again.

Notes

1. Martin Heidegger, *Nietzsche*. Vol. I. Trans. David Farrell Krell, (San Francisco: Harper & Row, 1979), 75.
2. *Ibid.*, 77.
3. *Ibid.*
4. *Ibid.*, 78.
5. *Ibid.*, 160.
6. *Ibid.*, 163.
7. *Ibid.*,152.
8. *Ibid.*, 209-210.
9. *Ibid.*, 185.
10. Plato, *The Republic*. Trans. Desmond Lee, second edition rev. (London: Penguin Books, 1987), 361.
11. Martin Heidegger, "Plato's Doctrine of Truth" *Pathmarks*. Trans. Thomas Sheehan. Ed. William McNeill, (Cambridge, UK: Cambridge University Press, 1998), 177.
12. *Ibid.*, 168, 171.
13. *Ibid.*, 177.
14. *Ibid.*
15. *Ibid.*, 178-179.
16. Martin Heidegger, "On the Essence of Truth" *Pathmarks*. Trans. John Sallis. Ed. William McNeill. (Cambridge, UK: Cambridge University Press, 1998), 150.
17. *Ibid.*, 147, 144.
18. Heidegger, *Nietzsche*, 164.
19. *Ibid.*, 165.
20. *Ibid.*, 164.
21. Philippe Lacoue-Labarthe, *L'imitation des modernes. Typographies II*. (Paris: Galilée, 1986), 190-194. See also the English translation of some of the essays of this volume, Philippe Lacoue-Labarthe, *Typography*. Trans. Christopher Fynsk, (Stanford, California: Stanford University Press, 1998), 297, 299-300.
22. Heidegger, *Nietzsche*, 159.
23. Plotinus, *The Enneads*. Trans. Stephen MacKenna, (London: Penguin, 1991), I.6, 45, 54.
24. *Ibid.*, 49, 46, 47.
25. *Ibid.*, 424.
26. *Ibid.*, 411.
27. *Ibid.*, 412, 413, 419, 420.
28. Heidegger, *Nietzsche*, 186-187.
29. Lacoue-Labarthe, *L'imitation des modernes. Typographies II*, 194.

The Neoplatonic Dimensions
of Skovoroda's Aesthetic Theory

Roman T. Ciapalo

Whenever I attempt to grapple with one or other of the many *aporiai* in the writings of Hryhorij Skovoroda, the 18th century Ukrainian philosopher, writer, and poet, I turn for inspiration and context to the following words of the historian Dmytro Chzhevskyj:

> The figure of Skovoroda stands at the end of the baroque period in the history of Ukrainian letters. Although he himself was part of the culture of the Ukrainian baroque, his period represented a transition to a new form of culture. He was therefore seen by many of his contemporaries as an "archaic," even decadent representative of the past. He stood in the shadow of a growing giant—the rationalism of the Enlightenment. For Skovoroda, however, this new spirit was without a soul, a monstrosity, the child of the devil, goliath, the Beast of the Apocalypse! Thus he could not and would not become part of his times. Although Skovoroda managed during his lifetime to assemble a small circle around himself, for which he had neither the intention nor the will to create any external cohesion, it could never assert itself after his death against that "monster," the spirit of the Enlightenment, and disappeared beneath the waves of those tempestuous times. And with this, Skovoroda himself fell into obscurity.[1]

In recent decades, however, interest in Skovoroda's thought has experienced a renewal. My own interest in his writings is due to several factors, not the least of which is my curiosity about the affinities between his views and ancient Greek thought. So it is to his so-called and often maligned "archaic" roots that I wish to turn in this brief paper in order to see what, if anything, his aesthetic theory (consisting of his observations on love, beauty, and God) owes to the ancients, in general, and to Neoplatonism, in particular.

Let me begin with some background on the "Ukrainian Socrates," as Skovoroda has frequently been labeled. The historian V.V. Zenkovsky has argued that Skovoroda "was a profound believer, but at the same time he was marked by unusual inner freedom. This inner freedom, his bold, sometimes audacious, flights of thought, stood in opposition to traditional ecclesiastical doctrines; but he feared nothing in his burning desire for truth . . . He had the genuine insight of faith; he was a mystic, in the best sense of the word, but his reason was unconstrained in its free inspiration, and there were often rationalistic features in his thought."[2] Furthermore, "Skovoroda became a philosopher because his religious experiences demanded it; he moved from a Christian consciousness to an understanding of man and the world. In general, Skovoroda allowed nothing to impede the movement of his thought. For him the spirit of freedom was a religious imperative, not the tumult of an incredulous mind."[3] In short, although Skovoroda considered himself a Christian and a member of the Christian Church, he remained a free ecclesiastical thinker, firmly preserving his freedom of thought.

We know from his friend and pupil, Kovalynskyj, in whom we find many parallels to Plotinus' Porphyry, that Skovoroda often experienced a spiritual exaltation, a specific kind of ecstasy. Skovoroda himself wrote to his young friend concerning one such mystical experience as follows:

> I went for a walk in the garden. The first sensation which I felt in my heart was a kind of release, a freedom and cheerfulness... I felt within myself an extraordinary emotion, which filled me with incomprehensible strength. A momentary but most sweet effusion filled my soul, and everything within me burst into flame. The whole world vanished before me. I was animated by a single feeling of love, peace, eternity. Tears poured from my eyes and suffused a tender harmony through my whole being...[4]

One only has to read a sample of Skovoroda's works to be convinced that this is not simply rhetoric, or an imitation of some other mystic, but a genuine and unique experience. And eventually one more thing will become clear: if Skovoroda is to be compared with the mystics, it is not with those of the West—although there is an astonishing similarity between him and Angelus Silesius for example—but with those of the East."[5]

Thus, it is from his religious concentration and his constant immersion in prayer, that Skovoroda developed a new understanding of life and the world, a new perception of man, and his theory of the ways of knowing. And as a result of his mystical experiences, Skovoroda became haunted by the thought, as he often put it, that "the whole world sleeps"[6] In his writings, many references can be found to this so-called hidden life of the world, a life which can be felt only religiously. Skovoroda felt very deeply the world's "secret sadness" and its "hidden tears." And long before Schopenhauer, who himself felt the sufferings of the world so acutely (under the influence of Hinduism), Skovoroda was constantly concerned with the world's affliction.

And thus, on the basis of this religious feeling Skovoroda came to feel alienated from the world. The life of the world appeared to him as a fundamental duality. The reality of being was different on the surface from what could be found in its depths; and this led Skovoroda to the epistemological dualism central to his philosophy. There was cognition which glided over the surface of being, and there was also cognition "in God." Accordingly, Skovoroda insisted on the psychological priority of sensory knowledge, from which it was necessary to rise to spiritual knowledge. "If you wish to know something truly," he wrote, "look first at the flesh," *i.e.*, at its outward aspect, and you will see there the divine traces which reveal an unknown and secret wisdom. This higher cognition, this beholding of the "divine traces" comes from a spiritual illumination, but is accessible to anyone who can tear himself away from the bondage of an exclusive reliance upon the senses.[7]

Skovoroda, then, seems to argue that the way to this deepened form of contemplation of being is to be found first of all in man's relation to himself. It is our self-knowledge, in its capacity to reveal to us two 'strata' of being, *i.e.*, a spiritual life behind our psychological experiences, that permits us to see everything in this duality of being. "Self-knowledge, therefore, is the beginning of wisdom: 'If you have not measured yourself first,' Skovoroda remarks, 'what benefit will you gain from measuring other creatures?' 'Who can discover the design in the materials of earth and heaven if he has not first been able to look into his own flesh?'"[8]

This thesis is, of course, highly reminiscent of the spirit of Platonism, the recognition of a world of ideas which duplicates being, however imperfectly. What Skovoroda adds is the tendency toward a mystical interpretation of what is revealed to the "spiritual eye"—thus for him "to know oneself and to understand God is a single enterprise."

Let us leave this brief sketch of Skovoroda's epistemology and turn to his anthropology. The problem of man, his nature, his destiny, and the meaning of his life stood at the very focus of Skovoroda's reflections. The basic concept which Skovoroda analyzed exhaustively in his doctrine of man is the concept of the heart.[9] What is central and essential in man, according to Skovoroda, is his heart. "As a man's heart is, so is he," he wrote.

It is important to remember that according to his principle of "seeing all things double," Skovoroda teaches that in addition to the earthly body, there is a spiritual body, which is mysterious, hidden, and eternal. Accordingly, there are two hearts. Concerning the "spiritual" heart, Skovoroda says that it is "an abyss which embraces and contains all things," but which nothing can contain.[10] In a dramatic and revealing passage, Skovoroda asks,

> "What is the heart, if not the soul? What is the soul, if not a bottomless abyss of thought? What is thought, if not the root, the seed and the grain of all our flesh and blood, and of all other appearance? ... Thought is the secret spring of our whole bodily machine."[11]

In thus characterizing the "heart," Skovoroda employs a conception which had come into use (first in mystical, and later in general, literature) from Meister Eckhart: the conception of a "divine spark," which is "buried in man."[12] "Skovoroda asserts that not only is there a 'divine spark' (Eckhart's *Funklein*') in man, but 'the Holy Spirit is also hidden there.'"[13]

All of this represents quite an original metaphysics of man, with unmistakable echoes of a variety of sources, including to some extent, anthropology of Philo. But, his views are also close to those 18th century doctrines which culminated in the concept of an "unconscious" sphere in man. What is clear when reading Skovoroda is that he is primarily an investigator of human nature, although in his various statements one continually finds echoes of other thinkers.

Thus, we can also find in Skovoroda traces of a Platonic and Neoplatonic anthropology, specifically, of the doctrine of the "erotic" nature of our aspirations. For him, "[t]he heart does not love unless it sees beauty." To this aesthetic formula, which we shall revisit later, is added the doctrine which is basic to Skovoroda's ethics: that we love deeply only what is "akin" to us and precisely because it is akin to us. Skovoroda's ethics thus enjoins obedience to the "secretly inscribed law of human nature."[14] And this, of course, comes very close to the Stoic principle of "living according to nature."

The key to understanding Skovoroda's theory of beauty seem to be to see it within its broader context, namely, his discussion of love, and it is to this topic that I shall now briefly direct our attention.

What we find in Skovoroda is an understanding of two sorts of love: the lower and the higher, or, as he usually puts it, earthly love and heavenly love. The sources of this view are many: ancient philosophy, medieval philosophy, especially Byzantine humanism, and the philosophical views of the Renaissance period. As he elaborated on the theme of love, what is obvious is that he tried to take into account all of the positions that preceded him. For example, he was particularly close to the Empedoclean conception of Love as a cosmic force, the cause of the production of things, the principle of their unification, and the countervailing power to Strife, the cause of destruction in the sensible world. It is not surprising, then, that Skovoroda once wrote that "everything began with love and love is to be found everywhere." He was also quite sympathetic to the ideas of Epicurus, particularly when the latter spoke of love as a pleasure that is found on both the corporeal and the spiritual levels.

But, on this theme Skovoroda appears to be particularly fond of Plato and the Neoplatonists, especially with regard to his understanding of idealized love, and his treatment of Aphrodite as an explanatory device. In the dialogue entitled "Narcissus: An Essay of Self-Knowledge" we find Skovoroda offering the following admonition:

> Do not be puzzled, my soul! All of us are lovers of dust and ashes. Whoever has fallen in love with his incarnate appearance cannot stop chasing after that appearance in all heavenly and earthly domains. But why, really, does he love it? Isn't it because in it he recognizes brightness and pleasure, life, beauty, and strength?

In this dialogue, Skovoroda "asserts that empirical man is a 'shadow' and 'dream' of the true man. In every man the 'Holy Spirit—a divine energy—is concealed,' and often it seems in reading Skovoroda that the 'true' man, whom we all have in our depths, is 'one' in all men."[15] He avoids the charge of pantheism, however, since he does not teach that god is the "substance" in every man. Rather, the above remark refers to the Son of God—the Logos—made flesh and man. The Logos is individual in its being as man, and at the same time it is every man. The "true man" in each of us is the guarantee of our individuality, but it is not to be separated from the "heavenly man," from the Lord.[16]

In his dialogue "Narcissus," written in the style of Ukrainian Baroque, Skovoroda quite precisely and in greater detail paints a picture of the theme of love. In it we find a combination of several ancient Greek and Christian elements. The theme of the ancient myth of Narcissus, the young boy who falls in love with himself and dies as a result of his self-love, is treated in a highly original and surprising manner. Skovoroda comments on this in the prologue to his dialogue as follows:

> This is my first-born son. Born in the seventies of this century. Narcissus is both the name of a certain flower and a certain young man. Narcissus—a young man who was gazing upon himself in the mirror of a spring's clear water and has fallen into a deadly love with himself—is an ancient parable from ancient Egyptian theology and of Hebrew history. His image exhorts us to the following: Know yourself! As if he had said: Do you want to be pleased with yourself and fall in love with yourself? Know yourself! Examine yourself vigorously. For how can one fall in love with something that is unknown? Does hay burn without touching fire? So, too, a heart doesn't love without seeing beauty. It is obvious that love is Sophia's daughter. Where wisdom has cast its gaze, there love has been ignited. Self-love is what is truly blissful, and it is saintly, yes, saintly, and it is true, yes, I say, true, and it has acquired and beheld that one beauty and truth: It is standing in your midst, and you are not aware of it.

Even this brief excerpt from Skovoroda's dialogue "Narcissus" helps to illumine somewhat his notion of love. Skovoroda refers to Narcissus autobiographically as his first-begotten son. He has himself in mind here, that is, a human being who is striving to understand the world. Only by coming to understand the world, and through this, to understand himself as a part of this world, can a human being come to love himself or herself. Obviously, Skovoroda is not talking here about any sort of egoism or egocentrism. Rather, he is putting into practice the Stoic idea of life in accordance with nature. Love, for Skovoroda, is not a passive human state; but an active endeavor, and it is inseparably bound to knowledge and cognition. Thus, it is not an accident that he refers to love as "the daughter of Wisdom." Love, then, is neither unwise nor blind. Rather, when it is joined to wisdom it is among the most sacred of things.

It is here that Skovoroda weaves into his discussion of love yet another theme—beauty. In his view, beauty and love are always found together. He takes great pains to point out that Narcissus fell in love with himself only *after* he saw and experienced his own beauty, the very beauty of the world of nature, of which he was a part. Narcissus understood perfectly well the fact that he, having emerged from Nature, would eventually return to it, thereby obeying one of the fundamental principles in Skovoroda's theory, namely, that "whatever one falls in love with, one eventually becomes," that love inevitably involves a transformation of profound dimensions.

As he did with love, Skovoroda divides beauty into two kinds: the earthly and the heavenly, drawing from the ancient distinction between Aphrodite-Ourania, representing higher celestial love, and Aphrodite-Gaia (or, more properly, Aphrodite-Pandermos), representing the love of the whole people: lower sexual love, in other words. The heavenly one (Aphrodite-Ourania) can be traced back to the Phoenician queen of heaven, while originally Pandermos was literally the one who embraces the whole people as the common bond and fellow feeling necessary for the existence of any state.[17]

It certainly appears to be the case that Skovoroda was able to appreciate the value of earthly beauty, the beauty of nature, and the sort of love that it evokes. His contemporaries spoke of his love of fine things, that he was very pleased when someone gave him a pipe carved from ivory, and that he appreciated gold ornaments and jewelry. Consequently, we cannot assume that Skovoroda completely denigrated earthly beauty. His remark that "A heart is not moved to love without first seeing beauty" can certainly be applied first to the world of sensible things. Thus, it is not accurate to maintain that Skovoroda was entirely alienated from this world and that his *sole* interest was the ideal world. Even the earlier quotation from his dialogue "Narcissus" rather clearly bears witness to the fact that, for Skovoroda, it is through the material world that the ideal world is reached. Thus, Skovoroda argues, it is only through by observing closely and learning from nature that we can reach beauty, truth, and love.

In addition to what has already been noted, what else, if anything, does Skovoroda's theory of the beautiful have in common with Neoplatonism? Let me turn to Plotinus for a few points of reference, in particular to his first treatise chronologically, I, 6 "On Beauty." As John Dillon, among others, has correctly pointed, but treatise I, 6

> ...appears at first sight to be an essay on aesthetics, since it begins with a critique of existing theories of beauty, or *to kalon*, but in fact for Plotinus there is no independent sphere of aesthetics, and the subject matter is primarily ethical.[18]

It is here that we find one of several parallels with Skovoroda, for whom it is not so important to discuss aesthetic theory as such, or the merits of competing theories of beauty in themselves, as it is to define the good life, the ideal way for a human being to live.

What is important in Plotinus, of course, is his contention that (I, 6, 2, lines 13-14) things in this world are beautiful because of their participation in form. Using the imagery of the *Symposium* (206d), Plotinus is able to speak of the soul's instinctive recognition of the presence of form in matter as kalon, but shrinking away from instances of its imperfect domination of matter as aischron (2.I-8). As Dillon later points out,

> ...this whole essay is shot through with reminiscences of Diotima's speech in the Symposium, the central myth of the Phaedrus (particularly the regrowing of the wings of the soul, 250eff.), and the Cave Simile of Republic VII. For Plotinus, the role of beauty can only be to recall us to a knowledge of the forms. VII. For Plotinus, the role of beauty can only be to recall us to a knowledge of the forms.[19]

Here, too, fruitful connections to Skovoroda may be noticed, since for him the awareness of earthly beauty is but an initial, quasi-inductive step in a human being's ascent to that true beauty of the divine realm. For Plotinus, the ascent to the forms, namely, to true beauty, is accomplished through the mastery of the virtues, particularly those with kathartic dimensions.

This is ultimately what makes Plotinus' stance on beauty an ethical one, as is obvious from his simultaneously self-centered and other-worldly remarks in chapter 7 (lines 1-12) of treatise I, 6, where he says the following:

> So we must ascend again to the Good, which every soul desires. Anyone who has seen it knows what I mean when I say that it is beautiful. It is desired as good, and the desire for it is directed to the good, and the attainment of it is for those who go up to the higher world and are converted and strip off what we put on in our descent—just as for those who go up to celebrations of sacred rites there are purifications, and strippings off of the clothes they wore before, and going up naked; until, passing in the ascent all that is alien to the God, one sees with oneself alone That alone, simple, single and pure, from which all depends and to which all look and are and live and think; for it is the cause of life and mind and being. [20]

What Skovoroda seems to have attempted, and what I have sketched briefly here is an adaptation of various Neoplatonic themes, along with the Stoic depreciation of the passions and bodily concerns in general, to an essentially Christian theology. So, wherever Plotinus, for example, encourages us to a life of union with our ultimate source, the supreme reality which is sheer unity, Skovoroda substitutes somewhat awkwardly, but largely successfully, the Christian notion of life in Christ.

By way of conclusion I shall return to Skovoroda's view of man's relationship to god. For Skovoroda, it is ultimately through creatures that we can come to understand God's nature and existence. So, as Walter Burkert has noted,

> However impious the apotheosis of sexuality may seem in light of the Christian tradition, modern sensibility can nevertheless also appreciate how in the experience of love the loved one and indeed the whole world appears transfigured and joyously intensified, making all else seem insignificant: a tremendous power is revealed, a great deity.[21]

The process of coming to know God, according to Skovoroda, is unusually complex and difficult. It is not surprising, then, that he describes Narcissus as "burning, kindling with the coals of love, bursting with jealousy, rushing about and suffering, and getting heart-sick" until finally he feels God's presence in his heart and finds peace and repose in Him. Thus, the beginning of the journey towards wisdom begins with our attempt to understand God. If one doesn't know God, Skovoroda writes,

> he is like a prisoner thrown into a dungeon. What can a person understand in such darkness? The most significant and the first element of wisdom is knowledge of God. I don't see him but I know and believe that he exists. And if I believe, then I am afraid: I am afraid to anger him; I am looking for what pleases him. This is love! Knowledge of God, belief, fear, and love of God - it is all one chain, knowledge in belief, belief in fear, fear in love, love in keeping commandments, and keeping of commandments in love of one's neighbor...

For Skovoroda, those who cannot recognize this higher path are like prisoners living in a dark cave who can never recognize the light of truth. We find here, of course, a classic parallel with the Allegory of the Cave in Plato's *Republic*, where the truth will never become available to those who continue to be imprisoned and paradoxically, those who manage to escape to freedom and by the power of their reason arrive at the beauty of the world, will have no credibility with the imprisoned. Consequently, if Skovoroda, like Plotinus and other Neoplatonists, disparages earthly life, then it is because it ultimately involves darkness, gloom, ignorance, foolishness; and if he decries people who emphasize only sensory pleasures, it is because they don't care at all about their internal spiritual world, about their higher origins.

For this reason Skovoroda writes with such irony in his dialogue "Narcissus" about the fact that it is the foolish and shallow person who accepts the Sun only as a heavenly body that gives off light and heat, and the fountain (or well-spring) only as a source of drinking water and the origin of brooks, streams, rivers, and seas. Such people do not see that in the sun and in the fountain there exists the very origin of life, they do not see the footprints of divine grace, they do not see in them love and hence genuine beauty. For Skovoroda, only the person of deep spirituality, the person who has turned within and found there the true source of his own beauty and life, is capable of reaching God.

And here we may notice in the thought of Skovoroda yet another echo of Plotinus' ethics. Man's quest for "likeness to God" is for Plotinus, as it is for Skovoroda, the goal of ethical activity. For both thinkers, human actions must be evaluated principally in terms of their ability to assimilate us to the divine. All earthly concerns ultimately must be discarded in the process of purification and ascent to the divine realm. And even though some attention must be paid to the body's needs, both Plotinus' "serious man" (*ho spoudaios*) and Skovoroda's "true Christian" might well be described by the following passage in treatise I. 4 ("On Well-Being"):

> He knows its needs, and gives it what he gives it without taking away anything from his own life. His well-being will not be reduced even when fortune goes against him; the good life is still there even so. When his friends and relatives die he knows what death is – as those who die do also, if they are virtuous. Even if the death of friends and relations causes grief, it does not grieve him.[22]

Thus, it is through the achievement of this highest sort of love that a human being becomes wise, indestructible, and unmoved by all unwanted situations and dangers. Such a person is calm with regard to his or her fate and enjoys blessedness. In Skovoroda's own words in "Narcissus,"[23] perfect love, for such an individual

> is calmness of soul and the breath of the Holy Spirit. It is like a beautiful garden, soft wind, sweet-smelling flowers, delight in something completed, in which

the imperishable tree of life is forever in bloom. And its fruits are well-wishing, mildness, a calm disposition, gentleness, sincerity, loyalty, safety, pleasure, spiritedness, and the like. For one who has such a soul, peace is with him, and mercy, and eternal joy.

Notes

1. Dmytro Chyzhevskyj, "An Introduction to the Life and Thought of H. S. Skovoroda," in Richard H. Marshall and Thomas E. Bird, Hryhorij Savic Skovoroda: An Anthology of Critical Articles (Edmonton: CIUS, 1994), 3.
2. Zenkovsky, 53-54.
3. *Ibid.*, 57.
4. *Ibid.*, 58.
5. This is an argument made quite cogently by Zenkovsky, 58.
6. Zenkovsky, 59.
7. *Ibid.*, 59-60.
8. *Ibid.*, 60.
9. *Ibid.*, 61.
10. *Ibid.*, 61.
11. *Ibid.*, 61.
12. *Ibid.*, 62
13. *Ibid.*, 62
14. *Ibid.*, 62
15. *Ibid.*, 62.
16. *Ibid.*, 63.
17. Walter Burkert, *Greek Religion* (Cambridge, Mass.: Harvard University Press, 1985), 152-155. Hereafter, "Burkert."
18. "An Ethic For the Late Antique Sage," 310.
19. *Ibid.*
20. The translation here is by A.H. Armstrong.
21. Burkert, 152.
22. The translation here is by A.H. Armstrong.

Neoplatonism and American Aesthetics

Jay Bregman

In his essay "the Poet," Emerson remarks that "men have lost the perception of the instant dependence of form upon soul. There is no doctrine of forms in our (*i.e.* Locke's) philosophy."[1] We are made of noetic stuff, at two or three removes yet ignorant of it. To strengthen his argument, Neoplatonic texts are sprinkled throughout the essay. New and higher beauty is expressed through the poet's announcement and affirming of things; thereby the poet opens phenomenal objects to Platonic Forms. "Being used as a type a *second wonderful value appears in the object far better than its old value*—as the carpenter's streched cord, if you hold your ear close enough, is musical in the Breeze"[2] — a phrase with Pythagorean overtones. Emerson's "proof text" for this notion is not out of Plato's Symposium *or any of the Dialogues*. Nor is it taken from *Enn.* I.6, V.8 or other, where Plotinus discusses Art. Rather it is from Iamblichus: "things more excellent than every image, are expressed through images."[3] For Emerson, referring back to his conception of Nature, "things admit of being used as symbols, because *nature is a symbol* in the whole and in every part."[4] As the soul makes the body (Spenser),[5] so the Universe is the externalization of the soul. Wherever the *life* is, that bursts into appearance around it. "We stand before the secret of the world where Being passes into appearance and Unity into Variety."[6] But we (*i.e.* Locke) treat the physical world as self-existent, rather than dependant on Being.

Then out of Proclus: "The mighty heaven exhibits in its transfigurations, clear images of the splendour of intellectual perceptions, being moved in conjunction with *the unapparent periods of intellectual natures.*"[7] The entire cosmos exhibits intellectual perceptions, because its motiion is aligned with the intellectual or noeric realm. (thoughts as active rather than as "noetic"objects.) The true poet or artist operates in Imagination, "a very high sort of seeing: ..."

As the eyes of Lyncaeus were said to see through the earth (*Enn.* V.8.4, Thomas Taylor, *Select Works of Plotinus*, contains I.6; V.8: on the pelucid and interpenetrating, all:part:part:all—Noetic realm[8]), so the poet "turns the world to glass..." This only happens "by the intellect *being where and what it sees: by sharing the path or circuit of things through forms, and so making them translucid to others.*"[9] In a celebrated passage from *Nature*, the one he "never quite lived down" Emerson reveals: "I became a transparent eyeball; I am nothing; I see all: the currents of the Universal Being circulate through me."[10]

Compare Plotinus' description of intellect in Taylor's translation: "There, however, everybody is pure, and each inhabitant is, as it were, *an eye*. Nothing likewise is there concealed, or fictitious, but before one can speak to another, the latter knows what the former intended to say."[11]

The poet properly names things after their appearance or their essence. The daemon or soul which stands over everything is the true *arbiter elegentiae*: "as the form of the thing is reflected by the eye, so the soul of the thing is reflected by a melody."[12] Indeed, sublime natural wonders, as well as every flower bed, have a pre- or super- existence in "pre-cantations" — apparently ur-Harmonies. Those who have ears to hear these "which sail in the air" can transcribe their notes, as it were, grasping the forms through Nature. The ultimate purpose of Nature is "ascension or the passage of the soul into higher forms."[13] The poet accompanies the divine aura which breathes through forms. Beyond conscious intellect resides new energy, " as if an intellect doubled on itself."[14] where the poet abandons himself to the nature of things. He becomes a universal force: "his speech is thunder, his thought is law and his words are universally intelligible..."[15] The poet who speaks adequately, speaks "wildly, or with the flower of the mind."[16] The *anthos tou nou* is a Procline/Chaldaen conception of super-noetic perception "near the One." Here, says Emerson, the intellect "released from all service," takes its direction from celestial life; thus the intellect "inebriated by nectar" is freed from practical activities and the poet sees with the "eyes of Lyncaeus."[17]

Emerson's adaptation of the *anthos tou nou* is striking and demonstrates a grasp of the theurgic Neoplatonist privileging of super-noetic intuition; only the "beyond-intellect" allows us to grasp form imaginatively and express it with artistic spontaneity.

In a passage about intimations of the immortality of our essence, Emerson thinks it appears when famous philosophers and company express their characteristic "thing," *e.g.*, when Socrates in *Charmides, tells us that the soul is cured of its maladies by certain incantations, and that these incantations are beautiful reasons,*[18] from which temperance is generated in souls. "This occurs also when Proclus calls the universe the "statue of intellect..."[19] Neoplatonic ideas adapted to Emerson's purposes are central to his conception of the poetic process, poetry and the poet; by extension the artist *per se.* His ideas provided a framework for many subsequent artists and thinkers.

Among American artists influenced by the Transcendentalists is the Hudson River school's Frederick Church. His "Rainy Season in the Tropics" has been called a "lightscape" in which he "sees through" matter, as Lyncaeus. A religious syncretist, it is likely that Church derived Neoplatonic aesthetic notions from Coleridge. M. Weinstein connects Church's vision of light to Plotinus and Iamblichus, "who spoke of the soul being known by its light."[20]

In the late 19th century French Symbolists Neoplatonized Schopenhauer, whose aesthetic theories have much more in common with Plotinus than with Plato: the artist does not imitate, but realizes Form; the work of art is something that wasn't there before. "We made a singular mixture of Plotinus, of Edgar Poe, of Baudelaire and of Schopenhauer," wrote M. Denis (Davezac, 258) They shared many key ideas. For Plotinus as for Schopenhauer, "the soul gives the realm of sense something of its own." "It is Plotinus view of art that the symbolists share: the faith in art's ability to redeem nature by discovering in phenomena its positive links with Idea"(Davezac, 260). In V.8.2 Plotinus says "... the arts are not to be slighted on the ground that they create by imitation of natural objects, ...we must recognize that they give no bare reproduction of the thing seen but go back to the ideas from which nature derives; and ..that much of their work is all their own; they are holders of beauty and add where nature is lacking;" the arts can transform nature into idea — "for the soul includes a faculty peculiarly addressed to beauty"(I.6.3). "Consider even the case of pictures-those seeing by the bodily sense the production of the art of painting...are deeply stirred by recognizing in the objects depicted to the eyes.. the representation of what lies in the Idea and so are called to recollect the truth."(II.9.16) This is very close to Schopenhauer, who, however, differed from Plotinus in his notion of Art as Temporary Nirvana. For Plotinus, as Fred Schroeder has shown in his eloquent article on Plotinus's *Symposium* of Plato, "Prophecy and Remembrance in Plotinus," there is still pain in the recognition of the Beautiful, and the Beautiful is thereby distinguished from the Good.[21] Still, for Schopenhauer the Idea is distinct from the reasoned Concept, always an object of perception.. entirely within the sphere of intuition"(Davezac, 261).

Plotinus was often quoted by Symbolist scholars and artists of the 1890's; according to M. Denis, in order to counter Auguste Comte's Positivism, P. Serusier "held forth on the doctrine of Plotinus and the school of Alexandria."

In America, Symbolism had few advocates. Arthur B. Davies painted mythological, almost surreal scenes such as "Full-Orbed Moon," whose luminous female figure under the orb of the moon, suggests mysteries connected with Selene. Elihu Vedder's Symbolist Mythological canvasses, Pre-Raphaelite in style, suggest a Neoplatonic inspired "mysteriosophy." Maurice Prendergast was influenced by the Nabi painters. Among John Singer Sargent's depictions of the evolution of religion for the Boston Public Library, noteworthy is his syncretistic "Astarte," with its mysterious diaphanous forms and "Near Eastern Style Occult Symbols"[22]—it seems to be a "theurgic" image of the goddess providentially bringing harmonic order as an Avatar of Universal Soul.

The American modern artist and sometime expatriate Marsden Hartley was perhaps the real heir of the Symbolist aesthetic. He was influenced by the Transcendentalists and Santayana. His favorite reading included writings of the Christian mystics and Plotinus.[23] An "irreligious mystic," he he sought Santayana's realm of essence- pure Being in its infinite implications. This essence was graspable only by intuition. Plotinus was his idea of a true thinker who presented "a modified mysticism through mind processes that suit me perfectly..."[24] I think it must be [that] PLOTINUS HAS REFINED MY MY SENSE OF ESSENCE DOWN TO THE LAST DETAIL..."[25] He adhered to G. de Nerval's doctrine of *correspondences*—Baudelaire's "Foret de Symboles"—in Nature. This symbolist notion implies overtones of Proclus's idea of the universal correspondences of images to archetypes and the *seira* or chains of Being; *e.g.*,"The Good" as Sun of the Intelligible World - Helios-Mithras, the Intellectual god, Visible Helios, Solar Daimons, Solar Heroes, Solar initiates(*Heliodromoi*) the Lion, the Cock, the Heliotrope, the Sunstone.

For Hartley the divine was "*NOUS*, the fourth dimension"—that which is more than ourselves—the 4th dimension that Cezanne tried to paint, the thing which exists between me and the object.[26] For a Neoplatonist this is "the Idea." His best canvasses, *e.g.*, Oriental Symphony—the Kandinsky influenced Indian Fantasy, the quasi-cubist constructions, with their geometric shapes, circles pyramids and mystic graphic signs, display this sensibility. Gertrude Stein approved of his first "mystical abstractions."

Noteworthy of Hartley's Landscapes of New England and Maine are his views of Mt. Katadhin, where he comes close to achieving the essence of Form through the object—the visible fourth dimension—his *NOUS*: "I know I have seen God now. The occult connection that is established when one loves nature was complete—and so I felt transported to a visible 4th dimension—and since heaven is...a state of mind. I have been there these past ten days."[27]

Contemporaries of Hartley, the Canadian "Group of Seven," became aware of Plotinus through the perrenialist Theosophy of Mme. Blavatsky. Their Transcendentalist landscape canvasses appear as a super-real or symbolic search for the "thing" between painter and object; they attempted to paint the Symbolic Idea, the essence of the North American landscape.

Hilary Armstrong insisted on the importance of the sense of the One and the Beautiful in Nature, almost in the manner of an enviromental theologian. For him the poet William Blake, despite his criticisms of Plato and company, remained close to Neoplatonism and W. B. Yeats was a "theurgic neoplatonist."[28] Among the poets who knew Yeats and company, Ezra Pound had a serious interest in Plotinus and Platonic connections with the Eleusinian mysteries, a notion he probably got from Thomas Taylor;[29] also, according to Pound, its medieval and later continuations. Perhaps historically naive, even delusional, Pound's ideas were poetically fruitful.

In Pound's syncretizing of Greek mythology, the Mysterries and Philosophy, Odysseus sets the standard of heroic action in the *Cantos*, the mysteries of Eleusis are connected with the beatific vision: "the beatific vision of the mystic is preceded by darkness and bewilderment equivalent to the darkness and confusion experienced by the initiate at Eleusis."(Surette, 256; *cf.* Plutarch, "On the Soul" 2).

In canto 98:

> no more black shawls in the Piazza
> *more sabello*, for Demeter
> *"Ut facias pulchram"*...

The black shawls according to Pound, were still worn in his "young" time in Venice, for Demeter (canto 102).

They represent a persistence of Eleusis into modern times, that is of the cult of beauty—*ut facias pulchram*.

In Byzantium, the Eleusinian awareness continued:

> "The body is inside" Thus Plotinus
> But Gemisto: "Are Gods by hilaritas;"

Here is Plotinus' notion that body is actually in soul and not vice-versa (Surette, 257).

Aphrodite and Persephone are manifestations of the Nous-the Divine Mind. The former is the seen form par excellence/beatific vision

> ...Cythera potens, Kythera deina
> no cloud but the Crystal body...

The luminous and/or diaphanous bodies of the gods seem to be based on Iamblichean theurgy. On a more mundane note, Pound records Porphry account of Plotinus's' stomach problems as "Plotinus bellyache..."[30]

Pound's hero, Odysseus is presented as an Eleusinian initiate who could brave both the terrors of the Underworld, and the bed of the goddess—a figure uniting the three major subjects of the poem: the descent, the repeat in history, and "the bust thru from the quotidien to the divine."

The poet also read Eriugena and thought his doctrines significant for the medieval Albigensian heretics, whom he saw as adepts of a pagan cult. He didn't understand the Manichaean issue very well: "I have...the text of Erigena... Johnny had a nice mind *Omnia quae sunt lumina.*" All things which are, are lights—the phrase appears in Pisan Cantos 74, facing the Chinese ideogram for "bright:" "in the light of light is the *virtu/sunt lumina,*" said Erigena (74/ 429:455) and lower on the same page:

> Light tensile immaculata
>   the sun's cord unspotted
>   *sunt lumina,* said the Oirishman to King Carolus
> *Omnia*
> all things that are are lights

The light is ultimately the light of Eleusis, Pound's synoptic and Neoplatonic tinged Eleusis (Taylor's influence), which persists in the 12th century love cult or religion of Amor and down to modern times; it represents the conquest of beauty leading to revelation.

It is not surprising, then , that Pound was also interested in the Neoplatonic Lichtmetaphysik of the 13th century Oxonian Robert Grosseteste.

C. Terrell has connected Pound with Medieval Latin Platonism;[31] *lux enim,* the primal light of Grosseteste is related to the spiritually charged lights of

Eriugena and Grossesteste's *"transitus per plura... diaphana..."* is in one place connected with Plotinus:

> *Nous* to *ariston autou*
> as light into water compenetrans
> that is *pathema*
> *ouk aphistatai*
> thus Plotinus
> *per plura diafana*

Nous and Light are equated. Grossesteste seems to distinguish *lux*, light as simple being, the source, from lumen, light as "spritual body," reflected or radiated light.[32]

Terrell points out, however, that what Plotinus and Grossteste assumed to be philosophy and/or science, Pound uses as metaphor: Says Pound, "Grosseteste may or may not be scientific but at least his mind gives us a structure..." Sharon Mayer Libera, a student of the Neoplatonic elements in Pound's poetry thinks that Pound's sense of pervasive light is *Nous* and linked with his love of myth (Libera, 355). He is a modern Neoplatonic polytheist:

> When is god manifest?
> When the states of mind take form
> When does a man become a god?
> When he enters one of the states of mind

And a theurgic Iamblichean Neoplatonic polytheist at that:

> By what characteristics may we know the divine forms?
> By beauty
> And if the presented forms are unbeautiful?
> They are demons.
> If they are grotesque?
> They may be well minded genii. (Libera, 258)

Gods appear formed "to the sense of vision and formlessly to the sense of knowledge"

In Canto 25/119:124, the wise man of Gilgamesh, Napishtim, amid "forms and renewals, gods held in the air, Casting his gods back into the νοῦς."

Reflecting Iamblichus *DM* (Taylor, 125) in his guide to Kulchur's (223) chapter on the Neoplatonics, etc.: "Iamblichus on the fire of the gods, *tou ton theon pyros*, etc., which comes down into a man and produces superior ecstasies, feelings of regained youth, super-youth and so forth." The lines: "Iamblichus light, the souls ascending" appear in a depiction of Egypt in Canto 5/17:21.

Pound's magical gods of mythology-the light imagery of his "magic moments" that break into eternal states of mind is reminiscent of the luminous *plasmata* of Iamblichus.(Libera, 360) Canto 23/107:111 includes the "divine fire" of Iamblichus in a Byzantine Neoplatonic context:

> *"Et Omniformis."* Psellos, *"omnis*
> *Intellectus est."* God's fire. Gemisto:
> Never with this religion

(*El Th* 176: all the Intellectual Forms are both implicit in each other and severally existent)

> Will you make men of the Greeks
> But build a wall across Peloponnesus
> And organize, and...
> damn these Eyetalian barbarians.

In the Malatesta Cantos, Gemisto, that is, Pletho ambassador to Ferrara, in Florence, because the "pest" is:

> ...Talking of the war about the temple at Delphos,
> and of POSEIDON, concret Allgemeine...

Pound caps Poseidon, who in Pletho's system corresponds to NOUS, Zeus to the ONE... Milton Anastos, in his classic paper on Pletho's Calendar and Liturgy indicates that for Pletho "Each god has a special province of his own. But all are subordinate to Poseidon, the eldest and most powerful of the children of Zeus"(see also Libera, 372). Pound saw Pletho as a seminal figure in getting Ficino his position as Cosimo de Medici's Neoplatonist translator and in respect of the genealogy of the gods, compared to Pletho, Ficino was perhaps a mere valedictorian.

ὕδωρ
Hudor et Pax
Gemisto stemmed all from Neptune
hence the Rimini Bas-Reliefs

(quasi-pagan temple of Malatesta-where Plethon's remains were moved from Mistra") and in Guide to Kulchur (224-Libera 373): "He (Gemistus) was not a proper polytheist, in this sense: His gods came from Neptune, so that there is a single source of being, aquatic (*udor*, Thales, etc. as you like, or what is the difference)." According to Iamblichus, light reflected in water is also a means of divination.

For Pound, Neoplatonically, the key is Mind, Intellect, perception of beauty to which Mind is specially fitted as if the forms one admires or creates were the thoughts of a greater whole in which one fleetingly participates. The old gods are present in "magic moments" to him who is "ready to look."(Libera, 377).

Since the Transcendentalists and their interest in Thomas Taylor, Hellenic Neoplatonism as such has formed a backdrop to elements in American thought and art. Despite quite literally damning the Absolute, William James, in *The Varieties,* seriously analyzes the Pseudo-Dionysian mystical tradition and counts Neoplatonism as an important strand of mystical thought.[33] In a book praised by James and recently popular, *Cosmic Consciousness*, the Canadian friend of Walt Whitman, the Psychiatrist, Dr. R.M. Bucke placed Plotinus high on the list of those possessing "cosmic consciousness," he tries to analyze his "mystical mentality," albeit from a not clearly reliable source.[34]

We should also remember that Pythagoreanism was also part of the package right along. This is not surprising, given the ancient Neoplatonist idea of the congruence of Neoplatonic and neopythagorean thought. Gregory Shaw has discerned a Pythagorean form of Theurgy in Iamblichus and even in Plotinus. Furthermore, there has been a modern revival of neopythagorean musical thought, music theory, and the pratice of music itself. Leonard Bernstein, Derycke Cook, Paul Hindemith, and H. Schenker among others, have argued for a "natural pentatonic scale" as the basis of Western tonality which followed musical law as Pythagoras conceived of it. Rather than an arbitrary convention, they thought, the Western scale has its source in the natural order. (Storr, 52). Bernstein wrote: "I believe that from the Earth emerges a musical poetry which is by the nature of its sources tonal. I believe that these sources cause to exist a phonology of music, which evolves from the universal known as the harmonic series. And That There Is An Equally Universal Musical Syntax, Which Can Be Codified And Structured in terms of symmetry and repetition." ("The Unanswered Question"—"coda"— Harvard, '73.) He thought all music past, present and future, and of all types and all cultures—"all of it has a common origin in the universal phenomenon of the harmonic series." (Storr, 57, 61).

The innovative 20th century composer Charles Ives in his *Essays Before a Sonata* — a kind of reflection on his Transcendentalist backround and intro to his Concord Sonata in four movements: Emerson, Thoreau, Hawthorne, The Alcotts—invokes Plotinus to back up his idea of individual expression—though Plotinus himself would perhaps find this a bit strange. The composer should not be afraid to express himself: "He can remember with Plotinus that in every human soul there is the ray of celestial beauty; and therefore every human outburst may contain a partial ray..."[35] And in another passage: "...each has in some degree creative insight and an interest desire and ability to express it..." in every human soul there is a ray of celestial beauty (Plotinus admits that), and a spark of genius (nobody admits that).[36]

Ives, who considerd Thoreau a great composer, if only for the rhythm of his prose, alludes to the natural Pythagoreanism expressed in *Walden's*, "accompanying undulations of celestial music,"[37] and the musical/mystical effect of Concord church bells, "At a distance over the woods the sound acquires a certain vibratory hum, as if the pine needles in the horizon were the strings of a harp... a vibration of the universal lyre."[38] The Transcendentalists read the ancient *Life of Pythagoras* as guides to life. Thoreau was especially attracted to Thomas Taylor's translation of Iamblichus *Life of Pythagoras* and *Pythagoric Sayings* from Stobaeus, especially when they displayed a Thoreau-like simplicity: "It is better to live lying on the the grass, confiding in divinity and yourself, than to lie in a golden bed with perturbation." His view of of nature seems at times to be influenced by the theurgic doctrine of correspondences of images to archetypes: the *seira* or "chains" of being on which plants, animals, human souls, daemons and cosmic bodies are "suspended" from higher realities. Hence "the sunflower moves in a circular dance towards the sun... if one could hear the pulsation made by its circuit.. he would perceive a sound..., in honor of its kind, *such as a plant* is cabable of...."[39] The Transcendentalist periodical *The Dial* also featured Pythagorean music criticism.

The Pythagorean tradition in music and musical speculation has been revived in the present (see J. Godwin).[40] In *The Pythagorean Plato*, Ernest G. McClain suggests that the number of the "tyrannical nature" in Plato's *Repub-*

lic translates (in the western scale) to the "tritone" most distant from the lowest note on the piano keyboard. In short, approaching the most dissonant interval we can imagine—or better perhaps the tritone may be understood as neither clearly consonant or dissonant and thus pure *apeiron*, indefiniteness — unresolved in any sort of *harmonia*.[41] European Jazz critc and producer J.E. Berendt opens his book, the *World is Sound on a frontespiece* in which a Pythagorizing Plotinus is quoted first: "All music, based upon melody and rhythm, is the earthly representative of heavenly music" Though his major interest is the recent influence on the West of Eastern philosophical and musical ideas, he includes a thorough discussion of speculative music, including modern Pythagoreans such as Marius Schneider, Hans Kayser and Rudolf Haase, as well as Pythagoras and the Pythagorean tradition including Kepler: "This book keeps making the statement that the world is sound. Not: the world is vibration. Of course, one could say *that* as a well—it is true and everybody says so. But it isn't precise enough. From the standpoint of physics, there billions of different possible vibrations. But the cosmos—the universe—chooses from these billions of possibilities with overwhelming preference for those few thousand vibrations that make harmonic sense (and in the final analysis; that makes musical sense): these translate to the proportions of the overtone scale, the major scale, (and less frequently the minor scale), the Lambdoma and certain church music and Indian ragas."[42] Plato knew the (seven) laws of harmony demonstrated by the Pythagoreans on the monochord (Berendt, 62) and referred to by Plato in *the Timaeus*, in which he recognized that the soul of the world is a musical scale.

One contemporary Platonic, or at least in part Platonic American visionary, who has not been widely recognized as such, is the late Sci/Fi author Philip K. Dick, whose stories "Blade Runner: Do Androids Dream of Electric Sheep?" and "Total Recall" have been made into Hollywood movies. Anyone who has seen these or has read him knows that the author is adept at playing with the perception of appearance and reality. During a conversion experience —to an idiosyncratic "Christian/Gnosis," he experienced a beam of laser-like pink light as "an invasion of my mind by a transcendentally rational mind, as if I had been insane all my life and suddenly had become sane."[43] This mind became in his last novels VALIS standing for *Vast Active Living Intelligence Systems*. (Kinney, 7-8). In addition to these novels he filled notebooks with millions of words, in the manner of a "gnostic." Among his 10 articles, which define "Gnosticism:" "But the Savior (Valis) is here, discorporate; he restores our memory and gives us knowledge of our true situation and nature. Our real nature-forgotten but not lost-is that of being fallen or captured bits of the Godhead. His nature—the Savior's—and ours is identical; we are him and he is us. The Creator of this world is irrational and wars against the Savior who camoflouflages himself and his presence here. He is an invader. Thus it is a secret that he is here, nor do we recognize the irrationality of this world and its frauds: that it lies to us. It is us and the Savior vs. this irrational world."

In order to modify this somewhat bleak picture Dick adds nine ammendments, some of them long and with complicated qualifications of his position. *e.g.*, "I say, this world in a more ultimate sense (unglimpsed by the Gnostics) serves a benign purpose: it teaches us and we either learn or we do not. If we solve the moral and epistemological puzzles we get to return to the Godhead from which we came. I say, this world is a maze. We may have built it ourselves (while we were in a higher unfallen state) and entered it voluntarily to test our powers (abilities). However, we have become trapped and so a fail-safe device—the Savior Valis—has automatically gone into action to aid us. And final example, I say, this world is not so much evil as a mystery. What may have originally been conceived by us as a challenge has turned out to be a prison (or trap?). Fortunately we anticipated this: thus the Savior who invades this irreal world (Maze) and restores our memory and knowledge and state *is* our own selves; the Salvator Salvundus: our supra-temporal discorporate Original and final Self."(*Gnosis* 13) Here we may think of Emerson in *Nature* perhaps intentionally reflecting the Hermetic myth of the Fall of Primal Man, the Anthropos, saying that man is the dwarf of himself, he used to fill the heavens, but now he fills only a small space, and you get the sense that Philip K. Dick is a sort of Gnostic Transcendentalist—of course "pessimistic" compared to the Transcendentalists "optimistic" visions, if we allow *mutatis mutandis,* for the differences between 19th century Ivy League New England Liberal Unitarian culture and post-1960's San Francisco Bay area Syncretistic "Hippy" culture. There *are* continuities as well as differences.

A most interesting and easily intelligible example of Dick's convictions about apparent and true reality can be found in his discussion in an interview in which he describes experience in Platonic terms: He is at the assasination of Lincoln. But the assasination ITSELF becomes a stage show in which the furniture and other elements of reality are seen to be what they really are: stage props. And then he perceives the stage where this is going on, as just that, a stage, in a theater building. The building itself is more than the stage and immediately "behind," the backdrop behind the curtains and the stage is some kind of initial darkness that is, however, connected to some higher or greater

Reality. The "show," whether the participants are aware of it or not, is basically a Projection of that Reality onto an apparent stage set. The show was nothing more than a "derivative illusion," of something deeper. Given the scene one assumes that the show is at least in part a representation of human History as well as empirical reality as such. After explaining his vision Dick said that it was *that experience he underwent* that enabled him to understand what Plato was talking about in his "Allegory of the Cave" in the *Republic*.

In his farewell lecture at Yale in 1972 "The Rationality of Mysticism," where he presented his avowed neo-Neoplatonic views J. N. Findlay asserted that mystical art displays "interpenetration," by which he meant something like what Proclus meant in *El.Th.* Prop 103, "Πάντα ἐν πᾶσιν, οἰκείωσ δε ἐν ἑκάστῳ'" "All things are in all things, but in each according to its proper nature: for in Being there is life and intelligence; in Life, being and intelligence; in Inteligence, being and life; but each of these exists upon one level intellectually, upon another vitally, and on the third, existentially." Thus according to Findlay, for example, Dante is mystical (and Neoplatonic). Mozart is deeply mystical in "The Magic Flute" and *not* mystical in "Don Giovanni." The implication is that the music *itself* would have to have a feel of "interpenetration" to qualify as mystical, in Findlay's sense.

Plotinus said that "symmetry itself" cannot explain why something is beautiful, else why is a flash of lightning (with no parts) beautiful.[44] He is of course working up to his argument that Beauty is dependent on Form. From another angle, we may add that neither does symmetry make a work of Art "mystical." Hard to define "ways of seeing," "ways of hearing" and "ways of knowing" are somehow more important in this regard.

I have attempted to give some examples of Neoplatonic influences on American art and thought. In addition to the admirable advances to Neoplatonic scholarship achieved in North America, Europe, and other places, especially in the last three odd decades, there has been since the 19th century, a stream of Neoplatonic toned ideas, sometimes flowing underground, that has significantly shaped, from the New England Transcendentalists through certain contemporary thinkers and artists, what has been for the most part an American aesthetic.

References

A.H. Armstrong, "The Divine Enhancement of Earthly Beauties;" "Platonic Mirrors," *Hellenic and Christian Studies* (London, 1990), 49-81; 147-181.

A.H. Armstrong, "The Escape of the One," *Plotinian and Christian Studies* (London, 1979), 77-89.

J.E. Berendt, *Nada Brahma: The world is Sound* (Rochester, VT., 1989).

J. Bregman, "The Neoplatonic Revival in North America" *Hermathena* no. CXLIX, Winter (1990), 99-119.

R.M. Bucke, *Cosmic Consciousness* (New York, 1969 ed.)

Philip K. Dick, "The Exegesis," *Gnosis* Fall/Winter (1985-1986), 12-15.

Shehira Doss-Davezac, "Schopenhauer according to the Symbolisis: the philosophical roots of late 19th century French Aesthetic theory," *Schopenhauer, Philosophy and the Arts* (Cambridge, 1996), 249-76.

R.W. Emerson, *Essays, Second Series* (Boston, 1903).

R.W. Emerson, *Nature, Addresses and Lectures* (Boston, 1903).

Joscelyn Godwin, *Cosmic Music* (Rochester, VT., 1989).

P. Hadot, *Plotinus and the Simplicity of Vision* (Chi 1993).

Charles Ives, *Essays Before a Sonata*, third ed., (New York, 1970).

William James, *The Varieties of Religious Experience* (New York, 1909).

Jay Kinney, "The Mysterious Revelations of Philip K. Dick," *Gnosis*, Fall/Winter (1985-1986), 6-11.

Sharon Meyer Libera, "Casting His Gods back into the *Nous*: Two Neoplatonists and the Cantos of Ezra Pound," *Paideuma* vol. 2 no. 3 Winter (1973), 356-77.

Edward Lucie-Smith, *Symbolist Art* (London, 1972; New York, 1985).

Townsend Luddington, *Marsden Hartley, the Biography of an American Artist* (Boston, 1972).

Ernest G. McClain, *The Pythagorean Plato* (Maine, 1978).

F. Schroeder, "Prophecy and Remembrance in Plotinus." Boston Area Colloquium in Ancient Philosophy 12 (1996), 1-28.

Leon Surette, *A Light from Eleusis* (Oxford, 1979).

Thomas Taylor, *Select Works of Plotinus* (London, 1911).

C. Terrell, "Mang Tze, Thomas Taylor and Madame YLH," *Paideuma*, vol.7 nos. 1 & 2, 141-54.

C. Terrell, "A Commentary on Grossteste with an English Version of *De Luce*." *Paideuma*, vol. 2 no. 3, Winter (1973), 447-62; latin text, 463-70.

Norman Weinstein, "Rejoicing in the Light of Paradise" *Parabola* vol. 21 no. 2, May (1996), 76-79.

Notes

1. R. W. Emerson, *Essays, Second Series* (Boston, 1903), 3.
2. *Ibid.*, 13 (emphasis added).
3. *Ibid.*
4. *Ibid.*
5. *Ibid.*, 15, paraphrasing Spenser.
6. *Ibid.*, 14.
7. *Ibid.*, follows Thomas Taylor's translation of Plato.
8. P. Hadot, *Plotinus and the Simplicity of Vision* (Chicago, 1993), 36. Hadot suggests that to "see through" matter to Form: "We might call this procedure the Lynceus method, 'since the latter could even see what is within the earth,'" (quoting Plotinus, *Enn.* V.8,4,25).
9. Emerson, *Essays*, 8 (emphasis added).
10. Emerson, *Nature, Addresses and Lectures* (Boston, 1903), 10.
11. Plotinus, *Select Works of Plotinus*. Trans. Thomas Taylor, (London, 1911), *Enneads*, V.8,4.
12. Emerson, *Essays*, 25.
13. *Ibid.*, 24.
14. *Ibid.*, 25.
15. *Ibid.*, 26-27.
16. *Ibid.*, 27.
17. See note 8 above.
18. Emerson, *Essays*, 30-31 (emphasis added).
19. *Ibid.*, 31.
20. Norman Weinstein, "Rejoicing in the Light of Paradise" *Parabola* vol. 21 no. 2, May (1996), 79. See note 8 above. In concert with the "Lynceus method" Weinstein says of Church: "He anticipates the discoveries of twentieth century physics in "seeing through" supposedly stable and solid matter, realizing as a recurring pattern of light and energy in constant flux."
21. F. Schroeder, "Prophecy and Remembrance in Plotinus" Boston Area Colloquium in Ancient Philosophy 12 (1996), 4.
22. Edward Lucie-Smith, *Symbolist Art* (London 1972; New York 1985), 142-45.
23. Townsend Luddington, *Marsden Hartley, the Biography of an American Artist* (Boston 1972), 16.
24. *Ibid.*, 18.
25. *Ibid.*, 20.
26. *Ibid.*
27. *Ibid.*, 23.
28. A. H. Armstrong, "The Divine Enhancement of Earthly Beauties"; "Platonic Mirrors," *Hellenic and Christian Studies* (London 1990), 68, 164-165, on Blake.

Also, A. H. Armstrong, "The Escape of the One," *Plotinian and Christian Studies* (London 1979), 89, in note 2 "...the great Pagan neoplatonist Poet W.B.Yeats."

29. C. Terrell, "Mang Tze, Thomas Taylor and Madame ΥΛΗ," *Paideuma*, vol. 7 nos. 1 & 2, 146-148 and 151-153.

30. C. Terrell, "A Commentary on Grosseteste with an English Version of *De Luce*." *Paideuma* vol. 2 no. 3, Winter (1973), 452.

31. *Ibid.*, 451-462.

32. *Ibid.*, 451 and 453.

33. William James, *The Varieties of Religious Experience* (New York, 1909), 416-417, 419 and 420.

34. R. M. Bucke, *Cosmic Consciousness* (New York, 1969), 121-125. Bucke includes a letter of Plotinus to one Flaccus, unknown to Plotinus scholars and derived from Robert Vaughan's *Hours With the Mystics: A Contribution to the History of Religious Opinion* (London, 1893). Bucke takes the letter as genuine, but it is a *"jeu d'esprit"* of Vaughan, who in vol. 1, page 82, refers to words he himself invented for Ammonius Saccas (74-75) as "this imaginary fragment from Ammonius Saccas." Bucke also includes material from A. Harnack's entry under "Neoplatonism" (*The Encyclopedia Britannica, A Dictionary of Arts, Sciences, and General Literature*, ninth edition, [Edinburgh, 1884] vol. 17, 332-9), which presents a fair summary of Plotinus' account of the return of the soul to the Good. I am indebted to Frederic Schroeder for this reference.

35. Charles Ives, *Essays Before a Sonata*, third. ed., (New York, 1970), 97.

36. *Ibid.*, 126.

37. *Ibid.*, 53.

38. *Ibid.*, 68.

39. See J. Bregman, "The Neoplatonic Revival in North America" *Hermathena* CXLIX, Winter (1990), 106.

40. Joscelyn Godwin, *Cosmic Music* (Rochester, VT, 1989), *Passim*.

41. Ernest G. McClain, *The Pythagorean Plato* (Maine, 1978), 23*ff*. For a discussion of the complex harmonic ratios involved and their ethical implications, see McClain, chapter 3, "The Tyrant's Allegory" (Republic), 33-39.

42. J. E. Berendt, *Nada Brahma: The world is Sound* (Rochester, VT, 1989), 90.

43. Jay Kinney, "The Mysterious Revelations of Philip K. Dick," *Gnosis*, Fall/Winter (1985/1986), 6*ff*, this section depends on this article.

44. Plotinus, *Select Works of Plotinus. Enneads*, I.6,1,34-35.

The Role of Aesthetics
in Plotinus' Ascent of the Soul

J. Noel Hubler

Although he did not write a single systematic work, Plotinus is nevertheless a systematic thinker. His many treatises reveal themselves as parts of a
great systematic understanding. The issues he addresses in metaphysics, physics, logic, and ethics all work together in his systematic vision. Aesthetics are
no exception. They form part of his overall system. This in no way diminishes
their importance, because aesthetics play a crucial role in the central concern
of Plotinus' philosophy: the ascent of the soul to the One.[1]

According to Plotinus, aesthetics both begin and perfect the soul's ascent
to the One. The One is the source of all being, intelligence, life, and beauty. It
is the soul's ultimate fulfillment, but it is not found external to the soul. Rather
the One is found at each soul's core.[2] A true understanding of aesthetics first
turns the human soul into itself and begins its ascent. True aesthetics teach the
soul that souls are the source of all the beauty in the external world. The world
soul creates the beauty of the natural realm, while humans are capable of producing technological beauty. This understanding directs the soul's natural desire for beauty inward. Once drawn into itself, the soul then needs to learn that
its core is the One. The trained soul learns to rest in and love the beauty of the
One. The aesthetic discovery is the soul's ultimate fulfillment.[3]

The One is the ultimate source of all things. Out of its perfection, the One
emanates the divine Intellect. The divine Intellect perfectly contemplates the
One and becomes perfected by it. When the Intellect contemplates the One, it
comes to its true understanding. The Intellect's perfect understanding is the
being of all things. Its understanding is truth itself, which is a unity of knower
and known. The Intellect's unity is an image of the unity of the One, but it is

not as perfect in its unity as is the One. Unity in intellection implies a subject/object dichotomy (6.9.2.36). The Intellect must gain its unity through contemplation, rather than being unity itself, as the One is. The One is fully present to itself and requires no intellection in order to present itself to itself (6.9.6.49, 6.5.10.16, 6.7.38.24). It is beyond both intellect and being.[4]

Out of its perfect contemplation, the Intellect emanates Soul. The eternal hypostatic Soul introduces motion into the universe. It produces sensation, nature, and matter, all of which are in motion. The eternal, hypostatic Soul includes the world soul, human and animal souls, and even plant souls as its various species (5.1.1, 4.9.4.15).[5]

Aesthetics play a two-fold role in the ascent of the human soul. 1) They show the soul that it is the source of all external beauty and thus direct it inward and begin the soul's ascent. 2) They lead the soul to discover its true internal beauty which is its core. The soul's core is the One and the One is beauty. We can call the two aesthetics external and internal. External aesthetics begin the ascent of the soul. Internal aesthetics perfect it.

External aesthetics

Plotinus' aesthetics dramatically depart from his inherited tradition. Plotinus quickly undoes the old Stoic definition of beauty as a "symmetria of parts to each other and to the whole" (1.6.1.21 f.). Plotinus points out that under the Stoic definition, no simples could be beautiful: neither colors nor sounds; neither virtues nor understandings. Neither would the parts themselves be beautiful, because only their composition would make them so. Therefore, the Stoics would have us believe that beautiful things could only be made from ugly parts (1.6.1).

Plotinus does agree that symmetry can make things beautiful (6.7.30.38), but I think it is fair to say that according to Plotinus' theory, symmetry is an imitation of true beauty. True beauty comes in unity and completeness. Symmetry is beautiful because it brings agreeable unity to its parts, but symmetry is merely a likeness of more fundamental unities. Symmetry is posterior to the unity of the forms. The forms are themselves secondary and gain their unity, perfection, and beauty from the One, which is the fount of all being and beauty (1.6.6.25, cf. 5.9.2).

For Plotinus, beauty lies in completeness, perfection, and unity. In the visible world, a beautiful thing is perfect and complete in its form. Its form unifies it and makes it beautiful. Plotinus explains that the form and completeness of the universe make it beautiful,

> Things become beautiful because of a cause. Since even now something is beautiful, because it is a whole—for "the whole" names this present thing and its form—and because it controls matter. It controls it if it leaves nothing of it unformed. It leaves something out if any form is lacking, for example an eye or something else (6.7.3.9-13 cf. 1.6.2.22-25).[6]

If a sculptor were to leave out an eye, the statue would lack beauty. It would fall short of its completion and perfection. Likewise, to remove a required part from a sculpture would diminish its beauty, as if one were to knock off David's nose. Leaving matter unformed and chaotic leaves it ugly. It is like the ugliness of a completely untidy room, which lacks the proper order. Form brings completion and unity to matter and makes it beautiful.

Form is beautiful to the extent that it completes and perfects, but form ultimately is merely an image of a greater beauty. The One itself is beautiful in its ultimate, self-sufficient completion and perfection. It is beauty without form, because it is in no way limited by form or by anything else,

> The power of all is the crown of beauty, beauty which makes beauty. For it generates beauty and makes it more beautiful by the abundance of the beauty from itself, such that it is the beginning and end of beauty (6.7.32.31-35).

The One is beauty in itself although it has no form, because it is complete and whole in itself and lacks nothing (6.7.10.9, 6.7.23.7). Form is not the ultimate beauty. Ultimately, perfect, complete unity is beauty. Form is only beautiful to the extent it mirrors the unity of the One.

Unity explains the human soul's desire for beauty. According to Plotinus, the soul is reviled by ugliness because an ugly thing is unlike the soul. It is unlike the soul because it lacks form and unity which the soul possesses. By contrast, the soul is drawn to that which is like it and it rejoices in it,

> If it sees anything that is of its kind or is a trace of its kind, it rejoices and is excited and comes to itself and it remembers itself and its own (1.6.2.8-11).

Material things are like the soul to the extent that they are informed. Form gives material things unity, akin to the unity of the soul. The soul recognizes that a beautiful thing has form just as it does (1.6.2).

Therefore, external aesthetics begin the soul's ascent. In seeing the beauty in the outside world, the soul is reminded of itself. The beauty of externals reminds the soul of its own unity. Plotinus uses the Platonic term "recollection" to indicate the process by which the soul recognizes its own unity in its appreciation of external beauty (1.6.2, cf. 5.8.2). Plotinus calls the process "recollection" because it draws the soul back to a recognition of the unity from which it originated (5.1.1.27, 5.8.2.46, cf. 2.7.16.48).

The process of recollection is critical, because human souls can be ugly or beautiful. They can have greater or lesser unity. It is evident to Plotinus that ugly souls are governed by passions. They are drawn to the outside world and are enslaved by desires for external, material things. The ugly soul mixes itself with the external world. The debased soul mixes with external evils which the body brings it through pleasures, desires, and fears (6.4.15.32-40). Plotinus borrows his expressions of the soul's sad state from Plato, but Plotinus carries the analysis of the problem deeper than his master. He points out that the soul is ultimately responsible for its own debased condition. It is the agent of its own misery,

> This is the evil of a human who has in himself a mob of overpowering plea-
> sures, desires, and fears and who gives himself over to such a mob (6.4.15.32-
> 35).

The soul is the one who gives itself over to the body and makes itself subject to its needs. Thereby, the soul subjects itself to the vicissitudes of the material world. In itself it is impassible from bodily changes, so only the soul's own action can afflict the soul. It suffers from its excess sympathy with the body (1.2.6.27, cf. 1.2.3.16).

By contrast, the beautiful and virtuous soul turns inward. It withdraws from desire for external things and purifies itself. Thereby, it finds the truth within itself and the truth beautifies the soul. It becomes a unity governed by intellect and not by external goods (1.6.5,6).

For its reasoning and activity the soul does not depend upon the body. Intellect grasps things not as they are materially, but as they are in their universal forms. It does not function materially or with a material organ,

> He will not err who asserts that the reasoning part of the soul does not need any corporeal organ in order to reason, but has its own operation in purity, so that it can reason purely. It is independent, unmixed with body, and in the first Intellect (5.1.10.13-18).

By turning away from the external material world, the soul comes to know itself as it truly is: independent and pure from the body. Ontologically, the body depends on the soul for its existence, not the soul on the body. The soul can exist and thrive without the body, but the body needs the soul to give it unity, otherwise it decomposes into a myriad of disparate parts. As an immaterial being with immaterial power of reason, the soul functions best when detached from the body (1.6.6).

The soul's inward turn leads the soul to pure understanding, undefiled by sensation,

> His own soul must become intellect and must trust and be established upon Intellect, so that what the Intellect sees, it will receive because it has been attentive. Thereby, he must behold the One without adding anything sensible and without receiving anything from sense into the Intellect, but must behold the most pure with a pure intellect and with that which is the first of the Intellect (6.9.3.22-27).

By turning inward the soul becomes like the divine Intellect which contemplates fully, completely, and eternally. The beautiful soul imitates the divine Intellect in self-sufficient contemplation. The divine Intellect needs nothing from the outside, but rests in eternal, perfect contemplation. An ugly soul which spends itself in pursuit of external sensation and activities is most unlike the Intellect.

As it turns inward the soul achieves its true and natural unity. The soul's true actuality lies in self-knowledge. In self-knowledge it achieves happiness (1.5.9.22 ff.) and freedom. It is unhindered by any external forces and is free to contemplate the divine Intellect and the One (5.5.9.14 ff., 6.8.7.1 ff.). It is unified and governed by the Intellect which gives it the light of understanding. The light from the One beautifies the soul,

> Since everything is beautified by that which is before the present things [the One] and has light, the Intellect has the luster of noetic activity by which it illuminates nature, while soul has the power to live because the fuller life has come to it (6.7.31.1-4, cf. 1.6.6.25-29).

A true understanding of aesthetics leads the soul to understand souls are the true source of beauty in the external world. Its role in bringing unity to the outside world could even lead someone to mistakenly think that the soul is the One itself,

> Therefore, since Soul drives everything into unity by crafting, making, forming, and ordering, must they who consider it say that soul supplies the One and is itself the One? (6.9.1.17-19, cf. 1.6.6.27-29).

Plotinus goes on to affirm that the soul does bring unity to the lower order of matter, but not by being the One itself. It is a dependent and secondary unity.

The world soul, individual human, animal, and plant souls are all species of the eternal, hypostatic Soul. Together they create the visible world and all that is in it. They create matter, sensation, and nature. Thus, they are the immediate sources of all the beauty which is in the world. When the soul understands that souls bring order and beauty to the material realm, it reflects back on its own beauty (5.8.2.40). External aesthetics turn the human soul from the distractions of the outside world and into a life of self-reflection and contemplation (1.3.1.26). The soul begins its ascent by becoming unified and self-sufficient in intellection, which makes it a likeness of intellectual beauty. Nevertheless, the human soul still needs internal aesthetics to become like the One and complete its ascent.

Internal aesthetics

True contemplation leads the good soul to know itself. In coming to know itself, it knows its own source (6.9.7.33, 6.7.34.12). True philosophical reflection shows the soul that its ultimate source, the One, is beyond understanding. Its source cannot be understood by intellection, because the One, which is the ultimate source of the soul and the Intellect, is beyond any intellectual likeness. It is the cause of intellection, it is not intellection itself (5.4.2). All intellection involves duality of subject and object. As such intellection is a plurality and must be caused by the ultimate unity, the One (5.1.4.27-30).

Therefore, to know the One the soul must transcend both sensation and intellection (5.5.6.18, 6.8.21.25). According to Plotinus this can only happen as the soul attains a rest and a love which transcends intellection in a presence in the One beyond intellection (6.9.4.3, 6.9.8.27). The One cannot be known sensibly or intellectually because it is beyond all sensible and intellectual images. To know it intellectually is to know it only through an intellectual likeness of the One. Plotinus does admit this kind of knowledge of the One, but it is a knowledge of the One only through its effects, as intellectual likenesses are effects of the One (3.8.11,19, 34). If a person knows the One intellectually, a person knows only its effects and not the One itself. But according to Plotinus, a person can know the One itself (6.7.39.1).

Direct knowledge of the One is possible, because the One is both transcendent and immanent. Many times Plotinus states that the One transcends being (5.1.10.2, 1.7.1.8, 1.8.3.1, 5.1.8.7, 5.5.6.11, 6.6.5.37). It is the source of all beings and as source, it is distinct from any being. It emanates being out of its perfection without diminishing its own perfection in any way. It transcends all its effects.

No being is the One. The sum of all beings do not constitute the One, because it is prior to them all. Yet the One is immanent.[7] Plotinus expresses the transcendence and immanence of the One in a spatial metaphor. Plotinus first explains that immaterial things are not separated by space as are bodies. Rather immaterial things are separated from each other by difference,

> They are not divided from each other by place, but by difference and distinction. When difference is not present, the undifferentiated things are present to each other. Therefore, that which has no difference is always present, although sometimes we do not possess it (6.9.8.31-35).

Therefore, if two incorporeals lack a difference, one can be said to be present to the other. In the immediate context, Plotinus does not give any examples of immaterial presence other than the One, but it is useful to consider an example. An isosceles triangle differs from a scalene because it has two equal sides and the scalene has none. But they do not differ from each other in having three sides. Therefore the isosceles triangle is separated from the scalene in virtue of having two equal sides, but the concept of triangle is present in both the scalene and isosceles. They do not differ in this respect. Neither differs from being a triangle.

Plotinus explains a one-way presence whereby the One is present in all, but they are not present in the One, "Therefore that which has no difference is always present, although sometimes we do not possess it." In Plotinus' sense of incorporeal presence, this means that the One does not differ from all things, although they all differ from it. This is problematic because we usually think of difference and presence as reciprocal relationships. If x differs from y, then y differs from x. If x is present to y, then y is present to x. But Plotinus argues that among immaterial beings, presence and difference are non-reciprocal and hierarchical. The greater can be present to the lesser, but the lesser may not be present to the greater. Likewise, the lesser may differ from the greater, but the greater may not differ from the lesser.

To see how this works, an example is again useful. We could say that "triangle" is present in the concept of isosceles, but "isosceles" is not present in the concept of triangle. To be isosceles, it must be a triangle, but a triangle is not necessarily isosceles. Isosceles contains the notion triangle, but triangle does not contain the notion of isosceles. Or in Plotinian terms, triangle is present in isosceles, but isosceles is not present in triangle. The greater, more universal term is present in the lesser, more particular term, but not vice versa. Conversely, isosceles differs from triangle, because isosceles introduces a specific difference which triangle does not include. But triangle does not differ from isosceles, because an isosceles is necessarily a triangle.

Plotinus uses this same distinction with regard to the One and all beings. The One is present in all things, because it has no difference. It does not differ from things, because whatever they are they are still unities, or they would not exist (6.9.1.3). To be is to be a unity (6.4.11.18). There is no difference in the One which prevents its presence in any being. But every being contains a specific difference from the One. No being is the One. They all include differences which are not found in the One itself. Whatever they are, they do not attain the perfect unity of the One. They can neither escape the One, nor can they contain the One. Rather the One contains all things (5.5.9.33). The One is present in all, but they are not present in the One.

The soul is also a unity and its unity is the One, although it does not always recognize this. It only recognizes its true unity by leaving behind all plurality. Sensation takes the soul outside itself into the plurality of the outside world. In intellection the soul begins to rest within itself (4.4.23.6), but still a plurality persists. The soul remains in the plurality of subject and object. When it leaves behind sensation and intellection, the soul discovers the unity immanent at its core (1.2.4.21).

To further explicate the immanence of the One, Plotinus relies upon one of his most used illustrations. He compares the One to a point and the universe to a sphere which radiates from the One as its center (5.1.11.7). [8] The whole universe depends upon the One as its point of origin (2.2.2.9). The universe is the divine Intellect. Being and intellect are co-terminus, so the divine Intellect knows all and is all. The universal sphere contains all beings in the perfect contemplation of the divine Intellect.

Plotinus builds on the illustration by comparing the universal Soul to the sphere as it revolves around the center,

> If someone assigns the Good [that is the One] to the center and the Intellect to the unmoved circle, then he will assign the Soul to the moving circle. It is moved by seeking. The Intellect immediately possesses and has received that which is beyond being, while the Soul seeks it. The sphere of the all is moved by that which naturally is sought because it possesses the seeking soul (4.4.16.23_29).

The Soul introduces motion to the cosmos. The Soul moves as it seeks the One. The One is the good which all things naturally seek (6.2.11.26, 1.7.1.5). The Soul introduces motion into the cosmos because it seeks after the One less perfectly than does the Intellect. The soul must seek the One rather than possess it in contemplation as does the divine Intellect. Seeking implies motion, so the seeking soul is a moving image of the intellectual universe.

Plotinus further develops the illustration by comparing individual human souls to circles within the universal sphere,

> We come to rest as we join our center to the center of all, just as the centers of the biggest circles join the center of the sphere which contains them (6.9.8.19-22 cf. 6.9.10.16).

The largest circle inscribed on the surface a sphere necessarily has the same center as the sphere. Smaller circles have different centers. To see how this works, imagine slicing a sphere. Each slice produces a circle on the surface of the sphere. If one begins at the edge, one can make a point size slice. As one progresses to the center, the slices become larger and larger, until one reaches the center. At the center, the slice is the largest. After passing the center, the slices get progressively smaller. The largest slice forms a circle co-centric with the sphere.

At its greatest perfection, the soul comes to know its own center as the center of all, it comes to rest in the One as its own center. The soul is only a circle, but it is co-centric with the sphere of the all. The soul's center is its unchanging core (6.8.15.14 ff.). It is the part of the soul that is neither changed by sensation nor even by intellection. The soul only discovers its core by ceasing from intellection and sensation. It then discovers that its unchanging core is the One and comes to rest in a unity with the One.

The soul comes to a unity with the One beyond all intellection,

> Since there are not two, the beholder is one with that which is seen. It is no longer that which is seen but is unified with the beholder (6.9.11.4-6).

The soul comes to be one with the One by falling into a rest which transcends all intellection. It leaves behind any subject/object distinction (5.3.5.15). Plotinus describes the soul in the state of rest,

> Even he is one and has in himself no difference with himself in any way—he sets nothing in motion. Neither wrath nor desire for another is present in him once he has ascended—neither reason nor any intellection nor himself at all, if one can say this. But he has become as if seized or inspired by quiet in a calm and untrembling stability. He never slips away from his own substance nor revolves around himself, but stands so completely still as if to become stillness itself (6.9.11.6).

The soul has come to complete unity with itself, by becoming still in the source of all. It experiences no more outward movements, but comes to complete rest in its center. It becomes a little unity, fully whole and complete in itself, an image of the One itself (6.9.11.43).

To describe the final ascent of the soul as the ceasing of intellection is to describe it in purely negative terms. Plotinus does not stop there. Plotinus also describe union with the One as the unmeasured love of the soul for the One. The One itself is unmeasured. No measure or limit can be applied to it because there is nothing greater than it. The soul becomes like the One and joins the One in unmeasured love,

> The love here is not bounded, because neither is the beloved, but the love of this one would be infinite, so that its beauty is otherwise and is a beauty above beauty (6.7.32.26-29).

The soul which leaves behind all measure found in reason and intellection releases itself in an unbound and unfettered love. Neither ideas nor images bind the soul any longer. Neither forms nor shapes contain it. It finds release into the pure unbound unity and beauty of the One.

The soul's love for the One is unlike that of the lover who pines by the door, outside the beloved's,

> This is the lover that stands by the door, present but always outside, seeking the beautiful and is content if he is able thus to share in it. Since the lover here does not receive beauty, but only has it by lying before it. But the One remains in itself and the many lovers of the One, love it entire, and possess it entire thus when they have it (6.5.10.3-8).

Unlike the lover of things below which seeks love external to itself, the lover of the One finds the true beauty within herself. It is a beauty of ultimate completion and unity. That true beauty of the soul is the beauty of the One which the soul discovers at its own core.

In the end, true aesthetics show the soul not just that it is the source of the beauty of the outside world. It also shows the soul that the beauty at its own core is the beauty at the core of all things. Its core is the One. When it discovers the One within itself, it comes to love its beauty.

Notes

1.   Gary Gurtler's study, *Plotinus: The Experience of Unity,* Lang: 1988, shows that
    Plotinus' psychology and metaphysics work together in a system. Gurtler op-
    poses the common twentieth century view that Plotinus' psychology stands in
    opposition to his metaphysics. In Blumenthals' terminology, Plotinus' metaphys-
    ics are static and eternal, while his psychology is dynamic and changing. See H.
    J. Blumemthal, *Plotinus' Psychology,* Nijhoff: 1971.
    I agree with Gurtler's results, but try to take them beyond the unity of the Intel-
    lect and into the unity of all beings within the One.
    J.M. Rist in *Plotinus: The road to reality,* Cambridge: 1967 argues that aesthet-
    ics are of secondary importance in Plotinus' system based upon Plotinus' state-
    ments in *Ennead* 5.5.12. There Plotinus argues that the Good is more universal
    than Beauty because Beauty is accessible only to the sophisticated mind. But as
    will be seen, Plotinus describes the ascent of the soul to the One as both an ap-
    proach to the Good and to Beauty. Plotinus describes the One as Goodness and
    Beauty and it is hard to see how to prioritize one over the other without making
    the One complex. If they are both the One, then they must be one reality.

2.   Gerard O'Daly calls it the "unintellectualizing root of the soul" in
    Plotinus"Philosophy of the Self, Harper and Row: 1973.
    O'Daly's view that the true self is the One is endorsed by A. H. Armstrong in
    "Form, Individual and Person in Plotinus," *Dionysius 1,* Dec. 1977, 49-68, esp.
    59, 65.

3.   For background in Plotinus' aesthetics see Gary Gurtler, S. J., "Plotinus and
    Byzantine Aesthetics," *The Modem Schoolman* 66, May 1989, 275-284.
    F.P. Hager, 'Métaphysique et axiologie de l'oeuvre d'art chez Platon et Plotin,"
    Diotima 14,1986, 130-137.
    D.N. Koutras, "The Essence of the Work of Art according to Plotinus," *Diotima*
    14, 1986, 147-153.

4.   The One does not lack intellection in the sense that it is missing something. It
    has a greater perfection than intellection. John N. Deck calls it the
    "superknowledge" of the One in *Nature, Contemplation and the One,* Univer-
    sity of Toronto Press: 1967, 17-21. Because greater knowledge comes in greater
    unity, the One has a "knowledge" as transcendent as its unity.
    Others deny even this sort of knowledge of the One. See O'Daly, *op. cit.*, 92.
    Rist, *op. cit.*, 48, focuses on Plotinus' use of the term *epibole* from which he infers
    that "The 'knowledge' of the One is by implication wholly different from any
    other knowledge that we can imagine."

5.   For an explanation of the relation of the hypostatic Soul to individual souls as
    the relation of genus to species, see Gary Gurtler's careful analysis in *Plotinus:
    The Experience of Unity,* 26-30. See also Deck, *op. cit.,* 32-34.

6.   Translations throughout are by the author.

7.   Deck, *op. cit.*, 116, expresses the immanence of the One as the "identification of the cause and the effect." He thereby overstates the case, because none of the effects are the One itself. Even though the One is immanent, it still transcends its effects.

8.   *cf.* 6.5.5, 6.8.18.6, 1.7.1.23. Plotinus also uses a circle to illustrate the unity of substance 4.2.1.24 and of the soul 4.2.2.38.

Creation or Metamorphosis?
Plotinus on the Genesis of the World

Panayiota Vassilopoulou

The Setting

In Chapter Nine of the first treatise 'On Difficulties about the Soul' (*Enneads* IV.3 (27)), Plotinus raises the issue of the relation between soul and body and immediately draws a distinction between two fields of enquiry. On the one hand, there is a set of problems concerning the way in which a particular soul relates to a particular body; on the other hand, there is the issue of the way in which soul as such relates to body in general. Plotinus introduces both problems with the help of the same familiar metaphor: in both cases, the question concerns the way in which the soul "enters" or "penetrates" (εἴσοδος, εἴσκρισις) the body and thus "takes upon itself a bodily nature" (12-3).[1] In the context of this metaphor, the difference between the two problems acquires a temporal dimension: the general problem is presented as the "first communication" (πρώτη κοινωνία) between soul and body, soul's original "passage from bodilessness to any kind of body" (8-9); the particular one concerns the subsequent movements of souls which, already embodied, pass from one body to another.

Given this way of framing of the issue, Plotinus naturally announces his intention to start with the most fundamental problem. At this level of generality, the issue could concern the relation of the soul considered as one of the Hypostases of the Plotinian system with matter as such. This problem is real for Plotinus and has been discussed, by him and his commentators, under the guise of the question of the origin and status of matter.[2] However, as will become apparent in what follows, Plotinus is not concerned here with the status of soul or matter prior to their postulated moment of intercourse. The temporal

207

formulation of the problem is a way to indicate that what interests him is not the origin of the soul or matter and whatever can be said about their separate existence, but rather the origin, through their interaction, of the embodied soul or the ensouled body of which the sensible universe is made.

It appears thus that the initial question ("How soul comes to be in body"?), when understood with the proper qualifications, is in fact a cosmological question presented in a cosmogonic manner: How are we to understand or explain the existing order of the world through a discussion of its origin? Anyone familiar with Plato will recognise the question animating the *Timaeus*.[3] The observation is corroborated by the way Plotinus proceeds to set up the problem:

> With regard to the Soul of the All—because it is perhaps <suitable> (εἰκός),[4] or rather it is necessary to start with it—we must of course consider that the terms 'entry' and 'ensoulment' are used in the discussion for the sake of clear explanation (τῷ λόγῳ ... διδασκαλίας καὶ τοῦ σαφοῦς χάριν). For there never was a time when this universe did not have a soul, or when the body existed in the absence of soul, or when matter was not set in order. But in discussing these things one can consider them apart from each other, because it is legitimate to analyse any kind of composition in thought and language (ἀλλ' ἐπινοῆσαι ταῦτα χωρίζοντας αὐτὰ ἀπ' ἀλλήλων τῷ λόγῳ οἷόν τε. ἔξεστι γὰρ ἀναλύειν τῷ λόγῳ καὶ τῇ διανοίᾳ πᾶσαν σύνθεσιν). For the truth is as follows. If body did not exist, soul would not go forth, since there is no place other than body where it is natural for it to be (ὅπου πέφυκεν εἶναι). But if it intends to go forth, it will produce a place for itself (γεννήσει ἑαυτῇ τόπον), and so a body (12-23).

Plotinus' claim about the starting point of the discussion makes clear that his interest is directed at the genesis and order of the sensible world, and not the nature and activity of the various Hypostases. The cosmic soul is distinguished from all the other souls precisely by the fact that it is the creator of the sensible world, the subject of the "first communication" between soul and body in which the "dwellings" of all other individual souls are "prepared;" thus it is indeed the appropriate starting point for an account of the creation of the world in the manner of the *Timaeus*, with the cosmic soul taking over the role of the Platonic Demiurge.[5]

The rest of Plotinus' remarks establish more specific relations with the project of the *Timaeus*. At a first level, they appear as an acknowledgement of Plato's own warning before his description of the construction of the cosmic soul, which in Timaeus' account takes place after the creation of the cosmic body. Plato warns the reader there that the order of the presentation of the activities of the Demiurge may be misleading, since the account, as an *eikos* mythos or logos, shares in the accidental or casual (προστυχόντος) element which characterises human existence and falls short of the desired rigour (34C). However, the problem is more complicated than the issue of the correct genetic order in an account of the creation of the world.

The question concerns initially the adequacy of the set of metaphors which so far has structured the issue. Terms like "εἴσοδος," "ἐμψύχωσις," and the like should not be taken literally because, although used "διδασκαλίας καὶ τοῦ σαφοῦς χάριν," may obscure the issue (or bring to it a deceptive clarity) by these aspects of their metaphoric logic which do not correspond with the reality they are supposed to render comprehensible. A term like 'entrance' brings into play a specific spatio-temporal 'staging' of what is to be thought or explained: A, initially outside B, will be finally inside B. Plotinus concedes that the reflective analysis (ἐπινοῆσαι) of a composite structure is allowed or possible (οἷόν τε, ἔξεστι) "in thought and language" and that such an analysis will take the form of a genetic narrative which will establish spatio-temporal relations between the constituent parts of this structure. However, he also warns his readers of the problems associated with the establishment of such spatio-temporal frameworks of analysis.

How are we to understand this warning? First, by examining Plotinus' literal claims in the closing argument of the passage, where the truth is explicitly to be stated. In this argument, in agreement with the starting point of the discussion (the cosmic soul) and the claim that body never existed in the absence of soul, the original synthesis of body and soul is accounted for in terms of the generative capacities of the (pre-existing) soul: body is generated by soul as its place (γεννήσει ἑαυτῇ τόπον). A first correction of the metaphoric framework becomes apparent: the cosmic soul does not 'enter' in a pre-existing body, but generates it. However, this generation can not be conceived, in this context, as an *act* of 'ordering' of a given material, since, as Plotinus states explicitly, "there never was a time...when matter was not set in order" (17-8).[6] Setting aside the possibility of generation *ex nihilo*, we are forced to conclude that, for Plotinus, the spatio-temporal framework is figurative: the creation of the world is not an event to be presented in this or that, correct or incorrect, order.[7]

The issue is obviously connected with the venerable and vexed question of the literal or figurative interpretation of the *Timaeus*.[8] Our claim that Plotinus' own cosmogony is to be treated figuratively is in agreement with the fact that

Plotinus followed the orthodox Platonic tradition, originating in Xenocrates and Crantor, which understood the account of the *Timaeus* figuratively, "σαφηνείας ἕνεκα διδασκαλικῆς." Within this tradition, he is credited by Proclus with the view "that it is [the world's] compositeness that is [in the *Timaeus*] called 'created', and to this is subsidiary the fact of being generated from an external cause."[9] Plotinus' own clearest statement of his position (although it does not refer explicitly to the creation myth of the *Timaeus*) is the following:

> But myths, if they are really going to be myths, must separate in time (μερίζειν χρόνοις) the things of which they tell, and set apart from each other (διαιρεῖν ἀπ' ἀλλήλων) many realities which are together, but distinct in rank or powers (τάξει δὲ ἢ δυνάμεσι), at points where rational discussions (λόγοι), also, make generations of things ungenerated, and themselves, too, separate things which are together; the myths, when they have taught us as well as they can, allow the man who has understood them to put together again (συναιρεῖν) that which they have separated (III.5.9.24-29).

This important passage clarifies Plotinus' understanding of the issue in a number of ways. First, it makes clear that the problems we have associated with a mythical genetic presentation of the order of the world cannot disappear in a literal or discursive account, since they are rooted in the nature of thought itself, at least when it turns to examine certain kinds of objects or processes.[10] Moreover, although the narrative primacy granted to the soul in the fictional account can be understood as a device signalling its superior 'rank' within the composite structure of the ordered world, this superiority cannot be translated straightforwardly into ontological relations of dependence between separate entities. In other words, the task of constructing or interpreting an adequate 'creation myth' is exhausted neither by deciding 'who comes first' or 'who is inside,' nor by translating these relations in ontological terms of priority or dependence, between, let us say, intelligible and sensible entities. After the analysis or the narrative has established the proper distinctions and the order of dependence, we are left with the question of "συναιρεῖν," of grasping the reciprocal "ὁμοῦ" of the elements in the composite structure; the primary task is not to show that, *e.g.*, intelligence is prior to necessity, but rather to account for their interaction.

Plotinus' closing argument in the passage we have been discussing above is quite instructive. In Plotinus' system there is certainly no doubt about the relative 'rank' of soul and matter as separate realities, and this rank is reflected directly in the claim that body is generated by soul. However, in the perspective established by the given composite structure of the world, the body is designated as the place "where it is natural for [soul] to be" (ὁποῦ πέφυκεν εἶναι). This designation turns body into both a product and a condition of the "coming forth" (προέρχεσθαι) of the soul, and hence, from the point of view of an account of the existence of the world, the body is both 'before' and 'after', 'inside' and 'outside' soul. With this designation, the simple order of dependence between the cause (the soul) and its effect (the body generated by an external cause) becomes a reciprocal determination, since the effect appears as a condition of the activity of the cause that generates it. As a result, what from an external point of view would appear contingent (the soul could or could not create the world at a specific moment) acquires a conditional necessity (if there is to be "going forth" of the soul, there has to be a place) in which, although the primacy of the soul is retained in a genetic account, the unity of the world as a composite structure can be "grasped together."[11]

The passage above, however, apart from legitimising the use of myths in discussing philosophical issues, can be also read as a recipe for writing good or effective myths: a myth about the genesis of a composite reality should be constructed in such a way as to make the "συναιρεῖν" of its elements more easy. We can turn now to the brief cosmogony which follows in our text and see how such a myth would look and how it can be effective.

A Concise Cosmogony

As we have already said, the creation of the world is fundamentally the generation of the place in which the soul "goes forth." The first of the three images that make up Plotinus' brief cosmogony tries to capture precisely the activity which leads to the emergence of this place out of soul's initial condition of rest. At its core there is an ordinary experience, but Plotinus formulates it in a very peculiar way:

> As soul's rest was, so to speak, strengthened in rest itself, a great light, we may say, shined forth from it and, in the outermost edge of the fire, there came to be darkness, which the soul saw, since it came into existence [as a substrate], and informed it (τῆς δὴ στάσεως αὐτῆς ἐν αὐτῇ τῇ στάσει οἱονεὶ ῥωννυμένης οἷον πολὺ φῶς ἐκλάμψαν ἐπ' ἄκροις τοῖς ἐσχάτοις τοῦ πυρὸς σκότος

ἐγίνετο, ὅπερ ἰδοῦσα ἡ ψυχή, ἐπείπερ ὑπέστη, ἐμόρφωσεν αὐτό. For it was not lawful (θεμιτόν) for that which borders (γειτονοῦν) on soul to be without its share of formative principle (λόγος) (23-28).

There are many striking features in this image, all directed to a calculated reversal of our ordinary experience of phenomena of propagation of light. There is, first, a spatio-temporal inversion. While we should normally say that light comes after darkness and takes its place by 'chasing it away,' while darkness perhaps 'resists,' Plotinus asserts that darkness comes into being after the shining forth of light (ἐγίνετο, ὑπέστη, ἐκλάμψαν) as its boundary. More precisely, darkness comes into being when light (for reasons left unclear, but *not* because it encounters darkness) stops at some point: at the border, darkness comes into being as visible darkness, as 'proximate' darkness ready to be seen in the light of the soul and be informed by it.[12]

The process that leads to the generation of darkness is quite peculiar, as evidenced by the complex syntax of the sentence. The centre of the construction is occupied by the clause "σκότος ἐγίνετο," as if the subject of the whole process is darkness, or rather the emergence of darkness, since "σκότος" is not the grammatical subject of an active verb. The central presence of darkness is countered by the fact that "ψυχή" is the subject of the only active and transitive verb ("ἐμόρφωσεν") of the entire sentence, which appears at the very end of it. Nevertheless, soul does not initiate explicitly the whole process: the event that precipitates the whole sequence, namely the "shining forth" of light, occurs as a consequence of the strengthening of soul's rest in the intelligible realm and is not presented as an intended action of the soul. Only after the soul 'overflowed,' so to speak, and in the presence of the light of this 'overflowing,' darkness emerged and was seen by the soul, did the soul take an active part. Moreover, we should note that this 'overflowing' is set apart from all the other 'events' in this story, by the fact that "ῥωννυμένης," which sets the temporal framework for the entire sequence, is the only participle in the present tense, and hence not an 'event' but a condition present for the entire sequence of the subsequent events.

The initial act of the cosmic drama is thus an 'event' that cannot be described easily within an ordinary framework; processes that can be described in terms of an interaction between distinct entities occur only at the very end of the whole 'event.' Two points should be particularly noted. First, throughout this whole process, there is a strong sense in which the cosmic soul remains separate and at rest in itself, suffering no alteration or relation, despite the 'overflow' caused by its 'strengthening.'[13] Second, darkness can be considered neither as intentionally generated by the soul (it comes into being as a side-effect of its 'strengthening' and 'overflowing'), nor as an effect of the activity of the soul in any normal sense (the proper effect of light is to enlighten); moreover, it is not merely encountered by the soul as an alien element (since it is soul's light that brings it into existence and makes it visible, by stopping at a certain point).[14] Thus the notion of proximity or neighbourhood (γειτονοῦν), which Plotinus introduces in order to account for the initial affinity between light and darkness which allows the soul to fulfil its function as a spontaneous transmitter of λόγος (like a diffusion process through a semipermeable membrane) falls equally and undecidedly between spatial contiguity and genetic resemblance: on the one hand, darkness 'occupies' a certain place, it happens to be there close to light; on the other, it comes into being by the light of the soul as its boundary.[15]

We should make a final note about the only intentional action in the image, namely soul's "ἐμόρφωσεν." Plotinus stresses, in almost paradoxical terms, its close connection with vision: the soul "ἰδοῦσα" (in seeing, by seeing, after seeing) darkness, informed it. This formulation should be juxtaposed with the way Plotinus describes elsewhere the process of 'information,' particularly the 'information' of matter. On these occasions, the activity of 'information' is described as the 'covering up,' the 'concealment,' the 'hiding' (περιτίθεμεν, κρυφθεῖσαν) of matter beneath form.[16] We may ask then: What exactly does the soul see? Does it ever see matter itself? Or does it always see 'informed' (i.e., 'hidden') matter and thus encounters only projections of itself?

At this stage, the soul has generated the place of its "going forth." In this clearing of luminous darkness,

> There came into being (γενόμενος) something like a beautiful and richly various house which was not cut off (ἀπετμήθη) from its maker (πεποιηκότος), but he did not give it a share (ἐκοίνωσεν) of himself either; he considered it all, everywhere, worth a care (ἐπιμελείας) which conduces to its very being and excellence (τῷ εἶναι καὶ τῷ καλῷ) (as far as it can participate in being) but does him no harm in his presiding over it, for he rules it while abiding above (ἄνω γὰρ μένων ἐπιστατεῖ) (29-35).

The transition from the first image to the second is really unexpected. In the original the effect is more pronounced since the innocuous "γενόμενος," which stands in the very beginning, has a double function: looking backward, it seems to describe the outcome of "ἐμόρφωσεν;" looking forward, it introduces us to the new image.

If we set aside this transition, we are temporarily on rather familiar Platonic ground, since the motivation behind this image and the role it plays appear easily recognisable. On the one hand, Plotinus has to account for the rich diversity and order of the sensible world considered as a whole and thus he has to invoke the image of a more complicated and intentional process than the mere propagation of light: the building of a house is a paradigmatic case of making a 'total' and complex artefact. On the other hand, he has to make clear both the transcendent status and the goodness of the maker and the dependent status and beauty of the creation. However, we should note that Plotinus passes over in silence the most salient points of the metaphor of building, the aspects which, after Plato's *Timaeus*, we would expect him to elaborate. As far as the motivation of the maker is concerned, Plotinus notes his general resolve to make the house as real and beautiful as possible. But the rational or technical aspect of building (the laying out of the plan, the determination of the objectives and the steps necessary for their realisation, the choice of the proper materials, the final execution) is never mentioned: the activity of building itself simply disappears in the gap of the transition between the first and the second image and there is nothing in this image to correct the metaphor of instant diffusion or imprinting carried over from the previous image.[17]

The transition between the second and the third image is punctuated with two remarks, one drawing the moral of the second image and the other announcing the claim that will be illustrated by the third image. Plotinus has depicted a world created and "mastered" (κρατούμενος) (36) by a soul which remains separate and external to it; the time has now come to show how this world, once created, does not remain a dead artefact, how "soul makes alive all the other things which do not live of themselves, and makes them live the sort of life by which it lives itself" (10.37-8):

> [The house] lies (κεῖται) in soul which bears it up (ἀνεχούσῃ) and nothing is without a share of soul. It is as if a net immersed (or soaked) in the waters was alive,[18] but unable to make its own that in which it is (αὐτοῦ ποιεῖσθαι ἐν ᾧ ἐστιν). The sea is already spread out (ἐκτεινομένης) and the net spreads with it (συνεκτέταται), as far as it can; for no one of its parts can be anywhere else than where it lies (κεῖτα) (36-43).

With this final and vivid image, we return to the imagery of natural elements with which we started. There are three points that we should particularly note here. First, Plotinus' insistence that the (informed) darkness-house-net is contained in soul or, rather, passively lies in it and extends with it as far as it can in the already spread-out soul. This claim raises again the issue of the proper spatial imaging of the relation between body and soul; the image of the net, which apparently contains and delimits what actually contains and permeates it, is a successful metaphor for the vexed dialectic of the 'inside-outside' we have already encountered.[19] Second, there is the aspect of movement, which in this context stands as a metaphor of life. The image of the net, which by being imperceptibly pushed by the sea which carries it, follows smoothly and passively the movement of sea and, on account of its agility, gives the appearance of being alive and determining its own effervescent movement on the inert background of the sea, is a perfect physical analogue of an animistic universe, even if it runs counter to the intuition that the soul directs things 'from the inside'. Finally, we should note that for the first time we learn something about the intentions and capacities of the body, which is thus personified at the very end of the account. The reference (οὐ δυνάμενον δὲ αὐτοῦ ποιεῖσθαι ἐν ᾧ ἐστιν) is formulated as a direct contrast with the creative capacities of the soul (the image follows the metaphoric logic of 'ποιεῖν' = 'περιτιθέναι' we have already noted) and captures the agonising and precarious nature of the life that the body lives: sustained almost indifferently in life by the soul, it is incapable of securing this life, which may slip away at any minute, as its own.

At this point, where the initial metaphor has been completely reversed and the 'entering' of the soul into the body has become the 'immersing' of the body into the soul, Plotinus' brief cosmogony ends. Before we move to the concluding section to discuss the character of this account, a few additional remarks are in place. In accordance with Plotinus' understanding of the function of creation myths, the next chapter starts with the following advice:

> Having then heard this, we must, going back again to that which is always such, grasp all as existing simultaneously (ἐπὶ τὸ ἀεὶ οὕτως ἐλθόντας ὁμοῦ λαβεῖν πάντα ὄντα) (10.1-2).

Presumably in order to help us to accomplish this task, Plotinus offers a concise reformulation of his cosmogony, in which the three consecutive images of his account are replaced with three contiguous (= simultaneously existing) 'parts' of the same image:

> so here there is soul always static, or the first, then the next in order, like the last gleams of the light of a fire (ὡς πυρὸς ἔσχατα); afterwards the first coming from this last gleam is thought of a shadow of fire (νοουμένου πυρὸς σκιᾶς), and then this at the same time is thought of as illuminated (ἐπιφωτιζομένου), so that it is as if form was diffused over what is cast upon soul, which at first was altogether obscure (ὥστε οἷον εἶδος ἐπιθεῖν τῷ ἐπιβληθέντι πρώτῳ γενομένῳ παντάπασιν ἀμυδρῷ) (10.5-10).

This image looks like a static snapshot of the first image of Plotinus' cosmogony, from which all the complicated temporal relations have been taken away. It can thus be considered as Plotinus' effort to undermine or even abolish altogether the temporal order of his account, in order to make clear that this order is only for the sake of "explanation." Alternatively, we may consider this image as a description of the composite structure of the sensible world in its final and permanent state, after everything that an account of the creation of the world may include has taken place. The spatial determinations (πῦρ-πυρὸς ἔσχατα-πυρὸς σκιαί) can be thus considered as indexes of the differences "τάξει δὲ ἢ δυνάμεσι" of the various components of the composite structure. We should note, however, that Plotinus cannot abolish all temporal determinations: the presence and the function of matter (the 'information' of which *is* the act of creation) can be grasped only with the help of a temporal differentiation between the πρώτῳ γενόμενον παντάπασιν ἀμυδρόν, and the πυρὸς σκιά which unavoidably gives a temporal colouring to the otherwise spatial ἐπιφωτιζομένου, ἐπιθεῖν, ἐπιβληθέντι.[20]

In the context of this synoptic image, a note should be also made about the expression πυρὸς σκιά, which presumably designates the status of the sensible world.[21] The word "σκιά" is repeatedly used by Plato in the *Republic* for similar purposes (*e.g.*, 500A, 515D, 517D, 532C) and the expression "τὰς σκιὰς τὰς ὑπὸ τοῦ πυρός" occurs in the story of the cave (515A). In the context of Plotinus' account, the genitive of "πυρός" seems to range over the entire spectrum of possible meanings: the shadow which emerges at the border of light as its privation, the shadow as an attenuated form of light, the shadow as a dim reflection of light. What is made clear, however, in the passage quoted above is, first, that the σκότος with which the soul comes into contact is 'always already' visible in the light of the soul and, second, that the final product, the sensible world, reflects back, even in an attenuated way, the light it receives. Both points have important consequences, which cannot be pursued here. The only thing we should note, in the perspective of the creation story, is that during its entire creative activity, the soul, in its movement from πῦρ to πυρὸς ἔσχατα and πυρὸς σκιαί, appears not to come into (direct) contact with something alien to itself, the "altogether obscure" or the "σκότος ὕλης" (see n.20 above). And this is as it should be, if we take seriously the literal claim that "there never was a time ... when matter was not set in order" (17-8).

Some Conclusions

Now that we have explored Plotinus' brief cosmogony, we may draw a few general conclusions. We saw that Plotinus followed the precedent set by Plato and responded to the issue of the order of the world with a creation story. The scale and the degree of elaboration of the two projects are of course very different; however, a broad comparison between the two will allow us to identify, rather briefly, the special character of Plotinus' enterprise and to determine the reasons which motivate it.

The myth of the *Timaeus* does not claim for itself the validity of a true account, always in all respects self-consistent and perfectly exact. However, Plato's intention was to create a coherent narrative whole, which places the 'events' of creation in a well-structured temporal order and unfolds in reasonably or plausibly connected steps.[22] From a literary point of view, the story of the *Timaeus* can be regarded as a piece of poetic art composed in a way which satisfies the most important conditions of successful poetry set by Aristotle in the *Poetics*.[23] The dramatic content of the myth is a mimesis of the actions of the Demiurge, whose well-defined character is substantiated in his actions. The story is obviously the mimesis of an important action (the making of the world), which is completed by events skilfully arranged by the most competent creator (whose rationality guarantees that nothing in the narrative is idiosyncratic or eccentric).

The presentation of events is based on the Homeric technique of beginning in medias res: presenting first the "works of reason," Plato opens a parenthesis in order to deal with "what comes about of necessity," and ends his story with a description of "the co-operation of reason and necessity."[24] This narrative device (in the temporal order established by the *Timaeus* itself necessity ought to have been presented first) enables Plato to attain maximum dramatic intelligibility, since a fully personified creative force is established first and all the other elements are incorporated in the story by direct reference to this single agent[25]. In this way, the dramatic interest is concentrated on the actions of the Demiurge, which in a natural manner succeed each other. The plot, the "soul" of tragedy according to Aristotle, is thus constituted by a specific set of actions and their internal relations (which correspond to the complex structure of the world they bring about): the internal disposition or any irrelevant action of the characters involved in the story is not allowed to interfere with this plot.[26]

In the perspective of Plato's practice and Aristotle's theory, our story appears rather odd, to put it mildly.[27] The most obvious question is the following: How are we to think of the *unity* of Plotinus' account? The question becomes more pressing if we take into account that our aim is to see how a myth may help us to "grasp together" the elements of the composite structure of the world. In general terms (which exceed the Aristotelian precepts for the unity of a plot), a narrative can be unified ultimately either on the basis of the characters that appear and act in them or on the basis of some framework established by the events that are being recounted. We may thus begin by considering these two options.

While the soul indeed assumes the leading role in Plotinus' narrative, the portrayal of its nature and activity is both complex and vague. As we have seen, the soul is personified as a maker in the second image, but Plotinus passes over the opportunity to present its character, capacities and actions; its creative nature is merely asserted by concentrating on its creation. Given its other appearances, as a source of light and its light and as a sea, the soul cannot be 'reconstructed' as a character in any ordinary way: we cannot attribute to it intentions directly and we cannot infer the existence of intentions from the data of its activity.[28] We are guided to understand the creative activity of the soul not as the externalisation of a subjective structure, but as the manifestation or appearance of a rational, but 'unconscious,' acting force; hence, the unity we are seeking cannot be expressed in subjective terms.

What can we say about the events narrated in the story? A first point is that, although, as we have seen, within the images themselves spatio-temporal relations are established in quite complex ways, there is no overall spatio-temporal framework which could provide some external sort of unity. If we examine now the natural phenomena or artificial activities which constitute the content of these images, we realise that there is nothing internal to them that would suggest any kind of normal continuity: a light is struck and, out of the darkness, a house emerges to become a net immersed in the sea. How are we to think the unity of this 'event,' which seems to transcend all the classical unities?

At this point it would perhaps be helpful to approach the issue the other way round: What are the requirements of a myth that could present effectively the "being together" of the elements of a composite structure? This myth would have initially to separate these elements and their activity and use an appropriate spatio-temporal framework in order to present their relative order of priority within the composite structure. However, if the final aim is the "συναιρεῖν" of these elements in their unity, we would expect a 'deconstructive' use of these devices: the spatio-temporal markers would unite as much as separate, and the activity of the elements would be described in such terms as to make these elements 'efface' themselves in the final product, *i.e.* lose their separate and distinct nature in the emergent dynamic unity of the composite, which would be thus presented as containing its own source of movement or development.

In the case of a generated, composite thing, such as the sensible world, the elements to be separated in this context are ultimately form and matter. As Plotinus puts it, echoing the discussion of chora in the *Timaeus* (50-1), the nature of such things can be thought of as a synthesis of an inert material and an active form which shapes it:

> for in some things, because of their bodily nature, individuality is fluid because the form comes in from outside and they have continual existence only according to specific form (τῶν σωμάτων τῇ φύσει τοῦ καθέκαστον ῥέοντος ἅτε ἐπακτοῦ τοῦ εἴδους ὄντος τὸ εἶναι κατ' εἶδος ἀεὶ ὑπάρχει), in imitation of the real beings; but in others, since they are not produced by composition (οὐκ ἐκ συνθέσεως οὖσι)...(IV.3.8.25-28).

The separation of the intelligible from the material has two senses, one absolute and one relative. From an ontological point of view, form and matter remain always separate and do not suffer any real change in their interaction. As Plotinus puts it, "νοῦς μόνος, ἀπαθὴς ἐν τοῖς νοητοῖς ζωὴν μόνον νοερὰν ἔχων ἐκεῖ ἀεὶ μένει" (IV.7.13.2-3), while matter "μένει οὂ ἐξ ἀρχῆς ἦν" (III.6.11.18); even soul, the agent of their interaction, "ἄνω μένει" (34). This absolute separation, however, does not belong to the perspective of a discourse dedicated to an account of the emergence of the composite, which would be impossible without some kind of interaction; such a discourse should separate these elements in a relative way, *i.e.*, with reference to their order in the composite structure.

In order to present this relative separation, Plotinus follows both models elaborated in the *Timaeus*. The second image belongs to the 'deliberate creation' model, which sets the framework of the *Timaeus*; the two other follow the 'instant interaction' model, which Plato developed in his discussion of the receptacle (49A-52D). In each case, in accordance with Plotinus' concrete narrative goals, the primacy of the active element is clearly presented or implied: the source of light which informs darkness, the architect who stands above the house built, the sea which imparts motion, and thus life, to the net. However, the specifically Plotinian contribution to the elaboration of these images within the models followed, lies precisely in an attempt to efface as much as possible the relative separation which underlies the hierarchy established. This tendency operates, as we have already seen, both in a passive and an active way. Passively, it guides, for example, the omission of all the details concerning the creative activity of the architect: when Plotinus had the narrative opportunity to present the operations of the maker on the material, he sent off-stage the maker (safeguarding his transcendent status), made no mention whatsoever of the material, and concentrated his attention on the house made. Actively, this tendency is expressed in the choice and elaboration of the two other images: the spatio-temporal frameworks and the natural phenomena described in both images tend to merge or collapse the separate elements into a single entity: the light-with-its-dark-boundary, the net-within-the-sea.

Similar remarks can be made if we examine Plotinus' literary device in shaping the entire account. The story appears as a collection of pictures that present the same tableau from different points of view; its oddness is a result of the fact that, so to speak, Plotinus turns off the light (breaks all narrative continuities) as he moves his camera from place to place in order to capture the different views. The overall effect of the narrative resembles the effect of a metamorphosis story: something becomes, in ways that cannot be explained in an ordinary way and point implicitly to some internal ability of self-transformation, something else. Instead of a narrative sequence of the form 'A and B interacted in such a way as to produce C' or 'A did B and as an effect there came to be C,' Plotinus' account appears to have the shape of 'A became B became C,' without differentiation between separate entities and reference to external determinations.

The major philosophical issue implicated by Plotinus' narrative strategy concerns the nature and the role of the cosmic soul. So far, not without justification (see n.5), we have treated the cosmic soul as equivalent to the Platonic Demiurge. A full discussion of the issue would have to include three dimensions: (a) the relation between the Demiurge and soul in the *Timaeus* (in the context of other late Plato's works, such as the *Laws*); (b) Plotinus' interpretation of Plato's position; and (c) Plotinus' own views on the issue. Here we cannot of course undertake this examination; we shall limit ourselves to a few remarks related to the cosmogonical context.

With regard to Plato, we should note that (a) the interpretation of the figure of the Demiurge (its status, its relation to the ideas (in particular the idea of good), or the soul) is still an open issue[29] and (b) the (cosmic) soul, on the one hand, is described as generated and, on the other, is characterised as the source of motion (and hence of any creative activity of generation).[30] Plotinus understands Plato's position in terms of a threefold distinction, associated with the three principal hypostases, in which the One is identified with the Good and is called "the father of the cause," the Intellect is identified with the Demiurge and is called the "cause," and the Soul is described as being made by the Intellect (V.1.8.1-8; cf. IV.8.1.40-51).[31] Hence, it would seem that Plotinus himself considers the cosmic soul as generated by the Intellect, which is thus the real Demiurge behind the creation of the soul and the world (ποιητὴν ὄντως καὶ δημιουργόν; V.9.3.26). In this case, we have to face two related questions: What precisely is the creative function of the cosmic soul in relation to the Intellect? Why does Plotinus not start his cosmogony from the creation of soul itself?

With regard to the first question, Plotinus seems, not surprisingly, to think in terms of a hierarchical continuum of creative principles, within which the (cosmic) soul plays an executive or ancillary function. Depending on the specific contexts, the description of this hierarchy is fluid enough to allow for formulations that, at least, seem to place the emphasis differently: sometimes the creative function of the soul is minimised, sometimes the creative principle is divided between the Intellect and the cosmic soul, sometimes the cosmic soul is designated as the properly creative or executive principle.[32] In any case, two points seem clear. First, the cosmic soul derives the principles which guide its creative activity from the Intellect: as Plotinus puts it, the ordering activity of the soul "depends on an abiding intellect of which the image is the order in soul" (IV.4.10.12-3).[33] Second, the auxiliary function of the cosmic soul can not be actually conceived in terms of a standard distinction between conception, planning, and execution. As we have already noted (see n.17), Plotinus thinks of the activity or effectiveness of form in its interaction with matter not in terms of planning and execution, but in terms of an instant and sudden attraction between two elements, one active and one passive, in the close proximity (γειτονείᾳ) generated by the soul's "going forth." In this context, apart from the potency of the active element, Plotinus is eager to point out the passive suitability of the inert element (*i.e.*, "ἐπείπερ ὑπέστη" in the first image); he will even attribute to it, although negatively, an active tendency (generated through reflection) to embrace form and thus become form in an active sense (*i.e.*, "αὐτοῦ ποιεῖσθαι ἐν ᾧ ἐστιν" in the third image). In this sense, the function of the soul would be to create a space, or rather a spacious proximity between the intelligible and the material, in which embodied forms can, so to speak, emerge spontaneously. In Plotinian terms, the soul is an "interpretative medium" which links the sensible with the intelligible domain[34]. From this point of view, we might say that the soul is both indispensable (no soul, no proximity, no sensible world) and superfluous (what indeed does soul add to the composite?): as long as the proximity is established, the interpreter 'disappears' (although it is everywhere), having brought into being (or being the order of) a unified composite of form and matter.[35]

Returning now to the issue of the form of Plotinus' account, we may draw a few concluding remarks. The task is an account which, respecting both the absolute and the relative separation of the elements of the composite structure, would try at the same time to establish the internal or immanent intelligibility of the sensible world. Plotinus' philosophical answer to this demand, which we have outlined in our discussion without examining it in detail, is the elaboration of a conception of the nature and mode of activity of the (cosmic) soul (in the context of a general account of the effectiveness of form or the activity of the Intellect) which transcends the standard distinction between deliberate (rational) action and 'blind' (mechanical) activity (as this can be found in the *Timaeus*). This conception informs his brief cosmogony, which assumes thus the form of a metamorphosis story, in which, to the extent that this is possible, creation or interaction is replaced by self-transformation. The genesis (and hence the order) of the sensible world is presented in terms of a single creative force, the cosmic soul, which, with all the relevant qualifications, acts upon itself; with the help of this entity, the interaction between two separate elements (matter and form) appears as a self-transformation which contains within itself the principle of its development. From this point of view, the fact that Plotinus does not start his cosmogony with a psychogony can be explained as a sign of his reluctance, in this context, to bring into account anything that would point outside this process of self-transformation.

Announcing the contents of his cosmogony, Plotinus talks about that "which happened, when the soul which was altogether pure from body took upon itself a bodily nature" (τὸ γινόμενο πάθος τότε, ὅτε ψυχὴ καθαρὰ οὖσα σώματος πάντη ἴσχει περὶ αὐτὴν σώματος φύσιν) (13).[36] The creation story has already been programmatically transformed into a metamorphosis story, the story of the soul which became the world, but the question is already facing us: Why did the soul transform itself?[37]

Notes

1. The text of Plotinus used is that of Henry and Schwyzer OCT *editio minor, Plotini Opera* (Oxford; 1964-82). Translations follow A. H. Armstrong's Loeb edition, *Plotinus with an English Translation* (Cambridge, Massachusetts; 1966-88), but are frequently modified by me. Passages from IV.3 are cited in the text by chapter and line numbers only; passages from IV.3.9 are cited by line numbers only.

2. Plotinus faces the issue in I.8 and in II.4. For a discussion with further references, see D. O'Brien, "Plotinus on Matter and Evil" in L. P. Gerson, ed., *The Cambridge Companion to Plotinus* (Cambridge; 1996), 171-195.

3. *Cf.* here Plotinus' program for a reading of the *Timaeus* in the context of an enquiry about soul outlined in IV.8.2; the questions concern (1) πῶς ποτε κοινωνεῖν σώματα πέφυκε [ἡ ψυχή]; (2) περὶ κόσμου φύσεως; (3) περὶ ποιητοῦ.

4. Inserted by Theiler; accepted by Henry-Schwyzer and Armstrong.

5. Plotinus mentions the special creative role of the cosmic soul in a number of passages; see, in particular, IV.3.6 (the metaphors quoted come from ll.14-5) and V.1.2. We will return to the issue of the relation between the cosmic soul and the Demiurge at the end of our discussion.

6. Contrast here the *Timaeus*. Plato claims both that the soul "is prior in birth and excellence" (34C) with regard to the body of the world and that one of the ingredients in its construction is the "being which is transient and divisible in bodies" (Περὶ τὰ σώματα μεριστὴ οὐσία) (35A). If we respect the narrative order (whether or not we want to interpret the *Timaeus* literally), this "being" can not be the sensible world, but is the chaotic "becoming" (γένεσις), which exists before the creation of the world (52D). In Plotinus' terms, that would be "not ordered matter."

7. That Plotinus thinks in terms of ordering, but not of an *act* of ordering is made clear in IV.4.10.9-11: "for the things it [the universe] ought to have have already been discovered and ordered without being set in order; for the things set in order were the things that happened, and what made them was the order (ἤδη γὰρ ἐξεύρηται καὶ τέτακται ἃ δεῖ, οὐ ταχθέντα· τὰ γὰρ ταχθέντα ἦν τὰ γινόμενα, τὸ δὲ ποιοῦν αὐτὰ ἡ τάξις)."

8. For an orientation in this issue, see the exchange between G. Vlastos ("The Disorderly Motion in the *Timaeus*" in R. E. Allen, ed., *Studies in Plato's Metaphysics* (London; 1965), 379-99), H. Cherniss (*Aristotle's Criticism of Plato and the Academy* (Baltimore; 1944), 421-431), G. Vlastos ("Creation in the *Timaeus*: Is It a Fiction?" in R. E. Allen, ed., *Studies in Plato's Metaphysics* (London; 1965), 401-419), and L. Tarán ("The Creation Myth in Plato's *Timaeus*" in J. P. Anton and G. L. Kustas, ed., *Essays in Ancient Greek Philosophy* (Albany; 1971), 372-407).

9. "τὸ σύνθετόν φασιν ἐν τούτοις κεκλῆσθαι γενητόν, τούτῳ δὲ συνυπάρχειν καὶ τὸ ἀφ' ἑτέρας αἰτίας ἀπογεννᾶσθαι" (*In Platonis Timaeum*, 85A; the reference is to *Timaeus*, 28B). The phrase "σαφηνείας ἕνεκα διδασκαλικῆς" comes from 89A. For reports of the ancient opinions, see A. E. Taylor's *A Commentary on Plato's Timaeus* (Oxford; 1928), 66-70 (ad 28B.4); J. M. Dillon, *Iamblichi Chalcidensis In Platonis dialogos commentariorum fragmenta* (Leiden; 1973), 303-7; and H. Cherniss, ed., *Plutarch's Moralia*, XIII.1 (Cambridge, Massachusetts; 1976), 168-71 (ad *De anima procreatione in Timaeo*, 1013A-B). For a discussion of this material, see R. Sorabji, *Time, Creation and the Continuum* (London; 1983), 268-283.

10. Thus it would be misleading to consider Plato's or Plotinus' use of 'myth' in this context as a regression to myth in its traditional sense; it is rather an attempt to specify the correct form of an account of the constitution of certain objects (*e.g.*, the sensible world as σύνθετον), in close connection to a rigorous philosophical specification of the nature of these objects.

11. *Cf.* here: "To ask why Soul made the universe is like asking why there is soul and why the Maker makes (τὸ δὲ διὰ τί ἐποίησε κόσμον ταὐτὸν τῷ διὰ τί ἔστι ψυχὴ καὶ διὰ τί ὁ δημιουργὸς ἐποίησεν). First, it is a question of people who assume a beginning of that which always is: then they think that the cause of the making was a being who turned from one thing to another and changed" (II.9.8.1-5).

12. *Cf.* here: "ἡ πᾶσα ψυχὴ οὐδαμοῦ ἐγένετο οὐδὲ ἦλθεν· οὐδὲ γὰρ ὅπου· ἀλλὰ τὸ σῶμα γειτονῆσαν μετέλαβεν αὐτῆς" (III.9.3.1-3).

13. Plotinus usually makes the point in terms of a distinction between powers or parts of the soul, as in the next chapter: "but one power belongs to soul which remains within it, and another which goes out to something else" (IV.3.10.33-4); *cf.* also, II.3.9.31-4; V.1.3.7-11 (in the general context of II.6.3.14-20 and V.4.2.27-34); and in particular II.3.18.8-14, where we encounter again the image of 'strengthening' and 'overflowing:' "δεῖ τὴν τοῦ παντὸς ψυχὴν θεωρεῖν μὲν τὰ ἄριστα ἀεὶ ἱεμένην πρὸς τὴν νοητὴν φύσιν καὶ τὸν θεόν, πληρουμένης δὲ αὐτῆς καὶ πεπληρωμένης οἷον ἀπομεστουμένης αὐτῆς τὸ ἐξ αὐτῆς ἴνδαλμα καὶ τὸ ἔσχατον αὐτῆς πρὸς τὰ κάτω τὸ ποιοῦν τοῦτο εἶναι."

14. Given this image one would expect that the darkness circumscribes light, *i.e.*, the familiar picture of a point-like source of light radiating in all directions. We shall see in the discussion of the third image that this is not the case.

15. *Cf.* here: "The only possibility that remains, then, is that all things exist in something else, and, since there is nothing between, because of their closeness (γειτονείᾳ) to something else in the realm of real being something like an imprint and image of that other suddenly (ἐξαίφνης) appears, either by its direct action or through the assistance of soul" (V.8.7.12-16). A. H. Armstrong notes *ad loc.*: "The insistence on the immediate and intimate relationship of the intel-

ligible and the sensible universes and the comparative unimportance of the mediation of the soul should be noted." We should note that a proper appreciation of the mediative role of the soul should take into account the fact that this "closeness" exists only in the light generated by the 'strengthening' of the soul; without soul there would be no "closeness." We will return to this issue at the end of our discussion.

16. *Cf.*: "καὶ ὁ κόσμος δέ γένοιτο ἂν ἄνευ μεταλλοιώσεως, οἷον οἷς περιτίθεμεν" (III.6.11.20-1); "ἀλλ' οὖν εἴδεσι κατέσχηται ἐξ ἀρχῆς εἰς τέλος, [the universe], ... ὅθεν καὶ χαλεπὸν εὑρεῖν τὴν ὕλην ὑπὸ πολλοῖς εἴδεσι κρυφθεῖσαν" (V.8.7.19-23).

17. Plotinus will make his position on the spontaneous nature of the creative activity of the soul clear in the next chapter: "For whatever comes into contact (ἐφάψηται) with soul is made as the essential nature of soul is in a state to make it; and it makes, not according to a purpose brought in from outside, nor waiting upon planning and consideration (ἡ δὲ ποιεῖ οὐκ ἐπακτῷ γνώμῃ οὐδὲ βουλὴν ἢ σκέψιν ἀναμείνασα)" (IV.3.10.13-16). The claim should be obviously read in the context of Plotinus' notion of intelligible creativity (*e.g.*, V.8.7).

18. The clause reads: "ὡς ἂν ἐν ὕδασι δίκτυον τεγγόμενον ζῴη." "ζῴη" is characterised "uix recte" by Henry-Schwyzer and is deleted (as "seltsam") by Theiler. Henry-Schwyzer conjecture without conviction "ἐρωῇ:" "as if a net immersed in the waters moved forth." In any case, the sentence makes sense under the assumption that the image refers to the passive movement of a net thrown in the sea, in a context where the existence of motion gives the appearance of life.

19. The situation is similar in the *Timaeus*. The soul is "set" (θείς) in the center of the body, but is extended in such a way as to envelop the entire exterior of the body (34B; 36D): the qualification neutralises the most obvious inference of the metaphor, namely that the soul is 'in' body; the soul is simultaneously 'in,' 'through,' and 'out' of body. *Cf.* Plotinus' comments in III.9.3.3-4 and V.1.10.21-4.

20. This image should be compared with a similar image from an earlier treatise, V.1.2.14-28 (10). There, "before soul it was a dead body ..., or rather the darkness of matter and non-existence (πρὸ ψυχῆς σῶμα νεκρόν, ... μᾶλλον δὲ σκότος ὕλης καὶ μὴ ὄν)" and we should imagine "soul as flowing in from outside, pouring in and entering it everywhere and illuminating (εἰσρέουσαν, εἰσχυθεῖσαν, εἰσιοῦσαν, εἰσλάμπουσαν): as the rays of the sun light up a dark cloud (σκοτεινόν νέφος), and make it shine and give it a golden look (λάμπειν ποιοῦσι χρυσοειδῆ ὄψιν διδοῦσαι) ...." From our point of view, the strength of this image, which understandably appealed to Sts. Basil and Augustine (see Armstrong's note *ad loc*), is its weakness: it derives from a number of stark antitheses (inside-outside, before-after, light-darkness) that, in our reading, Plotinus himself tries here to undermine.

21. The word "σκιά" appears for the first time in IV.3.9.48-9: "καὶ τοσαύτη ἐστὶν ἡ σκιά, ὅσος ὁ λόγος ὁ παρ' αὐτῆς [τῆς θαλάσσης ... τῆς ψυχῆς]."

22. *Timaeus*, 29B-D. The success of Plato in this respect does not concern us here.

23. The issue has been discussed by P. Hadot, in "Physique et poésie dans le *Timée* de Platon," *Revue de Théologie et de Philosophie* 115 (1983); cf. B. Κάλφας, ed., *Τίμαιος* (Athens 1995), 55-57. The relevant Aristotelian material comes mostly from Book VI of the *Poetics*. On the issue of mimesis in the *Timaeus*, see also, S. Halliwell, *Aristotle's Poetics* (London 1986), 117-19.

24. The headings are taken from F. M. Cornford's division of the *Timaeus* in *Plato's Cosmology: The Timaeus of Plato* (London; 1966).

25. Thus, for example, Plato is able to claim that the 'mixture' of reason and necessity which characterises the world should be described in terms of "necessity yielding to intelligent persuasion" (48A).

26. *Poetics*, 1450a 22-39.

27. We should merely note here, since we do not have the space to pursue it, that an analysis of Plotinus' story in terms of other Aristotelian concepts (such as περιπέτεια and ἀναγνώρισις) may lead to very interesting results.

28. Obviously some inferences can be drawn. We may, for example, attribute to the soul an intention to care for the house it builds. But recall Plotinus' exact formulation: "ἄξιος ἐπιμελείας νομισθεὶς [ὁ οἶκος]" (IV.3.9.31-2); even here Plotinus avoids active attribution to an agent.

29. For a discussion of the issue, see H. Cherniss, *Aristotle's Criticism of Plato and the Academy*, Appendix XI, 603-610.

30. Soul as generated: *Timaeus*, 34A-36E and *Laws*, 892C, 904A, 967D; soul as the source of motion: *Laws*, 896A-897B. For a discussion of the ensuing problems, see G. Vlastos, "The Disorderly Motion in the *Timaeus*," 390-9 and "Creation in the *Timaeus*: Is It a Fiction?," 414-9.

31. There is a passage where Plotinus seems to identify the Demiurge of the *Timaeus* with the cosmic soul, on the basis of the fact that the Demiurge "planned" (διενοήθει) and this is a function of the soul and not of the Intellect (III.9.1.35). As Armstrong notes *ad loc*, Porphyry identified the Demiurge with the cosmic soul and believed that this was Plotinus' view (Proclus, *In Platonis Timaeum*, 94A; Proclus disagrees with the attribution to Plotinus). Two things should be noted here: (1) As we have seen, Plotinus would not accept that the cosmic soul creates by "planning" (see n.17); (2) Plotinus criticises a similar position as a gnostic misinterpretation of Plato in II.9.619-25.

32. (1): "something like an imprint and image of [something in the realm of real being] suddenly appears [in the sensible world], either by [real being's] direct action or through the assistance (διακονησαμένης) of soul" (V.8.7.13-6); (2) "but since the ordering principle (κοσμοῦν) is twofold, we speak of one form of it as the Craftsman (δημιουργόν) and the other as the Soul of All (τοῦ παντὸς

ψυχήν)" (IV.4.10.1-3); (3) see n.5. The problem is more complicated, because Plotinus extends this hierarchy at the lower side in order to include both an immanent soul of nature (to be distinguished from the cosmic soul) and/or individual souls (cf. II.1.5; II.3.17-8; II.9.6.60-3; IV.4.10; and n.13).

33. Cf. II.3.17.13-18; II.3.18.8-14; II.9.4.9-10; V.9.3.24-37.

34. "This soul gives the edges (περατα) of itself that border on the sun to it [the sun], and creates by means of itself a connection to the sun there [the Nous], by becoming, so to speak, interpretative (καὶ ποιεῖ διὰ μέσου αὐτῆς κἀκεῖ συνῆφθαι οἷον ἑρμηνευτική) of what comes from that sun to this sun, and from this sun to that sun, as far as this sun can reach the other through soul" (IV.3.11.17-21).

35. Thus, given the mediating and unifying function of the soul, Plotinus can describe the sensible world without reference to the soul: "Then matter, too, is a sort of ultimate form; so this universe is all form, and all the things in it are forms; ... the making is done without fuss, since that which makes is all real being and form (ἐπεὶ δὲ καὶ αὕτη εἶδός τι ἔσχατον, πᾶν εἶδος τόδε καὶ πάντα εἴδη· ... ἐποιεῖτο δὲ ἀψοφητί, ὅτι πᾶν τὸ ποιῆσαν καὶ οὐσία καὶ εἶδος)" (V.8.7.23-25).

36. Note here the reversal of the theme of 'covering' (see n. 16).

37. I would like to thank Professors S. R. L. Clark, J. M. Dillon and S. Stern-Gillet for their comments on earlier versions of this paper. I am grateful to the Greek Foundation for State Scholarships (IKY) for currently funding my research project and the British Academy for a studentship I was awarded during 1997-1998.

Divinized and De-divinized
Conceptions of the World and of *Cosmos*

Leonidas C. Bargeliotes

Plato and Aristotle and, consequently, Neoplatonism and Aristotelianism, differ among themselves on account of their divinized and de-divinized conceptions of the world and of *cosmos*. Generally speaking, the former conception originates with the Italians, the latter with the Ionians. This, however, does not exclude a supplementary and interactive relation between them. The recognition of this distinction and the attempted interaction are important not only for the understanding of the Presocratic philosophy, but also for the particular tendencies and differencies between the two great philosophers and their adherents. This is manifest in considering Plato's and Aristotle's ways of approaching the world, as well as in the criticism that Neoplatonists have raised against Aristotle's own half de-divinized world and aesthetic approach. Examples are drawn from the long complex of divinizing tradition which includes, among others, Pythagoreans and Platonists, Neoplatonists and Neopythagoreans. They mostly follow the divine masters: Pythagoras and Plato, and understand the world as divine and harmonious. They also contrast their own religious like doctrines with those of the Ionians and of Aristotle and find them inferior and de-divinizing the world; the latter, according to their arguments, search for "material" causes, among other things, in order to give "physical" explainations and empirical arrangements to the world phenomena. In a word, they move from a divine mythical background and of *cosmos* to a "physical" or "natural" conception of the world.

Plato's aesthetic synthesis, as we shall see, is rooted in the conceptions of the world as *cosmos* of his predecessors, which he reshapes, transforms and enriches. "They express in words," as G. Mueller has put it,[1] "as sculptors do in stone, the vision of a beloved world." As a matter of fact, Eros, the love of the artist, is known to be the oldest divine artist, transforming chaos into *cosmos*. The blessed and happy *cosmos* is, therefore, the outcome of love for a balanced and harmonious achievement, but this "telos of love," stands in contrast to the unbalanced and disharmonious human existence. There is no doubt that behind the Platonic — and the Neoplatonic — conceptions of *cosmos* is, undoubtedly, Heraclitus' invisible harmony, "The invisible harmony is better than the visible."[2] But this invisible harmony is hard to find; it can only be found by the soul animated by an anticipating urge in the right direction.[3] Man will find the truth of the human affairs when he opens his psyche to the truth of God, which means a conversion, the turning-around from the untruth of human affairs to the truth of the Idea.[4] This, in turn, can be achieved by proper education and the replacement of the unseemly symbolizations of gods, as they were to be found in the poets, by the seemly symbols.[5] As E. Voegelin[6] has stated, "the validity of the standards developed by Plato and — partly — by Aristotle depends on the conception of man who can be the measure of a society because God is the measure of his soul." To this argument it is added the Platonic Eros — and its variants — toward the *kalon and agathon,* as well as their mathematical achievement and subordination of the forces in the soul. From our point of view, this interpretation is partly true regarding the conceptions of the world and of *cosmos* by both Plato and Aristotle and their adherents, because their reaction was different. Plato relies heavily on the divinized Pythagorean concepts of *Philosophia,* of *cosmos*, of *number* and of *harmonia,* which he reshapes, transforms and enriches in accordance with his Ideal World. Aristotle, based upon his own *entelechiac* and teleological conceptions of man and the world, rejects Pythagoreanism and partly de-divinizes the world. In what follows, the great Platonic and Neoplatonic conceptions of *cosmos* and of their aesthetic syntheses are extensively quoted and analysed to this effect.

In the first place, for the Pythagoreans philosophers are not only those who must inquiry into "a great number of things"[7] or those who are travelling θεωρίης ἕνεκεν,[8] but also those who are φίλοι of σοφία, in a deeper meaning of the word — such as "purification" and salvation through philosophy — those who consider man as an immortal god.[9] As Aristoxenus said of Pythagoras and of his followers,[10] "every distinction they lay down as to what should be done or not done aims at conformity with the divine. This is their starting point; their whole life is ordered with a view to following God, and it is the governing principle of their philosophy." This is the effort to escape through assimilation to God, ("φυγὴ δὲ ὁμοίωσις θεῷ κατὰ τὸ δυνατόν"),[11] in contradistinction with those who "think mortal thoughts," ("θνατὰ χρὴ τὸν θνατον, οὐκ ἀθάνατα τὸν θνατόν φρονεῖν").[12] Assimilation to God was for Pythagoras the goal of life, an aspiration rooted in the limit and order, of πέρας and of κόσμος. Plato's main concern, as we shall see, is the exploration of the human soul, and the true order of the soul turns out to be dependent on philosophy in the strict sense of the love of the divine σοφόν.[12]

For the Pythagoreans, *cosmos* unites the notion of order, arrangement and structural perfection with their beauty, things are interconnected and all nature is akin, and the human soul is intimately related to the living and divine universe. Pythagoras was the first to apply the name of *cosmos* to the world, in recognition of the order it displayed.[13] According to this religious doctrine, it is the "priests and priestesses concern to give a reasoned account"[14] of the nature of things, that is, all nature is akin, as the "wise men tell us that heaven and earth, gods and men are bound together by kinship and love and orderliness and temperance and justice.[15] The philosopher through association with what is divine and orderly (κόσμιος) becomes divine and orderly (κόσμιος).[16] The revolutions of our own thought, which is akin to the circuits of intelligence in the heaven, may profit by them by learning to know them and acquiring the power to compute them rightly according to nature; we might reproduce the perfectly unerring revolutions of the god and reduce to settled order the wandering motions in ourselves."[17] These men are the "best spectators," ("βέλτιστοι θεαταί"),[18] who take part in festival or fair. In short, the philosopher who contemplates the *cosmos* becomes *kosmios* in his own soul. *Cosmos,* for the Pythagoreans is the key to the whole.

Pythagoreans are also known for the important advances in the science of mathematics and its relation with *harmonia*. For the Pythagoreans number had a mystical significance and independent reality. As W. K. C. Guthrie[19] puts it, "Number was responsible for 'harmony,' the divine principle that governed the structure of the whole world." Numbers not only explained the physical world, but also symbolized or stood for moral qualities and other abstractions. They could express the love for the agreement of all things, and become the reconciling principle of the limiting form and the unlimited stuff, of the all-embracing Eleatic Being and the Herakleitean flux, better, the reconciling "force" of the things of sense-perception and the ordered soul, of the divine nature and the human art, especially music.

No one else save Plato and the Neoplatonists come so close to the Pythagorean religious character of mathematics. For Plato, in contrast with Aristotle, the acquisition of mathematical knowledge partakes more of the character of religious initiation than of mere instruction or research. For Plato, Arithmetic "draws the souls upwards...never allowing anyone to offer it for discussing mere collections of visible or tangible bodies."[20] Similarly, the objects of geometrical knowledge are "eternal, not subject to decay," and it tends to draw the soul towards truth and to produce a philosophic intelligence for the directing upwards of faculties which we wrongly turn earthwards."[21] Astronomy, too, as a pure mathematical science, must turn the soul's gaze upwards, not literally to the sky, but to the realm of "real being and the invisible."[22] This divinizing orientation of mathematics versus the de-divinizing observations of the empirical scientists who are discussing mere collections of visible or tangible bodies and are directing the faculties to turn earthwards and to the natural revolutions of heaven. The latter were seeking accounts and reasons to explain the phenomena, rather than forcing the phenomena and trying to fit them into arguments and opinions of their own. As Aristotle complained, they insisted on making the system coherent and they invented a non-existed planet to make up the total to the sacred number ten. Hence Aristotle's general rejection of their doctrine, that "things themselves are numbers," or that they "imitate" or "represent" numbers, or again, that they supposed the elements of numbers to be the elements of things and the whole heaven to be a harmony and a number."[23] Aristotle seems to express the spirit of Ionian thought, which, in the words of Guthrie,[24] was "less bemused by the religious associations of number and more rational in approach." Numbers are intimately connected with *harmonia*.

The word *harmonia* meant primarily the joining or fitting things together which the Pythagoreans equated with number and associated with music. The generalization of the number could apply to the whole heaven and become the harmony of the shperes,[25] while the numerical ratios could determine the concordant intervals of the scale."[26] Like *cosmos* which represented order and beauty the basic intervals of music could be represented by the ratios 1:2, 3:2 and 4:3, and be imposed on the chaotic range of sound by means of the four integers 1, 2, 3, and 4. These add up to 10, upon which the Pythagoreans have based their belief that this number "was something perfect, and contained in itself the whole nature of number."[27] It is this number that the Pythagoreans represented graphically by the figure known as tetractys, a sacred symbol for them, to which the followers of Pythagoras, were said to swear by him who handed down to them the tetraktys, "source and root of everlasting nature."[28] All these divinized Pythagorean conceptions, can be seen in Plato's great aesthetic synthesis.

Aesthetics for Plato are the arts and the ways of life inspired by the divine Muses, which constitute his divine—mythical background. In his own words, "the human soul, inspired by the Muse with 'divine madness' (μανία), creates 'music' (μουσική), the highest blessings of human existence—without which life would not be worth living."[29] This sort of madness is a gift of the gods, fraught with the highest bliss (ἐπ' εὐτυχίᾳ τῇ μεγίστῃ παρὰ θεῶν ἡ τοιαύτη μανία δίδοται). Both, aesthetic unity of soul and man, and symbolic fusion of body and soul, constitute the foundation of the true community and "of our national culture." It celebrates itself in the great national festivals and becomes aware of itself in the artistic glorification of its historical past. Hence, "the true Muse is the companion of reason and philosophy,"[30] for the aim of the philosopher is to discern the nature of soul, divine and human, its experiences, and its activities. Eros as aesthetic love, in respond to the call of the Muse, transfigures the given stuff into an expressive image of life,[31] motivates the true artist and distinguishes him from the ἄμουσον. This means that we have the technicians without inspiration, and those whose inspiration is impure and immoral; only the philosopher poet can unify these two conditions.[32] Love, then, is himself so divine a poet that he can kindle in the souls of others the poetic fire…we are everyone of us a poet when we are in love.[33]

The final end and consummation of the aesthetic life is, for Plato, a blessed union with the appearance of Beauty,[34] which means the production of dialectical contrasts between real and apparent beauty, between the outside and the inside illusion and, consequently, between Plato's condemnation of art from the practical point of view, and the unsurpassable heights of his art in which beauty is praised as the highest good. It also means the inadequacy and helplessness of a purely aesthetic culture, and that contemplation of beauty transcends the beauties of the earth, of the bodies, of practices and of sciences until one arrives at the knowledge of beauty itself and the essence of beauty, the "divine beauty," the "pure and clear and unalloyed…the divine beauty in its uniqueness."[35] Thus, every work of art is a concrete whole of opposites, made visible to imagination and philosophical self-comprehension, while "beauty in and for herself," which man enjoys, is the "only home he has in this world." For when man has brought forth and reared this perfect beauty, he shall be called the friend of god, and if ever it is given to man to put in immortality, it shall be given to him."[36] Man's soul is open to the transcendent Ideal Whole and is opposed to the charms of beautiful appearance. There is a need for it to go beyond beauty and art in order to evaluate beauty and aesthetic life with reference to the whole of reality. The ideal whole of reality without any visible embodiment, is "beyond (any given) being in power and dignity."[37] God too has been conceived as a self-sufficient organism whose life depends on nothing outside of itself. The divine whole has no sense-object against itself. As a matter of fact, this marks the culmination of Plato's thought and the beginning of Neoplatonism. In the end is the beginning. Plotinus, Proclus and Plethon will be respectively treated to this effect, in spite of their transformation they brought about in regard to their conception of *cosmos* and of divinity, and in opposition to the Aristotelian de-divinized strategy.

Plotinus, to begin with, in his conception of divine—physical beauty and the beauty of arts follows, in the main, Plato, but with variations. He preserves the divinization strategy in his hierarchical structure of reality and objects Aristotle's categories as completely inadequate, inapplicable and irrelevant for the κόσμος νοητός, but useful for the κόσμος αἰσθητός.[38] The dialectician, however, has the right to judge and use or ignore as his superior wisdom dictates.

Thus, the life of the organic unity which has its source beyond the world of forms, that is, in the Good, it is involved not only in the beauty which form gives to works of nature and art in the sensible world, but also in the beauty of forms themselves. It is by the *cosmos* of the world, its beauty and order that we are to know the divinity and be led to the contemplation of the intelligible. The work of art is beautiful in so far as it reflects the living organic unity of the whole which is the intelligible form. Plotinus, unlike Plato, puts the beauty of art on a level with the beauty of nature as a way to the intelligible beauty.[39] As the same author points out, Plotinus is only interested in the beauty of art, or of nature, as a help in our ascent to the intelligible beauty and beyond it to its source, the Good, which is older, not in time but in truth, and has the prior power—for it has all power.[40]

Plotinus, also, preserves Plato's view of the artist as copyist of sense objects, at two removes from the truth, although he considers the products of human art like those of the divine making, that is, images of forms in the intelligible world, to which the artist's mind, like all human minds, comes in direct conduct and which, in some cases, can improve on nature. He points out, that "Phidias did not make his Zeus from any model perceived by the senses; he understood what Zeus would look like if he wanted to make himself visible to us."[41]

Nature, too, though an image of wisdom (ἴνδαλμα φρονήσεως), is for him the appearance of the Over-Soul, which itself is derived from the archetypal Logos, and is divinized through its participation in the divine Beauty.

The divinity, says Plotinus, made the universe beautiful and harmonious throughout, which is its own aesthetic constitution.[42] He compares the movement of the heavenly bodies to a choral dance; they all aspire to the One. The moving and illuminating lights of the heavens are like the tones of a lyre. The natural harmony of the moving lights is like a musical symphony produced by instruments.[43] Even things that are less good or evil also contribute to the perfection of the universe. It follows that there is no necessity that all things be beautiful in the same degree because the very contraries (opposites) contribute to the perfection of the universe, and so the beauty of the world could not exist without them.[44] This, again, is illustrated by Plotinus' beloved instruments, the lyre and the shepherd's pipe. The assigned place of each string by the pitch of the sound and the weakest sound of the pipe can contribute to the total and perfect harmony. This leads us to recognize and appreciate that the world is a beautiful and brilliant spectacle—a magnificent and perfect image—that is beautifully formed by intelligible divinities.[45] The beautiful, then, even in that elementary stage, can only be known by the highest faculty which apprehends suprasensuous reality. This has led Plotinus to reject the classical concept of symmetry according to which there is a harmony of form and content, of soul and its embodiment, in the object. The conclusion is that symmetry is not beauty itself, but that it derives its beauty from a superior principle and, for that reason, cannot be scientific or derived from mutual agreement of these speculations. Plotinus goes beyond symmetry.

The Over-Soul, on the other hand, possesses the body of the universe. She contains all the souls in her breast, each distinct from her, but not separated. Entirely devoted to divine things and not withdrawn from her noblest contemplation, she governs the world by a single power whose exercise involves no anxiety.[46] Souls, therefore, are necessarily amphibians, since they alternately live in both worlds. The soul is the image of intelligence (Nous) and, as intelligence, is the image of the One. The closer we get to form, the greater the participation in divinity—and the assimilation to it. Analogous is the aesthetic ascent of the soul. When the soul is raised to intelligence, she sees her own beauty increased. Mathematics prepares for that achievement.

Mathematics, also, prepares the soul for the study of intelligibles and for purifying and strengthening it for the transition, to pure being.[47] When the soul is united to intelligence it is right in saying that "the soul's welfare and beauty lie in its assimilation to the divinity."[48] It is therefore only by intelligence that the soul is beautiful without any mediation and hence beautiful in itself.[49] This is the third stage of the Plotinian structure of reality. It is the stage of the third kind of citizens, the philosophers, the divine men, "τὸ τρίτον γένος θείων ἀνθρώπων," as Plotinus calls them, who, in their mightier power, are able to reach the beauty in the intelligible world and have a clear vision of the splendor above. In an almost lyric style Plotinus refers to these divine men as taking their flight above the clouds and darkness of this world and then, looking beyond all here below, they remain there and reside in their true fatherland, delighting in the unspeakable place of reality and truth, like a man returning after a long wandering to the pleasant ways of his own native land.[50]

The opposition between the two worlds, the divine and the material, the divinized and the de-divinized, can, also, be seen in Proclus, particularly, in his hierarchical arrangement of souls in their descent in the world, in his conceptions of mathematics and of arts, in his evaluation of physics and in his anti-aristotelianism, in general. In the first place, at the top of his hierarchy Proclus places the souls of the gods that do not descend into the world, and are not affected by any change, but govern it from their transcendent status of independednce. Below these come souls who do descend, but remain pure and unaffected by vice. And there are souls who do not only descend but also become corrupted by the material world.[51] Proclus uses Pythagorean and Orphic authorities to support Plato, while Aristotle, for him, occupies a subordinate place, in respect to his empirical approach,[52] to his image of the soul as tablet (γραμματεῖον),[53] as well as to his theory that numbers are mere abstractions from the material objects. The arguments which Proclus uses in a systematic way against this mundane derivation of mathematicals are directed against the Aristotelian theory of abstraction in order to a further strengthening of the anti-Aristotelian position. From the Neoplatonic point of view the accuracy that mathematicals possess cannot be derived from sensible objects. Neither immutable laws can be derived from a changing world, nor the general principles of demonstration can be posterior to sensible particulars. Almost all Neoplatonists are unable to understand the new possibilities that Aristotle's infinite indivisibility of mathematicals opens for the solution, among other things, of the old problem of the Atomists and of Zeno's paradoxes.

Proclus's concerns, however, are different. He is mainly concerned with showing the importance of mathematics for theology and the rest of the sciences, including the productive arts. For Proclus, mathematics prepares intellectual insight. His argument is worth quoted in length: "...thus Plato explains to us many wonderful doctrines about the gods by means of mathematical forms, and the philosophy of the Pythagoreans conceals its secret theological initiation using such veils. Such also is the entire *Sacred Discourse*, the

Bacchae of Philolaus, and the whole approach of Pythagoras' exegesis concerning the gods."[54] According to Proclus, as himself puts it, "productive arts 'mathematics' has the rank of paradigm, generating before in itself the principles and measures of what are produced."[55] Geometry, above all, reaches, as general mathematics do, up to true and divine being, "teaching us through images the special properties (ἰδιότητες) of the divine orders and the powers of the intellectual Forms…Here it shows us what figures are appropriate to the gods, which ones belong to primary beings…"[56] At the intermediate region of knowledge geometry unfolds and develops discursive principles (διανοητικοὶ λόγοι), while at the level below it examines nature, that is, "the species of elementary perceptible bodies and the powers associated with them, and explains how their causes are contained in advance in its own ideas."[57] For the Neoplatonist Proclus the structure of geometrical demonstrations, which rest on axioms and hypotheses, that is, the principles or 'causes' (both of the world and of scientific discourse) from which the conclusions are derived, must be transcendent, immaterial, and unchanging. Physics itself, then, must begin and derived from these meta-physical causes, the universal and unerring principles, if its mathematical-geometrical laws could be universally true. But when these laws are applied to physical bodies, which are of derivative ontological character and known through sense perception, such laws are deficient, probable and limited in scope. This means that physics has a 'dual' character. The one, the Pythagorean, either concerned with its transcendent 'divine' causes producing the world: the demiurge, the Forms, the lesser gods, soul (as in the 'theology' of *Timaeus)* or a science of the divine itself (as in the *Parmenides*), and the other rejected in the *Phaedo*, "which blinds the eye of the soul, holding as responsible causes as winds and ether according to Anaxagoras." The former, then, the true physics, must be attached to theology, "as nature depends upon the gods."[58] In the case of physics, Proclus claims that the physics of Plato, for reasons just explained, is superior to that of Aristotle. As he puts it, Aristotle concerns himself mainly "with immanent causes, matter and form in nature, and pays less attention than does Plato to the transcendent efficient, paradigmatic, and final causes …and to the extent he neglects the divine presuppositions of nature he diminishes that which gives physics what scientific value can have."[59] Plethon, as we shall see in what follows, will give more details of this "inferiority" of Aristotle.

Finally, George Gemistos-Plethon, who has declared the independence of Platonism and Neoplatonism from Christianity and identified them with Neo-Hellenism and true Humanism,[60] sought to make Plato a living philosophical fountain of truth. He was also eager to point out that Aristotle was inferior of Plato and far from agreeing with the Church. Through his religious, philosophical and moral ideas, Plethon attempted to revive Neoplatonism and Stoicism in order to re-divinize the world and, by appealing to their truth, preserve the eternal divinity of the world. Thus Plethon became the most active and outstanding philosopher dedicated to the revival of Neoplatonism and the survival of Hellenism during the last century of the Empire's existence.

In particular, Plethon, like his precursors Neoplatonists, endeavored to found his philosophical theology and metaphysics in the doctrines of Pythagoras, Plato and the Stoics, where science, philosophy and theology, along with ritualism formed an integral part of the Hellenic daily life. For a more reasonable formulation and justification of his metaphysical concepts, Plethon found it necessary to sanction them by attributing divine status to them.[61] To secure the divinization of his concepts, he appealed to "oracles" of antiquity and the "blessed name" of Zoroaster. On account of this Plethon despised any form of innovation and the introduction of the new metaphysical concepts.[62] The common "axioms," or "doctrines" or "ideas," as the philosopher calls the commonly accepted principles, are claimed to be as old as the universe itself, co-eternal with the *cosmos*[63] which ultimately gods have placed within man's soul in the best possible manner.[64] In his hierarchically arranged categories and attributes of Being which correspond to a parallel arrangement of deities, Plethon preserves the well-known tripartite division of cosmos:

> (i) The first super-essential and transcendental one (ὑπερούσιον τὸ "Ἑν) identified with Zeus and characterized as αὐτοόν, αὐτοέν and αὐτοαγαθός, the father and creator of all.[65]
>
> (ii) The principal agent of creation, the creative or demiurgic principle, Nous, corresponding to Poseidon, the first offspring of God the father; at once the eldest son and second god.[66]
>
> (iii) The third part of the hierarchy encompasses the individuals of the sensible world as well as the social beings. They are the phenomena of the sensible world, the rational and the irrational concrete beings, related to the eternal world of ideas as the copy is related to archetype.

Plethon conceives man as *methorion* in order to show that human soul, man'simmortal part, originates in the divine and it is carried to the human body by the celestial gods by means of the carrier of the soul (ψυχῆς ὄχημα). The souls enjoy preexistence as well as eternal life after death, since "they never cease from participating in mortal nature during all the successive stages in which the cycle recurs."[67] We proclaim," Plethon continues, "an eternity for the soul of man which is not half-measure or lame, but whole and complete...for it is plain that the eternity in both directions of which we speak is far greater and fine thing."[68] Immortality, therefore, for Plethon, means eternity of the soul, which thus is considered to be co-eternal with the Creator destined to assume and resume, alternately and indefinitely, a mortal nature.[69] Hence Plethon's definition of man: "man is an immortal animal, born to communicate with the mortal nature."[70] In other words, man is of composite nature, of the divine and of the bestial nature (θείου τε δὴ καὶ θηριώδους συντεθειμένος)."[71]

Man's composite nature is, according to Plethon, the outcome of a similar composition of the universe itself which is composed of immortal and mortal beings (ἀιδίων τε καὶ θνητῶν). Man has been devised so as to be a kind of bond (σύνδεσμος) between these two sorts of beings and, consequently, to be their μεθόριον.[72] Through this common limit and bond man is elevated above that which is mortal and can be united with the gods, through the line of kinship, in participating to their immortality and to their glorious beauty which man shares with them to a degree and is undoubtedly inferior, but, nevertheless, similar to divine beauty.[73]

Another important service of the admixture of the immortal with the mortal nature in man is its contribution to the harmony of the whole. In respect to this doctrine Plethon writes: "Our soul which is akin to the divine, as immortal and eternal, resides always in heaven which is the limit of the world. Then attached always to a mortal body, the soul is sent by the gods...in view of the universal harmony (τῆς τοῦ παντός ἕνεκεν ἁρμονίας) so that the union of the mortal nature with the immortal nature within us, may contribute to the union of the whole."[74] Plethon's conception of the human soul is an optimistic one; it takes us beyond the pessimism of the Orphic writings and the puritanism of Plato's *Phaedo* "Though the soul," Plethon writes, "is fastened to the mortal body, she feels no shame for it" (οὐκ αἰσχύνεται); on the contrary she boasts (αὐχεῖ) for the harmony, that is the union, in which the mortal body (βρότειον σῶμα) is involved; she takes pride in it as if she herself had produced such a function for the sake of the whole universe ...in the same way the universe has become one such harmony (οὕτω καὶ τὸ πᾶν εἰς μίαν τινα ἁρμονίαν συγκροτεῖσθαι).[75] The purpose of the union is again for the plenitude and the harmony of the great whole (τῆς τοῦ παντός πληρώσεως ἕνεκα καὶ ἅμα εὐαρμοστίας).[76] As a good Neoplatonist Plethon was convinced that the unequal distribution of good and happiness as well as our faults and vices —

which is impossible not to commit on account of our contact with the inferior nature (ὧν οὐχ οἷόν τ᾽ ἦν μὴ μετίσχειν τοὺς τῷ θνητῷ τῷδε κεκοινωνικότας)—does not affect the harmony of the whole; on the contrary, it contributes to it.[77] Man's contribution to the harmony of the *cosmos* is confirmed by the philosopher's theory of measure and harmony.

Beauty, according to Plethon, consists in measure and symmetry. He argues as follows: Beauty cannot be immeasurable or indefinite and constantly increasing. But it may be asked why this is so, when that which possesses more being is always superior? The answer is that that which possesses being in the highest degree is not that which is the greatest in number, volume, or quantity, but that which is most permanently durable; and that is unity, or what is relatively more completely unified.[78] The simple, Plethon points out, is more unified than the complex, the symmetrical than the asymmetrical, the proportionate than the disproportionate. What has a common measure or identical proportion is most completely unified. What lacks measure or proportion in its components lacks unity and consequently will fail to be permanent. So it is measure and definition that the greater degree of being, and therefore of beauty and quality, is to be found, rather than in the constantly increasing and wholly indefinite."[79] The divinized and aesthetic views of the philosopher of Mistra can be better appreciated in their anti-parathesis to the corresponding de-divinized views of Aristotle and particularly in his criticism of Aristotle's understanding of the first principle, the creator, and the object of art. Thus, in comparing Aristotle's views of God, the creator, with those of Plato Plethon argues as follows:

> Plato's view is that God, the supreme sovereign, is the creator of every kind of intelligible and separate substance, and hence of our entire universe...[80] It may be pointed out that Aristotle does make God the end and the final cause,[81] but even this must be regarded as a not very exalted claim and not one worthy of God, if he makes God the end not of the existence or essence of particular things but only of movement and change. If, on the other hand, his reason for not calling God anywhere the creator of the universe is simply that he does not believe him to be such, then he would be guilty of an even graver fault, in that he neither states nor even believes the noblest doctrine of all philosophy, which is common not only to philosophy but to all right-thinking mankind.[82]

The reasons the philosopher of Mistra gives to demonstrate his thesis and that Aristotle doesn't believe in this doctrine are worth to be quoted in full:

Now, I shall show that he does not believe in this doctrine. First, it would not be reasonable, if he accepted this noblest doctrine, that he should never refer to it anywhere in his work, when by contrast he goes on at unnecessary length about such things as embryos and shellfish. Secondly, he criticizes those who postulate a cause of the generation of numbers (meaning a cause as distinct from a time when they came into existence, as is clear from his exposition of their arguments); and he argues against them that 'it is absurd, indeed an impossibility, to suppose the generation of eternal entities.'[83] From this it is clear that Aristotle, like others no doubt, assumes that generation in time must be a necessary consequence of causal generation...But if Aristotle regards our universe as eternal,[84] he clearly could not presuppose its generation; and if not generation, then no creator of it either.[85]

But we, the Platonists, Plethon adds, "place God as universal sovereign over all existing things, and assume him to be the originator of originators, the creator of creators, and refer everything without exception to him...." [86]

Equally de-divinizing is Aristotle's use of the teleological argument concerning nature and art. Aristotle says,[87] Plethon argues, "it is absurd to think that what happens is purposeless unless one can see the agent of it exercising deliberation." On the contrary, says Aristotle, art exercises no deliberation; for if the art were inherent in a piece of wood, it would not be deliberating.[88] But how could, Plethon asks, an art continue to be so called if there were no deliberation prior to its exercises? What is the essential constituent of an art other than deliberation? If that were taken away, no art would remain. How could anything be carried through to an end of any kind without a mind exercising prior deliberation, and indeed preconceiving that end within itself? For if art imitates nature, as Aristotle himself holds,[89] then nature cannot be inferior to art: on the contrary, nature must long beforehand possess that which constitutes art in an even higher degree. And even though there is clearly an element in art which does not deliberate, such as an instrument or a laborer, it is not in them that the art lies but in the master-craftsman. Similarly, if one observes something irrational in nature, then the nature which effectively produces the result does not lie therein; for nature is instituted by God, and God's institution cannot be irrational.[90]

It becomes evident from the above that Plethon's conception of man as *methorion* is an outcome of his Neoplatonic world view. It is also evident that this conception is incompatible with and opposed to the Aristotelian—and the Christian—conception of soul and body. Plethon cannot accept the Aristotelian doctrine of soul, because Aristotle reduces its role to a simple element of man and ruins the Platonic doctrine of the immortality of the soul, in doubting about its pre-existence as well as its survival. Aristotle's doctrine of intellect is far from being in agreement with his concept of *methorion* because Aristotle contradicts himself in stating that the human intellect is immortal and also that man is ruined after death. Aristotle's conception of God, the creator, as moving cause only, as well as his teleology of nature and art clearly show, from Plethon's Neoplatonic point of view, his de-divinized inclinations. His conception of teleology in nature and art independently of the noetic cause could not but lead to such consequences. Besides, Aristotle contradicts himself when he affirms that nature acts without the intelligent agent (βουλεύεται), a thesis which, in reality, is not distinguished from that of mechanism—according to which nature acts accidentally or necessarily—which his teleology tries to avoid.

Notes

1. *Plato the Founder of Philosophy as Dialectic*, New York, the Philosophical Library, 1965, 143.
2. Fr. B 54: "ἁρμονίη ἀφανὴς φανερῆς κρείττων."
3. *Cf.* Eric Voegelin, *The New Science of Politics,* University of Chicago Press, 1952, 68.
4. *Cf. Republic, 518d-e.*
5. *Cf. Republic,* 378-379.
6. *Cf.* E. Voegelin, *op. cit.,* 70.
7. Heracl. Fr. 35.
8. *Cf.* E. Voegelin, *op. cit.,* 70.
9. Emped. Fr. 112.4.
10. Ap. Iambl. V.P. 137, DK, 58D2.
11. Plato. *Theaet.,* 176a.
12. Epich, 263 Kaibel (DK, 23B20, vol. I, 201).
12a. *Cf.* Phaedr., 278d: "Τὸ μὲν σοφόν...καλεῖν ἔμοιγε μέγα εἶναι δοκεῖ καὶ θεῷ μόνῳ πρέπειν."
13. Aet. II, I (DK, 14.21: "Π. πρῶτος ὠνόμασε τὴν τῶν ὅλων περιοχὴν κόσμον ἐκ τῆς ἐν αὐτῷ τάξεως").
14. Plato. *Meno,* 81 c.
15. *Cf. Gorg.,* 507e.
16. *Polit.,* 5005c.
17. *Tim.,* 47b-c.
18. DL, viii, 8.
19. *A History of Greek Philosophy,* Cambridge University Press, 1971, vol. I, 213.
20. *Polit.,* 525d: "ὡς σφόδρα ἄνω ποι ἄγει τὴν ψυχὴν καὶ περὶ αὐτῶν τῶν ἀριθμῶν ἀναγκάζει διαλέγεσθαι, οὐδαμῇ ἀποδεχόμενον, ἐάν τις αὐτῇ ὁρατὰ ἢ ἁπτὰ σώματα ἔχοντας προτεινόμενος διαλέγηται."
21. *Polit.,* 527b: "τοῦ γὰρ ἀεὶ ὄντος ἡ γεωμετρικὴ γνῶσίσ ἐστιν...Ὁλκὸν ἄρα, ὦ γενναῖε, ψυχῆς πρὸς ἀλήθειαν εἴη ἂν καὶ ἀπεργαστικὸν φιλοσόφου διανοίας πρὸς τὸ ἄνω σχεῖν ἃ νῦν κάτω οὐ δέον ἔχομεν."
22. *Polit.,* 529a-d: "ἀναγκαάζει ψυχὴν εἰς τὸ ἄνω ὁρᾶν καὶ ἀπὸ τῶν ἐνθένδε ἐκεῖσε ἄγει...τὴν ἀλήθειαν ἐν αὐτοῖς ληψόμενον."
23. *Metaph.* 985b23, 987b28, 986a1, 1078b21; *De Caelo,* 293a 25.
24. *Op. cit.,* p. 219.
25. *De Caelo,* 290b 12.
26. *Polit.,*531a.
27. Arist. *Metaph.,* 986a8: "τέλειον ἡ δεκὰς εἶναι δοκεῖ καὶ πᾶσαν περιειληφέναι τὴν τῶν ἀριθμῶν φύσιν."
28. Porph. V. P. 20, Iambl. V. P. 150.

29. Phaidros, 244b, 245bc: "...τὰ μέγιστα τῶν ἀγαθῶν ἡμῖν γίγνεται διὰ μανίας, θείᾳ μέντοι δόσει διδομένης...ἄνευ μανίας Μουσῶν...ἀτελὴς...καί ἡ ποίησις."

30. Polit., 548b-c.

31. Cf. Symp., 196e

32. Cf. Laws, IV, 719cd and VII, 801bc.

33. Symp.,196e: "πᾶς γὰρ ποιητὴς γίγνεται ... οὗ ἂν Ἔρως ἅψηται."

34. Cf. Polit., 403c: "δεῖ δέ που τελευτᾶν τὰ μουσικὰ εἰς τὰ τοῦ καλοῦ ἐρωτικά."

35. Symp., 211a-b: "αὐτό καθ' αὑτό μεθ'αὑτοῦ μονοειδὲς ἀεί ὄν, τὰ δὲ ἄλλα πάντα καλὰ ἐκείνου μετέχοντα."

36. Symp., 212a: "τεκόντι δὲ ἀρετὴν ἀληθῆ καί θρεψαμένῳ ὑπάρχει θεοφιλεῖ γένεσθαι, καί, εἴπερ τῷ ἄλλῳ ἀνθρώπων, ἀθανάτῳ καὶ ἐκείνῳ.

37. Polit., 509b: "ἐπέκεινα τῆς οὐσίας πρεσβείᾳ καὶ δυνάμει."

38. Enn.v, 1, 2, and 3; cf. Christos Evangeliou, Aristotle's Categories and Porphyry, E. J. Brill, ed. Philosophia Antiqua n.18, The Netherlands 1988, 13.

39. Cf. A. H. Armstrong, "Plotinus," The Cambridge History of Later Greek and Early Medieval Philosophy, Cambridge, University Press, 1970, 232.

40. Op. cit., 233.

41. Cf. Enn., v 8 (31) 1, 38-40: "ἐπεὶ καὶ ὁ Φειδίας τὸν Δία πρὸς οὐδὲν αἰσθητὸν ποιήσας, ἀλλὰ λαβὼν οἷος ἂν γένοιτο, εἰ ἡμῖν ὁ Ζεὺς δι' ὀμμάτων ἐθέλοι φανῆναι."

42. Enn., iii.2.3: "ὅλον γὰρ ἐποίησε πάγκαλον καὶ αὐτάρκες."

43. Enn., iv. 4. 8: "εἰς τὸν σύμπαντα οὐρανὸν ἐλλάμψει ὥσπερ χορδαὶ ἐν λύρᾳ συμπαθῶς κινηθεῖσαι μέλος ἂν ᾄσειαν ἐν φυσικῇ τινι ἁρμονίᾳ."

44. Cf. Enn., ii. 3. 16: "οὗ δεῖ πάντα καλὰ εἶναι...ἐπεὶ καὶ τὰ ἐναντία συντελεῖ καὶ οὐκ ἄνευ τούτου κόσμος."

45. Enn., ii. 9.8: "ἄγαλμα ἐναργὲς καὶ καλὸν τῶν νοητῶν θεῶν εἴποι ..."

46. Cf. Enn., iv, 8. 3.

47. Enn., I 3, 3, 8: "πρὸς τελείωσιν ἀρετῶν."

48. Enn., i. 6. 6. "Ψυχὴ οὖν ἀναχθεῖσα πρὸς νοῦν ἐπὶ τὸ μᾶλλὸν ἐστι καλόν. Νοῦς δὲ καὶ τὰ παρὰ νοῦ τὸ κάλλος...διὸ καὶ λέγεται ὀρθῶς τὸ ἀγαθόν καὶ καλὸν τὴν ψυχὴν γίνεσθαι ὁμοιωθῆναι εἶναι θεῷ...ὅτι ἐκεῖθεν τὸ καλὸν καὶ ἡ μοῖρα ἡ ἑτέρα τῶν ὄντων."

49. Enn., v.9.2: "ὃ παρ' αὐτοῦ καλόν."

50. Enn., v. 9. 1: "... ἔμεινεν ἐκεῖ τὰ τῇδε ὑπεριδὸν πάντα ἡσθὲν τῷ τόπῳ ἀληθινῷ καὶ οἰκείῳ ὄντι, ὥσπερ ἐκ πολλῆς πλάνης εἰς πατρίδα εὔνομον ἀφικόμενος ἄνθρωπος."

51. Cf. Commentary on the Timaeus, I 131, 28-132,5; II 112, 23-5; III 259, 11-27.

52. Cf. Commentary on Alcibiades II 277-281.

53. *Cf. De an.*430a1.

54. *On Euclid*, Prol. I. 22, 15-16.

55. *Comm.* 24,27-25,3.

56. *In Eucl.* 62, 5-10.

57. *In Eucl.* 62, 11-13; 19-63,1.

58. *Cf. In Tim.* I 204, 3-10ff; *In Parm.* 796, 26-39.

59. I 2, 15-3,20; I 295, 26-7.

60. *Cf.* B. Knos, 'Gemistos plethon et son souvenir,'*Lettres d' Humanite*, 9, 1950, 131, and A. E. Vakalopoulos, *Origins of the Greek Nation*, trans., Jan Moles, New York, Rutgers University Press, 1970, 171,

61. *Cf.* J. N. Taylor, *Georgius Gemistus Pletho's Criticism of Plato and Aristotle*, Menasha, Wisconsin, George Banta Publishing Co., 1921, 94.

62. PG.160, 928 B.

63. *Cf. Nomoi*, 252 Alexandre: PG. 160, 971A.

64. *Cf. Nomoi*, 252, Alexandre: PG. 160, 971A.

65. *Cf. Nomoi*, 94: "τῶν δ' ἄλλων ἀπάντων πατήρ τε καὶ δημιουργός πρεσβύτερος," 172: "ἀγένητος," "προαιώνιος."

66. PG 160, 973 B: "δεύτερος θεός;" *cf. Nomoi*, 34, 46.

67. *Cf. Nomoi*, 258.

68. *Cf. Nomoi*, 260: "Ἡμεῖς δ' ἀρτίαν τε, καὶ οὐχ ἡμίτομον οὐδὲ χωλὴν, τῇ ψυχῇ τῇ ἀνθρωπίνῃ τὴν ἀϊδιότητα ἀποφαίνοντες...Δῆλα γὰρ δὴ ὅτι ἐπ' ἀμφότερα αὕτη ἡ ἀϊδιότης τῆς ἡμιτόμου ἐκείνης πολὺ μείζων καὶ καλλίων..."

69. *Cf. Nomoi*, 252.

70. Πλήθωνος, Πρὸς ἠρωτημένα ἄττα ἀπόκρισις, ed. L. Benakis, Φιλοσοφια 4 (1974), 357, 95: "τὸν ἄνθρωπον εἶναι ζῷον ἀθάνατον θνητῇ κοινωνεῖν φύσει πεφυκός."

71. *Ibid*, 357, 114-120.

72. *Cf. Nomoi*, 142.

73. Πλήθωνος, Ζωροαστρείων τε καὶ πλατωνικῶν δογμάτων συγκεφαλαίωσις, 266.

74. *Ibid*,, 274.

75. *Cf. Nomoi*, 138.

76. *Cf. Nomoi*, 138.

77. *Cf. Nomoi*, 182.

78. *Cf. Nomoi*, 84..

79. *Nomoi*, 84 Alexandre. See F. Masai, *Plethon et le platonisme de Mistra*, Paris, 1956, 125-7.

80. *Epistles*, ii. 312E; *Timaeus*, 27 c-30d.

81. *Metaph.* xii. 1072b3.

82.   *De differentiis*, 321, 23 -322,4 (Lagarde, trans., C. M. Woodhouse).
83.   *Metaph.* xiv. 1091a 12-13.
84.   *Metaph.* xii. 1072 a 22 –23.
85.   *De differentiis,* 322, 4-19 (Lagarde, trans., C.M. Woodhouse).
86.   De differentiis, 342,14-24; *cf.* 342, 31-34, *cf.* also Timaeus, 29e.
87.   *Physics*,ii. 199 b 26-30.
88.   *Physics,,* ii. 194a 21-22; ii. 199a 15-17.
89.   *Ibid.*
90.   *De differentiis*, 331, 32-332,10, (Lagarde, transl. By C. M. Woodhouse).

The Contributors

Aphrodite Alexandrakis earned her Ph.D. from the University of Miami, Florida. She is Professor of Philosophy and Humanities at Barry University in Miami Shores where she teaches a variety of philosophy and humanities courses, and supervises four disciplines. She has been the recipient of two N.E.H. fellowship awards: in 1996 at the University of Tennessee at Chattanooga, and in 1997 at the University of Texas at Austin. She is a board member of the International Society for Neoplatonic Studies, and researches and publishes in Platonic and Neoplatonic aesthetics.

John P. Anton is a Distinguished Professor of Philosophy at the University of South Florida; has authored and edited twenty books and published over one-hundred articles. He is currently President of the International Society for Neoplatonic Studies; an honorary member ΦΒΚ, Corresponding Member of the Academy of Athens and an Honorary Doctorate at the University of Athens.

Leonidas C. Bargeliotes, born in Olympia of Peloponnese, attended the Gymnasium of Zacharo and the Theology and Philosophy Schools at the University of Athens where he received the corresponding diplomas. He pursued further postgraduate studies in philosophy at the Universities of Norma and Emory (USA) where he received his M.A. and Ph.D. respectively. Since 1975, he has been teaching philosophy at the University of Athens. He is the author, among others, of *Pletho's Criticism of Aristotle*, *Philosophy and Scientific Research* and *Philosophy of Science*. At the present he is President of the Olympic Center for Philosophy and Culture and is co-editor of the journals *Skepsis* and *Ifitos*.

247

Jay Bregman, Professor of History at the University of Maine, has written on the relationship of Platonism, culture and religion in the late antiquity. Recently, he has turned his attention to the influence of Neoplatonism in North America and is preparing a manuscript on the topic for the "Hermeneutics and the History of Religions" series, edited by Kees W. Bolle.

Liana De Girolami Cheney, Professor of Art History and Coordinator of Art History, Interdisciplinary and Intercollegiate Studies at University Massachusetts Lowell, is the author of *Botticelli's Neoplatonic Images*, *The Paintings of the Casa Vasari*, *Readings in Italian Mannerism*, *Self-Portraits of Women Painters*, *The Symbols of Vanitas in the Arts, Literature and Music*, and *Pre-Raphaelitism and Medievalism in the Arts*. Presently, she is completing a book on Edward Burne-Jones' Mythological Paintings.

Roman T. Ciapalo is a Professor and Chairperson of the philosophy department at Loras College, Dubuque, Iowa, and Director of the Loras College "Classical Philosophy Lecture Series," which he established in the Spring of 1990. He received his Ph.D. in philosophy from Loyola University of Chicago. He has lectured nationally and internationally in New Delhi, Bratislava and Ukraine. He has been the recipient (1991) of a FulbrightHays Summer Seminar Grant and in 1993-94 was a Fulbright Scholar in Ukraine. He has published articles on Neoplatonism and is currently working on a translation into English of the collected works of the 18th century Ukrainian philosopher, Hryhorij Skovoroda.

R. Baine Harris is Eminent Professor of Philosophy Emeritus at Old Dominion University in Norfolk, Virgina. One of the founders of the International Society for Neoplatonic Studies he served as its Executive Director for twenty four years and is the General Editor of its 13 volume series *Studies in Neoplatonism: Ancient and Modern*.

Robert Meredith Helm is a native of Winston-Salem, North Carolina. He holds a B.A. Degree from Wake Forest College and M.A. and Ph.D. Degrees from Duke University. He has been a member of the faculty of Wake Forest University for many years, where he is currently Worrell Professor of Philosophy. He has contributed a number of papers and articles to scholarly journals and is the author, co-author, or co-editor of several books. He and his wife Carol divide their time between a home in Winston-Salem and a home in the Blue Ridge Mountains of Virginia.

John Hendrix lives in Rome where he is an Adjunct Professor at Roger Williams University and is finishing his dissertation on Roman Baroque Architecture and Neoplatonic Philosophy at Cornell University.

J. Noel Hubler is an Assistant Professor of Philosophy at Lebanon Valley College. He is a student of Ancient and Medieval Philosophy and contemporary Philosophy of Mind. He lives with his wife, Mededyth, in North Cornwall, Pennsylvania.

Dimitrios N. Koutras, born in Patra, has a Degree in Philosophy obtained form the Philosophy School of University of Athens, and attended postgraduate studies in philosophy at the University of Heidelberg in Germany. In 1969, he was awarded Ph.D. for his dissertation, "The notion of light in the asthetics of Plotinus." He founded the Proceedings of the Conferences on Aristotle's Ethics and Politics, in 1994. He is currently a Professor of Philosophy in the University of Athens and is author of many books and articles regarding Aristotelian philosophy, ancient Greek and contemporary philosophy.

John Lachs is Centenial Professor of Philosophy at Vanderbilt University. He works in ethics, American philosophy and German idealism. His latest book, with Michael Hodges, is *Thinking in the Ruins* (Nashville, Tenn.: Vanderbilt Press, 1999).

Nicholas J. Moutafakis, Professor of Philosophy at Cleveland State University, has authored various articles on logic and linguistic analysis, and ancient Greek philosophy, and several book titles: *Imperatives and Their Logics* (New Delhi: Sterling, 1975), *The Logics of Preference* (Boston: Reidel, 1987), and the forthcoming "*Byzantine Philosophy by Basil Tatakis* (Indianapolis: Hackett).

Jean-Marc Narbonne is the Dean of the Faculté de Philosophie of Laval University and author of many monographies and articles on Plotinus and the Neoplatonic tradition. His most important works include *Plotin, Les deux matières: Trad. and commentary* (Paris: Vrin, 1993), *La Métaphysique de Plotin* (Paris: Vrin, 1994), *Plotin. Traité 25: Trad.and commentary* (Paris: Cerf, 1998) and *Hénologie, Ontologie et Ereignis* (Paris: Belles Lettres, 2000).

Kalomoira Polychronopoulou is currently finishing up graduate studies at the University of Patras in Greece. She has worked closely with Christos Terezis on their study of Proclus.

Constantinos Proimos was born in Crete, Greece where he now lives and works. After earning a B.A. in Sociology in Athens, he performed his graduate work as a Scholar of the Greek State in Philosophy and in Art History in Paris (E.H.E.S.S.) and in New York (New School for Social Research) where he completed his Ph.D. in 1998. He is now an independent scholar and has published critical essays on artists like Joseph Beuys, Yves Klein, Jannis Kounellis and on philosophers like Maurice Merleau-Ponty, Martin Heidegger and Jacques Derrida.

Patrick Quinn is Head of the Philosophy Department, All Hallows College, Dublin and has written extensively on philosophy and education, in particular, on philosophical issues in the writings of St. Thomas Aquinas. He is author of *Aquinas, Platonism and the Knowledge of God* (Haunts, UK: Avebury, 1996).

Frederic M. Schroeder, Professor of Classics at Queen's University in Kingston, Canada, was educated at the University of Toronto and has published widely on Plotinus, including *Form and Transformation. A Study in the Philosophy of Plotinus* (Montreal: McGill-Queen's Press, 1992).

Joseph Sen teaches philosophy at the City University, London. He wrote his doctoral dissertation on Plotinus under the supervision of Richard Sorabji at King's College, London. He has published several papers on Plotinus and post-Aristotelian philosophy.

Christos Terezis, with doctorates in philosophy and theology, is an Associate Professor at the University of Patras in Greece. His research interests include: ancient Greek philosophy and Byzantine philosophy and theology.

Panayiota Vassilopoulou graduated from the University of Athens in 1993 and is currently studying for the degree of Ph.D. in Philosophy at the University of Liverpool. The subject of her thesis is Plotinus' views on beauty and her research interests include ancient Greek philosophy, Neoplatonism and early Byzantine philosophy.

Index